INTERSPECIES ETHICS

Critical Perspectives on Animals

Critical Perspectives on Animals: Theory, Culture, Science, and Law

Series Editors: Gary L. Francione and Gary Steiner

The emerging interdisciplinary field of animal studies seeks to shed light on the nature of animal experience and the moral status of animals in ways that overcome the limitations of traditional approaches to animals. Recent work on animals has been characterized by an increasing recognition of the importance of crossing disciplinary boundaries and exploring the affinities as well as the differences among the approaches of fields such as philosophy, law, sociology, political theory, ethology, and literary studies to questions pertaining to animals. This recognition has brought with it an openness to a rethinking of the very terms of critical inquiry and of traditional assumptions about human being and its relationship to the animal world. The books published in this series seek to contribute to contemporary reflections on the basic terms and methods of critical inquiry, to do so by focusing on fundamental questions arising out of the relationships and confrontations between humans and nonhuman animals, and ultimately to enrich our appreciation of the nature and ethical significance of nonhuman animals by providing a forum for the interdisciplinary exploration of questions and problems that have traditionally been confined within narrowly circumscribed disciplinary boundaries.

The Animal Rights Debate: Abolition or Regulation? Gary L. Francione and Robert Garner

Animal Rights Without Liberation: Applied Ethics and Human Obligations, Alasdair Cochrane

Experiencing Animal Minds: An Anthology of Animal-Human Encounters, edited by Julie A. Smith and Robert W. Mitchell

Animalia American: Animal Representations and Biopolitical Subjectivity, Colleen Glenney Boggs

Animal Oppression and Human Violence: Domesecration, Capitalism, and Global Conflict, David A. Nibert

Animals and the Limits of Postmodernism, Gary Steiner

Being Animal: Beasts and Boundaries in Nature Ethics, Anna L. Peterson

CYNTHIA WILLETT

INTERSPECIES ETHICS

Columbia University Press / New York

Columbia University Press
Publishers Since 1893
New York   Chichester, West Sussex
cup.columbia.edu
Copyright © 2014 Columbia University Press
All rights reserved

Library of Congress Cataloging-in-Publication Data
Willett, Cynthia, 1956-
Interspecies ethics / Cynthia Willett.
pages cm. — (Critical perspectives on animals: theory, culture, science, and law)
Includes bibliographical references and index.
ISBN 978-0-231-16776-5 (cloth) —ISBN 978-0-231-16777-2 (pbk.)
—ISBN 978-0-231-53814-5 (e-book)
1. Human-animal relationships—Moral and ethical aspects. 2. Human-animal relationships—Philosophy. 3. Ethics. 4. Speciesism. I. Title.

B105.A55W56   2014
179'.3—dc23   2014001325

Jacket Design by Julia Kushnirsky
Jacket illustration by Sue Coe

For Stefan, Liza, Joe, and the cats

CONTENTS

INTRODUCTION:
New Ideals of Belonging and Africana Origins of Interspecies Living
1

1. CAN THE ANIMAL SUBALTERN LAUGH?
Neoliberal Inversions, Cross-Species Solidarities, and Other Challenges
to Human Exceptionalism
WITH JULIE WILLETT
29

2. PALEOLITHIC ETHICS:
Ethics' Evolution from Play, the Interspecies Community Selection
Hypothesis, and Anarchic Communitarianism
60

3. AFFECT ATTUNEMENT:
Discourse Ethics Across Species
80

CONTENTS

4. WATER AND WING GIVE WONDER:
Meditations on Cosmopolitan Peace

100

5. REFLECTIONS:
A Model and a Vision of Ethical Life

131

CODA; OR, THE SONG OF THE DOG-MAN:
Mourning in J. M. Coetzee's *Disgrace*

147

Acknowledgments 175

Notes 177

Index 217

INTERSPECIES ETHICS

INTRODUCTION

New Ideals of Belonging and Africana Origins of Interspecies Living

It is better to be a human being dissatisfied than a pig satisfied; better to be Socrates dissatisfied than a fool satisfied. And if the fool, or the pig, are of a different opinion, it is because they only know their own side of the equation.

—JOHN STUART MILL, *UTILITARIANISM*

I wish I had a tail and mobile ears.

—MARC BEKOFF, *THE EMOTIONAL LIVES OF ANIMALS*

Low-level warfare has been raging across Africa, India, and parts of Southeast Asia for decades, *New York Times* writer Charles Siebert reports after returning from Uganda's Queen Elizabeth National Park.[1] Adolescent males alone or in gangs have been attacking villages and plowing under swaths of crops in retaliation for the murder of their families and the destruction of their tribal lands. The rogue males terrorizing African parks and jungles are not the orphaned youths of the Lord's Resistance Army, those kidnapped children pressed into service for the Ugandan rebels. However, like child soldiers, these adolescents, too, are caught in downward spirals of destruction and self-injury triggered by decades of violence. They are among the last surviving members of the elephants of Uganda. Elephants are quickly diminishing in numbers and approaching extinction levels in some regions, which is alarming and yet, sadly, not surprising. What is surprising are the eerily humanlike responses of the elephant herds to their threatened demise.

The uncanny similarities have been documented by Ugandan refugee and Cambridge-educated ethologist Dr. Evelyn Lawino Abe, who has lived through the massacre of her Acholi people and witnessed first hand the impact of the destruction of family and community infrastructure for humans and elephants.[2] The chronic low-level warfare on elephant communities chronicles only a small part of the biopower unleashed since humans developed large, agriculture-based societies and state governments some five thousand years ago, amidst the Neolithic revolution.[3] Since that time, human populations have learned to band together in increasingly large groups and live like the handful of other ultrasocial species (wasps, ants, bees, termites, and naked mole rats) for which group members would not be able to know each other personally. Today we live ever more impersonally and apart from communities and yet also strikingly interconnected. Over the past decades, a technologically driven globalization ushers in once again that classical philosophical question, but, given its trans-species reach, this time with unprecedented urgency and unclear significance—*what might provide the basis for a life in common?* The work of ethologists like Dr. Abe, who are recovering insights on interspecies communities from small-scale African societies, joins with a larger movement among scientists, philosophers, and animal activists in search of alternative forms of belonging across human and nonhuman animal species. This book, as a speculative venture in social and political ethics, draws insights broadly from vast intellectual and social movements in the context of our unprecedented era to propose trans-species ideals of communitarianism and cosmopolitan peace.

Communitarian ethics has largely dropped out of the picture for progressive, modern humans, who are, first and foremost, defined as individuals. As individuals, we modern humans experience our lives as predominantly separate from ancestral and communal ties. Worse than irrelevant, unmodern communitarian idioms of belonging and a common life raise specters of retroactive state-based racism or cultural and religious nationalism. Against these threats, modern moral theory foregrounds the autonomous individual, who is expected to take ownership over her own well-being by exercising a capacity to make rational choices based on general principles of fairness. Some aspects of rational autonomy can be found in classical Greek and Hellenistic philosophies, which is not surprising given the rise of large city-states and empires during that time period. However, modernism's atomic individualism emerged and then intensified in capitalist, late capitalist, and neoliberal eras. Under these conditions, interdependence, although acknowledged in much of moral theory, retreats backstage as affect-laden, social ties play, at most, a supporting role for the entrepreneurism of professional, corporate, and state life. Of the complicated array of ethical norms and social practices that lend communities their affective textures and biosocial histories—including playful reciprocity, tragedy's intergenerational *hubris*, retribution, forgiveness, consolation, festive ceremonies of reconciliation, moral beauty, and sublime compassion—only a relatively attenuated form of reciprocity (a flattened "tit for a tat" style of exchange) takes center stage in moral theory from its capitalist through recent neoliberal applications. Today new technologies of electronic media and social networking (Twitter, Facebook, Instagram, etc.) promise to recharge communal-based networks. However, pressured by our entrepreneurial culture, the new social media may just as likely shift humans further away from that communitarian ethos that characterized our species along with elephants and other social mammals for eons, at least up until the rise of large-scale societies with the Neolithic revolution.

With increasing human atomization, moral theory consigns eons-old social practices of ethical life to personal and religious spheres, to the imaginary realms of the cathartic arts or comic entertainment, to biblical Jubilee or Buddhist sangha, and to the utopian dreams of social anarchists and third-world liberation movements. In the post 9/11 context, state and corporate bureaucracies recast earnest political confrontation as espionage or criminal terrorism and, riding waves of popular panic and diffuse consumerist dreams, shore up truly frightening conglomerates of power. Yet reemerging sources of political wisdom from Uganda and other regions of Africa and the world are challenging modern moral theory's grasp of the nuances of sociality (our own alongside other species). Documented studies attest not only to the tragic implications of punctured social bonds in elephants in Uganda but also for the exploited animal and human workers in our research labs, factory farms, and corporate theme parks. Paradoxically, modern humans are relearning the communal ties of our ancient species through the destruction of these relationships in other species.

In a vivid portrayal of devastation, published as the article "Elephant Break-up" in *Nature* (2005), brought to national attention by Siebert in the *New York Times Magazine* (2006), and subsequently expanded into the book *Elephants on the Edge* (2009), psychologist Gay Bradshaw alerts us to the soul-destroying terror experienced by orphan elephants.[4] She elaborates on this terror through trauma and attachment theories, theories originally designed to explain human behavior. It turns out that it takes a village to raise a child, for elephants and for humans. Elephant development is driven by a social desire to belong, as attachment theorists established for rhesus monkeys and human infants some decades ago.[5] Otherwise healthy individuals suffer trauma through the disruption of the particular bonds that hold them together in a social web. The systematic targeting of elders, as occurs in elephant poaching, tears apart the communal structure, which for these creatures is the air they live and breathe, the element of their social lives. When elephant orphans lose the elders that anchor communities and educate the youth in their culture, they act out as we might expect any gang of abandoned and traumatized adolescents to do. Disoriented and disconnected, these rogue males engage in social crimes—harassing older female elephants, mounting and murdering rhinoceroses, and self-injury—previously unknown among their species.[6]

Reflecting on this wrenching violence, Bradshaw explains the deliberately "injurious crime" as "more than an act of aggression."[7] The crime of these adolescent males is not the result of some brute animal force. Elephants are not at some elemental level savage. They are not possessed by a death wish. It is the "relational breach" and the "rending of the social fabric" among the tribes that unleash the social sickness of their societies and set in motion the downward spiral of emotional and social demise.[8] Nor does this social fabric retreat to the background with the maturation process. Maturation is not separation; it is achieving the connectivity of living with—the substance of ethical life. Living, feeling, thinking nodes in fleshly networks of overlapping sensibilities and relayed communications, elephants are, like humans, Siebert writes, "profoundly social creatures. A herd of them is, in essence, one incomprehensibly massive elephant: a somewhat loosely bound and yet intricately interconnected, tensile organism."[9]

Elephant social networks establish more than mere analogies between human and elephant societies. Webs of sentience and discourse entwine the two species in the biosocial ethos of common ancestors and shared habitats. Bradshaw characterizes this confluence of registers that she and others have documented in the national parks of Uganda as a "trans-species psyche" that is still poorly understood by science.[10] Yet, the stories of interspecies communities plagued by a malaise and torn apart through self-destructive revenge reek of what the dramatic arts have long portrayed as a tragic *pathos*. As in ancient drama, violations against individuals reverberate across families and communities, unraveling webs of trust and friendly interaction. In Uganda's national parks, the tragic generation of communal pathos—of communal suffering and its self-destructive forces—is not just a device of literary fiction. It is real. As portrayed in preclassical tragedy, destruction wreaks havoc over generations through repeated trauma until vital bonds are regenerated or repaired.[11]

Moral philosophy has much to learn from ancient wisdom traditions about the dangers of relational breach and the pathos that haunts interlocked species. Until the recent past, small-scale human and elephant societies passed on ethical practices that sustained their cohabitation. These practices have been nearly lost with modernization. Barbara Smuts, who spent years living with wild baboons and chimpanzees in East Africa, suspects "that reciprocal understandings . . . between people and at least some of our nonhuman neighbors were common during our time as hunter-gatherers, which constituted 99% of our history as a species."[12] After decades of colonization, poaching, trophy hunting, and civil war, with elders as prime targets for culling or murder, modern humans have forgotten how to live with other animals. *Are the deracinated elephants becoming modern too?* Reflecting on the trans-species tragedies, Abe, Bradshaw, and Smuts believe ancient practices might reveal a path out of modernity's chronic low-level warfare against other species, one moment of which is now measured statistically as the "Human-Elephant Conflict." The multispecies communitarianism of these ancient practices lays the ground for reflecting upon a postmoral, posthumanist ethics.

CHALLENGING HUMAN EXCEPTIONALISM: FROM ANCIENT WISDOM TO RENEGADE SCIENCE AND POSTHUMANIST IDEALS

In this book we explore the posthumanist, cosmopolitan ethics of alternative agencies and multiple belongings within and across human and nonhuman animal species.[13] The concluding chapters 4 and 5 offer a partial and tentative philosophical framework for interspecies ethics, guided by the preclassical anarcho-communitarianism of small-scale societies and models of network clusters in biology and neuroscience. These models expose trans-species layers of subjective and presubjective agency and communal norms of reciprocity, forgiveness, reconciliation, and spiritual peace. Modern, humanist conceptions of the self as autonomous, and, for the most part, their ongoing revision in notions of relational autonomy, consign the biopsychic social norms of species inter- and intrarelationships to background conditions for the maturation of the individual (typically restricted to the human) and to secondary processes and strategies for social justice. These modern social norms assume that moral subjects are structurally homologous rather than diverging fundamentally in their agential modes of interaction, biocultural styles of subjectivity, and complexity of biosocial relationships.

Much of modern science has reflected the same human exceptionalist ideologies. Theories that rely upon mirror metaphors, as in the measurement of self-awareness through the mirror recognition test and theorizing empathy through mirror neurons or abstract sameness, inadvertently reinforce atomistic models of the self as bound and separate rather than attuned to, and immersed with, others in a biosocial web with its larger energy flows (chapters 3 and 4). Adding insult to injury, creatures failing measures of selfhood based on humanist and legalistic ideologies are sentenced to a lower moral status and to conditions of solitary confinement or torture in research labs and the food production system. The oppressive dynamic of these research and food systems, rendering enslaved animals socially disconnected, psychologically friendless, and politically weak, fade out of the consumer's view. Even animal and human rights workers, given their narrow, negative focus on alleviating animal suffering, can lose sight of complex biosocial forms of solidarity required for meaningful existence as participants, if not *cocitizens*, of multispecies communities (Sue Donaldson and Will Kymlicka). A posthumanist lens ventures beyond modern and postmodern binaries, as in sympathy for the "other" or Nietzschean affirmation of whatever, to engage multilayered symbiotic agencies and biosocial communities. Social animals desire meaningful connectivity that they might live in a world not indifferent to them.

The postmodern inattention to biosocial agencies and communities of social animals inherits its weaknesses from modern and classical European thought. Any acknowledgment of nonhuman animal flourishing has been marginal among the canonical thinkers of modern or classical European moral theory, with the exception of Jeremy Bentham. Bentham's appeal to the common capacity for suffering provided the central philosophical justification for social movements against animal cruelty for the past two centuries.[14] However, his utilitarian welfarist approach to ethics obscures modes of animal (and human) agency and social life by narrowing the focus of moral concern to sentience or even to the negative states and passive features of vulnerability and suffering. The unquestioned assumption that language and reason mark humans as the moral animal or superior species blocks serious attention to animal agency, social intelligence, and community life that shapes them and us together.[15] The prejudice against "nonrational" animals rings loud and clear in John Stuart Mill's retort, "It is better to be a human being dissatisfied than a pig satisfied; better to be Socrates dissatisfied than a fool satisfied. And if the fool, or the pig, are of a different opinion, it is because they only know their own side of the equation."[16] Ironically, the same prejudice that grants superior moral status to the "rational" human over the mere animal blinds us to the biosocial basis of human flourishing. We may not be able to signal to cocitizens and coworkers with a wag of the tail or a wiggle of the ears. But, like the pig and the clown, we too are quintessentially social animals.

Since the 1960s and '70s, poststructuralists, inspired by Jacques Derrida and Michel Foucault, exposed the incapacity of reason or language to provide any reliable ground for ethics and knowledge claims. Abstract modes of reasoning and inherited linguistic categories too readily impose biases or prejudices onto others instead of opening us up to listen and respond to them. Freed by the poststructuralists from narrow modern theory, posthumanists took the next step and began to use the critique of reason and language to challenge human exceptionalism. Why should one species, the human, serve as the standard for measuring the capacities or determining the moral worth for all the other species?[17] Are species with alternative communication technologies or cognitive processes to be ranked higher or lower by the standards of some favored philosophical tradition of moral thought? Should we not instead recognize them and ourselves as diverse contributors to the complex biosocial communities of ethical life?

For thousands of years, humans have encountered other species under the dull conditions of agricultural domestication and, worse yet, the brutalizing condition of captivity and industrial food production.[18] As the social upheavals of large-scale societies set in, the thinkers of the Axial Age (roughly 800–200 BCE), Confucius, Buddha, Socrates, Plato, Aristotle, and the prophets of Israel entered on the scene. These figures, in lockstep with the accelerating abstraction of everyday existence, established what persists as our classical philosophical origins.[19] One wonders what ancient wisdom they displaced.

Over the past few centuries, industrialization and capitalism intensified the effects of the agricultural revolution on the social stratification of urban centers. Modern philosophers, increasingly unaware of interspecies communities compared to their more ancient forbears, have attended not to social roles and interdependencies but to autonomous subjects and abstract principles as the exclusive basis for moral life. These modern theorists do not question the atomic individualism and rule-bound bureaucratic regulation characteristic of large-scale societies. It was not until the twentieth-century's toxic mix of totalitarian and imperialist politics with penetrating technologies of power, surveillance, and domination that a philosophical movement, poststructuralism, would search for some alternative to modern moral law's abstraction and homogenizing sameness. Post-Holocaust thinkers wondered if an other-directed, or "heteronomous," *eros* might serve better than an individual autonomy anchored in language and reason, or *logos*, to awaken a sense of responsibility to others. "Response ethics," also known as "alterity ethics," turned philosophical attention from laws and principles examined through solitary reflection or rational argument to the *pathos* of an appeal from the vulnerable stranger—the Other whose singular identity exposes the epistemic poverty of language and concepts. As we will explore in detail, response ethics offers an important reaction to the rationalist biases in modern moral theory, but has yet to generate multifaceted norms or guideposts for the expansive biosocial structures required for an interspecies ethics. Response ethics may serve to urge humans to respond to the alterity of animals and animal suffering. But responding to alterity is not living with those other creatures. The question is, how can we enhance our ethical rapport with nonhuman creatures with whom we enjoy, suffer, and find meaning in evolving modes of earthly cobelonging and worldly cocreating? What basis is there for trans-species communitarianism and cosmopolitanism?

FROM RESPONSE ETHICS' VULNERABLE OTHER TO THE CALL AND RESPONSE OF INTERSPECIES COMMUNITIES

Born of the moral ordeals and political upheavals of twentieth-century Europe, response ethics (represented by Emmanuel Levinas, Jacques Derrida, and Julia Kristeva among many others) has emerged alongside deontological moral theory (Immanuel Kant) and utilitarianism (Jeremy Bentham, John Stuart Mill) of the modern period and classic virtue ethics (Aristotle) as a fourth major tradition in the philosophical canon.[20] The genocides of the Holocaust and the violence of colonization to which the intellectual and cultural centers of modern Europe shamefully lent ideological support prompted a profound critique of modern moral traditions. Surely it was not inevitable that European moral theories would be used to legitimate the crimes against those misfits, freaks, and subhuman types who were not recognized as rational and fully human. Yet it would be hard to deny that these moral theories lacked the soul-wrenching insights and norm-shattering reflections that might have served to heal the past century's traumas and to expose the tragically recurring blind spots in racist, ethnocentric, and normalizing European bureaucracies and cultures. After these failures, and profound soul-searching, post–World War II poststructuralists would turn, not to building new systems of morality, but to clearing the ground for the sake of an approach geared toward witnessing and listening to the claims made upon us by a docile, vulnerable, and, too often tragically, opaque Other. This Other, whose "alterity" or otherness in its distinct and unique singularity necessarily eludes the abstractions and misrecognitions of what Europeans have variously defined as the "reasonable" or "rational," appears in the work of Levinas through the figurative language of the Hebrew Scriptures as "the stranger, the widow, and the orphan."[21] This postmoral ethical orientation, as an ethic of eros in contrast with modern or classical philosophical ethics based on logos, turns attention from self-legislating reason and moral judgment to the pathos of the vulnerable Other. A response to the Other's ethical claims aimed to replace not only modern self-legislating reason but also classical virtue ethics' self-discipline and self-cultivation as the proper site for ethics. For response ethics, the direct and compelling source of obligation is not rational principle, individual preference, or character virtue, but the overpowering draw of the vulnerable other and is *erotic* in this nonreductive and nonsexual use of this ancient Greek term. Eros names a desire larger than the self.

If autonomy, moral law, and individual rights are key to modern moral theory, postmoral response ethics is an "ethics of response-ability," as Kelly Oliver explains in *Animal Lessons: How They Teach Us to Be Human* (2009).[22] Yet, while Levinas's original formulation of response ethics offered a profound challenge to the rationalist bias of modern moral theory, ironically, it dismissed our animal others as lacking sufficient otherness for ethical status. Modernists viewed animals as too different from us to merit full moral consideration, but early response ethics pronounced animals not other enough. Once again philosophers had failed to cross the species barrier. As Oliver explores in her groundbreaking critique, it was not until Derrida turned poststructuralism against its lingering humanist prejudices that the prevailing winds began to shift and paths opened for a multispecies ethics of response-ability.

Derrida's critique of the concept of the self (or "the subject") and its capabilities set in motion a centrifugal ethics that would unmask the ruses of the West's "carnophallogocentrism." His deconstructive attack on *carno*centrism "points to the impossibility of the sovereign subject of Western philosophy's 'I can'," whether it is the 'I can' of "I can train the others/animals' or of the 'I can love the others/animals,' which amount to the same thing if love is a matter of knowing, understanding, sovereignty, individuality, autonomy, possession, mastery, law—those values at the center of the Cartesian subject, not to mention Western ideals of citizenship, rights, morality, and politics."[23] The carnophal*logo*centric mix of traditions that have come to mark "the West" hark back to the classical Greek metaphysics of reason and language, *logos*, as the marker of superior moral status. Like animals, women too have been associated with inferior moral status by the *phal*logocentric pairing of maleness with reason. A relentless receptivity to others aims to resist any presumption that one can understand and thereby judge based in the last analysis on culturally limited and pseudological grounds. (Recall that in the poststructuralist analysis there is no concept or logic for ethics or politics that is not deformed by blind spots and epistemological distortions.)[24] Response ethics resides in a nonjudgmental stance of generosity and compassion. Still, Oliver warns, human "love" for animals has proven to be just as dysfunctional as Cartesian rationality. Any genuine ethics requires vigilance along with a generous response: "We cannot rest in our quest to love or give. . . . Vigilance requires questioning our history, our motivations, our sense of ourselves as sovereign agents in pursuit of these goals."[25]

Despite his animal-friendly reformulation of response ethics, however, Derrida retreats from science's provocative and radical new claims for a biological continuum between human and nonhuman animals.[26] Thousands of years of metaphysical prejudice—a chasm between the human and nonhuman arose only after the Neolithic revolution—recurs in Derrida's deconstructive project.[27] In contrast, Maurice Merleau-Ponty's underexplored suggestion, from his posthumously published lectures on nature, "that human consciousness is just one type, theme, or style of behavior among others" risks a "strange continuity" among human and nonhuman animals.[28] A phenomenological approach, once left behind by poststructuralists and their linguistic turn, recalls that experience occurs not primarily through the cognitive and linguistic capacities that set humans apart from other animals but through bodily and sensory immersion in a partly shared world.[29]

Merleau-Ponty enlists music metaphors to propose an "attunement" between creatures and their habitats (or *Umwelt*, understood as the perceptual world of a species).[30] He offers a romantic vision of nature's "melody singing itself" as a seductive counterpoint to Aristotle's classical depiction of the universe as a "god thinking itself."[31] "Already in the animal, in the ceremony of love, desire is not mechanical functioning, but an opening to an *Umwelt* of fellow creatures (possibility fixation on others), communication," as the published lecture notes indicate in abbreviated form.[32] This romantic *mythos* of a primordial *eros* (Merleau-Ponty likewise uses the Greek term for overpowering desire) evokes oceanic forces of a symbiotic world and projects a unified origin where all creatures are part of one flesh.

But this dreamlike life world does not provide all the ethical guideposts required to work through the wrenching drama of cross-species conflict and alliance. It does not explore the layers of subjectivity and intersubjectivity found in a comic social attunement or in tragic, political overreach within and across animal communities. And it does not foreground the agency and communication required for a biopolitical ethics of human and nonhuman animal solidarity. Any romance of cosmic attunement can be spiritually regenerative and politically revolutionary (chapters 4 and 5), but the agonistic politics of the rough-and-tumble social field of interspecies life requires as well a critical pragmatic approach (chapters 1, 2, and 3).

Key to this critical pragmatic approach is the role of affect-laden, but not necessarily irrational or noncognitive, attunement for the clusters or communal associations that compose a biosocial network. The unexpected

INTRODUCTION

agencies and communicative powers of creatures who may share overlapping habitats, histories, or communal structures with coevolving other species point beyond generosity or compassion to a more ordinary dynamic of "call and response." The horizontal reciprocity in this antiphonal calling, rather than the sublime verticality of compassionate response, articulates an ethical charge in the mundane ebbs and flows of biosocial communities. Antiphonal musical and singing patterns, well known in hip-hop, blues, jazz, gospel, and African American working songs, have a long history in sub-Sahara African cultures, where the call-and-response rhythm structures democratic participation in musical choruses, civic discussion, or religious rituals. Ethical and political insight into the rhythmic, tonal, or gestural patterns of animal communication can take cues from another front—well-established research on affect attunement among human infants and adults.[33] The claims of this psychological research cannot resolve the concerns that have turned poststructuralists away from theories of ethics and justice based on reciprocity to an exclusive focus on generosity or compassion for the stranger or outcast. My intent is not to set aside alterity ethics, but to join the vertical vector of this profoundly quasi-religious ethics and potentially revolutionary politics to the ordinary, horizontal practices that generate social codes and expectations for reciprocity and fairness within multispecies communities.

Any communitarian resituating of response ethics into histories and agencies rooted in communicative exchange will require critical vigilance against imperialist, predatory, and neoliberal modes of power. As response ethicists insist, the singularity of other persons or of creatures from other species brings attention to the need for engaging those who are far removed from ourselves in their sensibilities and biocultures and who may initially strike us as not only strange or inconsequential, but as disgusting or ridiculous and as ready targets of deadly neglect or annihilation. Moreover, social and political hierarchies, which structure human and nonhuman societies, inevitably warp perceptions of fairness and distort the registers of attunement or communicative technologies. These concerns no doubt prompt response ethics' appeal to the transcending force of compassion. Only through the transcendence of everyday life might one respond to strange or freakish ethical claims beyond the ordinary meanings of community or social attachment.

Still, the ordinary ethics of everyday life is a bit more nuanced than we might first think. Studies of the call-and-response exchanges between adults and infants demonstrate possibilities for reciprocity among those who are severely unequal or mismatched in agency and social power, and far from commensurate in cognitive and linguistic skills or in motives and desires. This social dynamic illustrates how adult humans can interact with an infant creature that lacks adult cognition or even a preliminary sense of self and yet asserts without fail biosocial claims to which adults may or may not appropriately respond. These infant-adult social exchanges point toward the possibility for communicative exchanges across a significant range of nonhuman species.

In particular, Daniel Stern, influenced by Silvan S. Tomkins, offers a concrete analysis of social engagement in the development of self and self-awareness among infants.[34] Specific features that Stern observes in adult-infant encounters can be viewed as structuring aspects of trans-species interactions as well (chapter 3). Stern borrows from poetic discourse the term *correspondence* to account for the attunements of nonverbal "proto-conversations." The poetic term highlights the (nonmirroring because non-imitating!) resonance of meanings communicated across distinct sensory modes, such as between a vocal sound and a physical gesture or a color and a sound. Proto-conversations may occur through the body below the level of awareness and without any necessary mediation through adult human cognition or language. These well-observed patterns establish a basis for cross-species communication and, thus, for ethical rapport without assuming the presence of human language and conceptual thought or even what we modern, adult humans would likely call a self.

The multimodal poetics of social attunement does not rely on mirroring, mimicry, or shared identity between conversation partners and thus serves to account for aspects of trans-species communication and shared perspective beyond modern moral theory's thin social glue of mimetic empathy or cold reason.[35] The modern formula of reason plus or minus empathy contributes but does not suffice to hold together complex societies. Moreover, the recurring binary of emotion versus reason reinforces other related binaries such as subject versus object, active versus passive, self versus other, and individual versus community. Chapter 4 argues that the mirror metaphor central for modernist theories of empathy as well as for conventional scientific and philosophical tropes of self-recognition should be replaced by attunement and resonance metaphors. The attunement metaphors, as used by phenomenologists, break out of the Cartesianism that lingers in modernity's active subject/passive object and sameness/difference binaries.

When the infant and adult are engaged in a song and dance of a playful exchange or irritated struggle, the one partner does not merely imitate or observe the other as a quasi-object. The social interplay opens as each partner feels its way into the experience of the other and responds through its own singular style. Encounters with other persons are not ontologically experienced as abrupt intrusions on, and discontinuous with, an originally asocial, prelinguistic, disorganized, or narcissistic and animalistic infant (as variously assumed by poststructuralists, modernists, and classical philosophers throughout the Western tradition).[36] For social animals, these everyday social encounters do not function to call (i.e., "hail" or "interpellate" in poststructuralist terms) the previously or hypothetically animalistic, asocial infant into the uniquely human world of language, intersubjectivity, and social alienation. Encounters among social animals with or without what humans term language are not essentially alienating processes that introduce an alterity abyss or ontological gap between human and other. The "call-and-response" vibe (to borrow a locution from Africana culture) lives and breathes in the consonant or dissonant dynamic of communicative exchanges. Through this vibe, the nonverbal, perhaps, but profoundly social animal may be vulnerable (like the infant), but is capable nonetheless of signaling desires. The communication of affects can be creative and expressive of diverging sensibilities and establishes a vital process for asserting agency and demanding acknowledgment and response. Call and response (more centrally than self-legislated autonomy or dependent vulnerability) should be understood as tracing the everyday dynamic of biosocial ethics.[37]

This insight culled from child development theory and phenomenological studies of affect attunement is crucial for understanding cross-species communication. If we human primates were to assume that a monkey's smile mirrored the function of our own, we would miss an opportunity to engage with this fellow creature beyond sentimental, mirroring projections of human styles and affects onto this other species. Primatologist Frans de Waal provocatively explains the dangers of an uninformed, as distinct from an informed, "anthropomorphism":

> Naturally, we must always be on guard. To avoid making silly interpretations based on anthropomorphism, one must always interpret animal behavior in the wider context of a species' habits and natural history. Without experience with primates, one could imagine that a grinning rhesus monkey must be delighted, or that a chimpanzee running toward another with loud grunts must be in an aggressive mood. But primatologists know from many hours of observation that rhesus monkeys bare their teeth when intimidated, and that chimpanzees often grunt when they meet and embrace. In other words, a grinning rhesus monkey signals submission, and a chimpanzee's grunting often serves as a greeting. A careful observer may thus arrive at an informed anthropomorphism that is at odds with extrapolations from human behavior.[38]

A romantic metaphor portraying an original animal submersion in a dreamlike world of musical harmony conjures up the specter of what traditional psychoanalysts would term a primary narcissism. For the most part (although not necessarily in all cases), this specter may be more projection than real. Such a specter may well account for energy flows and mystical experiences (chapter 4), but does not give full play to the conflicting desires and syncopated rhythms that regularly puncture animal societies. Our everyday life world does not ordinarily pose humans or other species as folds of a single flesh, but as distinct subjective agencies in uneasy alliances through networks of overlapping habitats and contested terrains. Merleau-Ponty's phenomenological approach may lack specific insights into animal political ethics.[39] Still, his attention to music metaphors prepares the stage for a multispecies communitarianism with cosmopolitan yearnings.

INTRODUCTION

A critical pragmatic approach to the motley ethics of everyday life borrows freely not only from phenomenological and poststructuralist approaches to strange kinships and animal vulnerabilities (David Abram, Ralph Acampora, Matthew Calarco, Leonard Lawlor, Patrick Llored, Eduardo Mendieta, Kelly Oliver, Peter Steeves, Chloë Taylor, Ted Toadvine, Cary Wolfe) but also from the Nietzschean-inspired "becoming-animal" wing of posthuman ethics (Rosi Braidotti).

FROM BECOMING-ANIMAL TO AFFECT CLOUDS OF BIOSOCIAL NETWORKS

"Becoming-animal" is for post-Nietzscheans Gilles Deleuze and Felix Guattari and posthuman ethicist Rosi Braidotti the route out of a cramped capitalist culture of abstract modern life. Modern lives, these provocateurs argue, are caught in what earlier Freudo-Marxist critical theorists such as Herbert Marcuse diagnosed as emotionally draining cycles of a guilt-driven compulsion to work and the consumer's allure of easy pleasure in owning and playing with things. Deleuze and Guattari update the critique by exposing capitalism's newest ruses for restricting desire production to the private property relations and the melancholic attachments of productivity machines.[40] This critique sounds a warning against conforming to work habits and personality structures through which citizens of the overdeveloped world are shaped as productive and valued, perhaps, but chronically anxious subjects. On the contrary, these post-Nietzschean daredevils open the prospect of breaking polymorphous eros out of structure, organization, and hierarchy in the worse kind of way. They hold out for an alternative life course, one in which we roll with the animals right into their zones of intensities.[41]

Donna Haraway, however, is not impressed with these animal antics, and in part for good reason. She explains in her book *When Species Meet* that the reckless bohemian abandonment of the confines of quotidian society never in fact accounts for any real encounter with other species.[42] Deleuze and Guattari treat the totem of animality as an inducement, if not to go native, at least to find layers of existence disruptive of social traps. They map these disruptions onto polymorphous preoedipal energies that are said to fuel animal desire, but that, in fact, as even they admit, tend toward impersonal forces of destruction and death. If Freud saw no way out of repressive cultural and personality structures to hold in check these brutal impulses for the sake of "peaceful civilization," Deleuze and Guattari find in deathbound drives a wildly liminal experience that amplifies the intensity of (sub)human life. Haraway's critique of Deleuze and Guattari is central for interspecies ethics as encountering and living with real others. Nonetheless, the intensities of affect beneath, beside, and superseding the self or the subject open pathways, not merely for disrupting subjectivity and society, as Deleuze and Guattari thought, but also for tapping into their biosocial core.

"Affects," in contrast with "feelings" or "emotions," here refer to waves that sweep across a biosocial field and not properties or states interior to bound subjects or nonporous bodies.[43] Contagious laughter, rage, or panic may be presubjective, but they are not asocial phenomena. These affects function as biosocial signals and shape the desire (eros) for attachment and social networks; they account for aspects of trauma that can disturb interspecies relationships across individuals and generations, as witnessed in elephant society. In interspecies habitats, waves of affect, for good and bad, spread through refracted networks of conceptually incommensurate perhaps, but nonetheless co-responding biosocial fields. Fear and disgust we animals smell, and why not also joy?[44] The post-Nietzschean provocation to become-animal throws off vital, burdensome dimensions of companionship or communal structure, but it brings attention to the waves of affect that cross species barriers and compose a tacitly biosocial scene.

Waves of affect, or "affect clouds," have been identified in any number of nonhuman species, including birds. Natalie Angier reports for the *New York Times* what might be called a journalistic sensation: "Recent research reveals that birds have a nose for news after all, that people are deeply affected by odors in ways they often are not consciously aware of, and that one class of odor that is likely to impinge on both humans and birds is the scent of a fellow's despair."[45] The chemicals in the sweat of a distressed creature signal fear to others, who respond with increased anxiety. These negative affects can spread like wildfire, casting onto entire cultures or societies a paranoid style or a virtually untreatable cultural malaise. Anxiety and paranoia, or the exaggerated perception of threats, psychologist Jonathan Haidt notes, are easily triggered in the human animal: "Most people's minds have a bias toward seeing threats and engaging in useless worry."[46] These readily triggered affects are agencies of social change and political movements. They can migrate within and, in all probability, across some unknown range of species boundaries.[47]

A climate of negative affect has saturated modern elephant and human societies with harsh social and political consequences. Bradshaw explains the "dramatic disruption of indigenous cultures by colonization—a disruption passed through successive generations and transmitted across species from human to elephant and back again to human, like a virus. Traumatic disruption takes on a life of its own, becomes a culturgen, redrawing a perceptual and moral baseline to define culture itself. . . . Cultural trauma replaces traditional ritual and leaves 'indelible marks upon their group consciousness, marking . . . memories forever.'"[48] Elephant society is normally oriented toward fostering affiliation through social rituals and events such as greetings, celebrating births, rites of passage of adolescents into adult society, and the mourning of the dead.[49] Matriarchs communicate to their affiliates through antiphonal calls and responses.[50] Ricocheting cycles of harm brought on by social trauma have been the tragic legacy of human societies in the wake of colonization. Now we know that the malaise spreads across interlocking human and nonhuman animal societies.

A post-Freudian celebration of preoedipal energies alone seems unlikely to heal these wounds. Haidt offers a refreshing set of insights into the unconscious eros that breaks out of the oedipal mythos by sidestepping it all together.[51] As he and others explain, Freud's first premise, that unconscious desire is incestuous, is a problem given that the social taboo against incest is not uniquely human, but found quite naturally in many animal societies.[52] Moreover, an oedipally oriented sexual desire can hardly explain the tender bond between a child and its parent for any mammal, including what some might describe as the sexually obsessive bonobo. Freud's postulated death wish likewise seems more a configuration of the modern imaginary and traumatized societies than an inevitable reality. But Haidt agrees with Freud and his followers that affect-laden motives and desires account for behavior while operating mostly behind the back of consciousness and apart from rational control.

Theorists of the psyche all the way back through the Axial Age have overvalued our intellectual capacities to the detriment of the unconscious processes and social connections that impact ethical well-being and moral decision making. As Haidt recounts, Plato's dialogue *Phaedrus* represents the structure of the conflict-ridden psyche through the image of a charioteer driving two horses. The charioteer symbolizes the capacity of reason (logos) to control good and bad desires (eros) as represented by the two harnessed horses. The spirited horse seeks honor and suffers from the shame and outrage of insults or other acts of what the Greeks called *hubris*, while the simple pleasures of food, drink, and sex drive the unruly horse. Note that among the pleasure centers, something so basic and simple as the tender need for touch, as a nonsexual element of eros, is absent. Note as well that the depiction of the psyche through the image of the rational driver and his horses has a long legacy with many variants, including Freud's theory of the id, superego, and ego.

Haidt challenges this age-old story by insisting that the "rational" self is in fact driven by those horses, not the other way around, and that the unconscious affects and desires that drive us do not (contra Freud) typically lead us astray. On the contrary, after a long evolutionary process, these horses pretty much know where to take us. In this sense, the unconscious processes operate, not like wild horses, but like a large and intelligent elephant with a relatively tiny rider attached to its back, Haidt suggests. The image of the tiny rider emphasizes the limited powers of conscious reasoning. Haidt's point is that while our rider-self might discipline some aspects of our unconscious elephant-self, we cannot rely very heavily on reason or verbal control to direct where our elephant-self takes us. Our higher-level cognitive processes may nudge the elephant here and there, but cannot command it. For the most part, our rider-self does well to trust the elephant's lead. Typically, we have little choice.

Yet, I think, the elephant metaphor should prompt us to remember what elephants never forget—that we social animals dwell not alone but in herds. "Recall a herd of them is, in essence, one incomprehensibly massive elephant: a somewhat loosely bound and yet intricately, interconnected, tensile organism."[53] In that shift—from Plato's charioteer and Haidt's single elephant to the elephant herd—lies the "between" of the interconnected organism, and the ground for ethical life.[54]

Imagining ourselves not merely like, or at one with, but also interconnected with other animal species is the final aim of this project. Elephants suffer not just from pain but also from assaults on their tribal structures. They thrive in a communal atmosphere, but they can also exhibit hospitality to strangers. Traumatized elephants seek revenge on innocent tourists and villagers or other bystander species. But, normally, elephants are careful to target retaliation against those specific individuals who have violated them. In short, elephants serve not just as tropes for the embodied soul. They are fellow creatures. Deleuze and Guattari's trope of becoming-animal flattens social encounters; however, zones of intensities unfurled in waves of vital affect or weighed down by heavy clouds of despair compose the biosocial landscape upon which these encounters ride.

TRANS-SPECIES COMMUNITARIANISM

In a remarkable essay, "Unspeakable Things Unspoken" (1988), Toni Morrison describes her struggle as a writer to capture the convulsive rhythms of communities under assault.[55] The social dynamic of community that structures African American culture may barely register in modern moral theory. However, Morrison discovers, it rings out loud and strong in ancient Greek drama and the communitarian religions and philosophies of Africa.[56] That "intense connectedness" provides the backdrop for the deep social vein of pushback against violation brought forth in the civil rights movement, and, more broadly, in what Patricia Hill Collins describes as the "visionary pragmatism" of the African diaspora.[57] During the 1960s, this spirit of connectedness reappeared in youth movements through the utopian ideals lived out in communes. Today these ideals, long ago heard through the Marcusean refrain "the fight for life, the fight for *Eros*, is the political fight," sound a mythic note of a bygone era. And yet the old revolutionary politics of eros lingers on in appeals from contemporary social groups such as the anti–Wall Street anarchists.[58] Now the pragmatic vision of connectedness takes on a new turn with the growing call for interspecies ethics and relational justice.[59]

Collins returns us to a classic essay by Audre Lorde, "The Uses of the Erotic" (1978), to pursue further Morrison's insights for an ethics of connectivity.[60] Collins explains that Lorde theorized that oppressive social systems "function by controlling the 'permission for desire'—in other words, by harnessing the energy of fully human relationships to exigencies of domination."[61] Collins locates this conception of oppression, and, by implication, a corresponding idea of social freedom, in Morrison's novel *Beloved*. In a central scene of the novel, a freed slave, after recalling his experiences on a chain gang in Georgia, declares that he knows what it means to be free: "to get to a place where you could love anything you chose—not to need permission for desire—well, now, *that* was freedom."[62] Collins explains that "freedom from slavery meant not only the absence of capricious masters and endless work but . . . the power to 'love anything you chose.'"[63] This power to love is not understood through the overly sexualized or sentimental conceptions that prevail in modern culture. This love is an "erotic" capacity for creative work and meaningful bonds that supersede both sexuality and subjective sentiments in external sources of identity. As Lorde notes, "the very word *erotic* comes from the Greek word *eros* personifying creative power and harmony."[64] Modern legal and moral debate anchored in theories of autonomy focus on the damage that oppression does to the individual's capacity to reflect and to make rational choices for himself, and no doubt oppression can and does inflict this kind of harm. The modern account, however, obscures the damage that oppression can do on the erotic energy at the self's biosocial core.

Still, Lorde, writing in the political climate of the 1970s, and under the sway of Marcusean critical theory and the sexual revolution, analyses libidinal sources of energy that fall short of the communal structures Morrison labors to portray in her novels. In the essay "Home" (1997), Morrison cautions that the "driving force of the narrative [of her novel *Beloved*] is not love . . . [but] something that precedes love, follows love, informs love, shapes it, and to which love is subservient."[65] The contrast between love and what precedes love indicates what is missing both from the free expression of the libido (Lorde) and, perhaps, from the unrestricted energies and intensities of becoming-animal (Deleuze and Guattari, Braidotti). Collins glosses freedom as "the power to 'love anything you chose,'" and yet Morrison had not written the word *power*. Morrison's text reads: "a *place* where you could love anything you chose. . . . *that* was freedom (emphasis mine)." More than a creative power and an individual agency, although no doubt these as well, she writes of freedom as though it were a haunted but still living place. Eros is not a bare striving for pleasure or wild intensity, but a meaning-laden yearning. Eros is a drive toward home.[66]

In earlier work, I explored the meaning of this drive for home beyond the context of the modern family, a context that flattens the role of the mother, the agency of the child, and the adventure of social life.[67] In this dull story, a passive mother nurtures a passive child. Its ethics of care secures the trust of a dependent for whom maturation equals separation and rational autonomy. This sentimental portrait of the home as a safe but uneventful place forecloses the social attunements and communicative structures that ground intersubjectivity for humans as well as for other species.[68]

The free-range habitats that biologists and environmentalists describe as necessary for animal well-being do not consist of shelter and nourishment plus sexual opportunities. "When we look through science's dark glass," Bradshaw observes, "the human-elephant conflict takes on a whole different meaning: aggression between the two species . . . is related through time and space with the disruption of *ancient social bonds*."[69] Similarly, the mad violence of an outraged species cannot be repaired apart from healing the breaches to social bonds that colonization, poaching, and civil war inflict on humans and other species. In her struggle against her homeland's devastation, Evelyn Abe is searching for clues from African stories and ancient sources of ecological knowledge on how modern African societies might restore the relationships that once existed between the Acholi people and elephants. Much of the old knowledge is gone, but rather than remain bereft of hope and vision, she insists: "Focus on the positive progression to old traditions of Acholi people and on the beauty of elephants and other animals that are not apart but PART and definitional to Acholi wellbeing."[70] In fact, there is some basis for hope amidst the continual devastation, Bradshaw observes: "Uganda shows signs of recovery. Camp residents [human and elephant] have started to return to their former homes. . . . Kampala [Uganda's capital] has acquired an air of energy and viability."[71]

These ancient sources resonate well with recent paradigm shifts in biology, neuroscience, and cognitive ethology.[72] The hubristic assault that punctured the bonds of community and of hospitality to strangers in ancient drama reappears as a biosocial phenomenon. What tragedians portray as the spiraling tragic cycles passed down from one generation to another finds supporting scientific evidence from research on the inheritance of trauma through the epigenetics of gene expression.[73] As "symbionts," part of a somewhat loosely bound and yet intricately interconnected, tensile organism, we either heed the "ecologies of all mortal beings, who live in and through the use of one another's bodies" or suffer, as Haraway warns.[74]

Animal species have developed "moral codes," which, along with ethologist Marc Bekoff, we struggle to translate into modern, human discourse. Bekoff writes that "the proper behavior of a person in society . . . [is known as] manners. In its most basic form, morality can be thought of as 'prosocial' behavior . . . and it exists as a kind of webbing or fabric that holds together a complicated tapestry of social relationships."[75] Yet the codes for this tapestry bear ethical weight and in this way differ from what we modernists conventionally call manners. At the same time, these codes spin complicated patterns of a communitarian and cosmopolitical ethos that similarly elude the abstraction of moral laws.

Pre-Socratic Greek tragedies with their choruses of satyrs (tragedies originated in these choruses) capture aspects of this social tapestry, but the focus on individual virtue and character in classical and Hellenistic philosophy obscures them. Aristotle's lectures on character and the *polis* (community) fail to elaborate upon the role of hubristic assaults and reconciliation ceremonies for community flourishing. Yet he does offer a tantalizing glimpse into an already attenuated trans-species ethos in his *History of Animals*. There he mentions in passing that natural forces are known to commit acts of hubris, as when animals wantonly destroy human crops.[76] Ancient drama depicts hubris as an assault and an insult on selves-in-communitis by the powerful. This drama warns of the excess of power and privilege accumulated by elites in a social realm warped by conflict and power differentials. In contrast, modern liberal law, aiming for a formal equality, abstracts from, rather than confronting, the sharp gradients in power that are ever the tragic source of blind arrogance. Ancient codes against hubris impose restraints on the asymmetries of power and provide rituals for reconciling differences through mourning and forgiveness, in this way differing from modern legal codes backed up by prison systems. They sustain home as a living place, tending the social fabric. Moreover, the ancient codes were acknowledged across species lines.

Clearly large-scale societies organized into state and corporate bureaucracies cannot fully reinstitute community-based forms of mediation for conflicts. Yet radically supplementing modern moral and legal theory with ancient communal practices of forgiveness and reconciliation would go far to redress the wounds ignored and exacerbated by modern legal and judicial processes on both domestic and international fronts. Modern processes, designed to yield moral judgments of right and wrong against individual agents, dismiss age-old practices for negotiating communal justice and restraining elites. Legal apparatuses and moral theory lack the symbolic rituals and communicative technologies that would heal species and inter-species divisions[77] and dampen the aftershocks of colonial and postcolonial tragedies that slosh across past and future generations.[78]

The raging elephants of Uganda are bent on a tragic cycle of destruction in which modern humans are implicated. Yet life is nothing if not resilient. Frans de Waal, who often finds himself enjoying the laughter of the chimpanzees outside the window of his office in the Yerkes National Primate Center in Atlanta, remarks that he cannot help laughing too.[79] Laughter, one of the most contagious of the affects, transmits its vital force across species. When laughter pops up unexpectedly, it can energize friendships as selves overflow their normal boundaries and spread out into the social field.[80] What does it mean when the laughter of chimpanzees overflows the boundaries of their captivity? Could this field of laughter signal home?

GUIDE TO THE CHAPTERS AND THE CODA

J. S. Mill showed little regard for the pig or the fool, but what does it mean if the subaltern can laugh back? Chapters 1, 2, and 3 take a comic detour around the politics of what Rosi Braidotti diagnoses as the "melancholic left."[81] The aim is to explore new idioms for multiplying agencies and solidarities across species, yet without leaving the tragic history of human exceptionalism far behind. Does the anarchic vision of an interspecies ethics through common laughter and social play renaturalize humans or spiritualize animals? Chapter 4 resoundingly responds yes to both sides of the equation as it slips outside the usual binaries to explore the magic of water and the ethical sublime among baboons, mystics, and anthropologists. Reflecting upon the horizontal and vertical dimensions investigated in previous chapters, chapter 5 offers a four-layer model of interspecies ethics. The coda closes with a musical vision of mourning and remembrance that might regenerate the eros of interspecies life.

CHAPTER 1. CAN THE ANIMAL SUBALTERN LAUGH?
NEOLIBERAL INVERSIONS, CROSS-SPECIES SOLIDARITIES,
AND OTHER CHALLENGES TO HUMAN EXCEPTIONALISM
(COAUTHORED WITH JULIE WILLETT)

Animals not only suffer from acts of cruelty but also assert a sense of their own defiant agency that at times takes a turn toward the comic. Might a shared capacity for friendship and laughter take us beyond witnessing vulnerable animal others and toward an everyday politics of solidarity instead? Histories of interspecies communities resisting unfair labor practices expose sources of oppression and shared world-making outside humanist categories.

INTRODUCTION

CHAPTER 2. PALEOLITHIC ETHICS: ETHICS' EVOLUTION FROM PLAY, THE INTERSPECIES COMMUNITY SELECTION HYPOTHESIS, AND ANARCHIC COMMUNITARIANISM

A November 2011 tabloid headline reads: "Occupy Wall Street animals go wild . . . ZOO-cotti," to which this chapter responds: why not reclaim for our human selves the animal trope, literally rather than just figuratively? The comical subversion of authority, and festive celebrations of solidarity, can be observed across animal species. Studies of social play among carnivores pose an evolutionary origin for ethics and an evolution-based argument for the continued relevance of anarchic communitarianism across species.

CHAPTER 3. AFFECT ATTUNEMENT: DISCOURSE ETHICS ACROSS SPECIES

Donna Haraway calls for a cosmopolitical trans-species ethics. But then on what biosocial basis might we tap into communicative capacities in a world that we inhabit together with other species? This chapter explores this question through preliminary clues from well-established research on the responsive, preverbal "proto-conversations" between human infants and adults. Social attunement, more powerfully than mirroring empathy, explains the communication of affects within communities and across diverse species.

CHAPTER 4. WATER AND WING GIVE WONDER: MEDITATIONS ON COSMOPOLITAN PEACE

An interspecies ethics flips the claim of human exceptionalism several times on its head. Here we consider not only our own species' animality but also the culture, technology, history, humor, and, finally, the sacred experiences discovered across a range of species. A meditation on worldly peace begins with an excursion alongside wild baboons who, as witnessed by Barbara Smuts, display a sense of wonder before a river's still pools of water. From there we travel up and down the vertical vector of spiritual experience. The disgusting and the ridiculous at the bottom end of this vector turn out to

INTRODUCTION

bear as much ethical relevance as elevated experiences of moral beauty and the sublime for ourselves and other animals.

CHAPTER 5. REFLECTIONS: A MODEL AND A VISION OF ETHICAL LIFE

A four-layered model is offered for an interspecies ethics. (1) *Subjectless Sociality*: the contagion of an "affect cloud" across a social field meets with the singular responses of unique living creatures. (2) *Face-to-Face and other intersubjective modes of attunement and companionship*: playful encounters between creatures with different modes of self-awareness are a source for the codevelopment of a biosocial self. (3) *A Sense of Home*: social bonds are interwoven not only between companions but more profoundly in a biosocial space—a place inflected by memories, histories, technologies, and biocultures of meaning. (4) *Worldly Spirituality and Compassion for Strangers*: induced states in various species may loosen the mundane boundaries of selfhood and communal attachment and open up expansive visions of moral beauty and compassion for strangers and outcasts through symbols of freedom and peace.

CODA; OR THE SONG OF THE DOG-MAN: MOURNING IN J. M. COETZEE'S *DISGRACE*

Predation and death are sewn into the fabric of life, leaving difficult questions unanswerable. How should we deal with the moments when death, tragedy, and unpardonable disgrace strikes? How do we respond to violation and destruction when the gods are dead, and play, affect-attunement, and communities are no longer possible? The coda turns to a moment of breakage when the world threatens to lose its meaning and exposes bare life to the cold exile of the absurd. South African Ubuntu communal ethics unexpectedly reappears at our story's end in the ancient ancestral bonds between an abandoned dog and a human protagonist.

1

CAN THE ANIMAL SUBALTERN LAUGH?

Neoliberal Inversions, Cross-Species Solidarities, and Other Challenges to Human Exceptionalism

There is a natural dislike of injustice.

—FRANS DE WAAL, *THE AGE OF EMPATHY*

If you tickle us, do we not laugh?

—SHAKESPEARE, *THE MERCHANT OF VENICE*

MONKEY BUSINESS

Could a comparative study of primates and other intelligent animals provide humans with that long-sought-after difference that makes us uniquely and superiorly human? Perhaps, but the big surprise is that studies of culture, technology, and communication within nonhuman animal species uncover ever more parallel capacities than expected.[1] Stephen Colbert's spoof on a monkey experiment currently underway illustrates the humor of endeavors to reestablish human exceptionalism, here in the context of the post-2007 recession: "Consumer spending is down and we're in danger of a crippling double dip recession. . . . But science has found the secret to getting this economy moving again: Monkeys!"[2] Colbert explains that a scientist has joined forces with an advertising firm to test whether capuchin monkeys trained to understand and use money will choose an advertised bowl of Jell-O over the other brand. This is, as the *New Scientist* headline proclaims, "the first advertising campaign for nonhuman primates" aimed to determine if commercialized images of female monkey genitalia and alpha males motivate consumer patterns among sub-apes.[3] As a member of the superior species, Colbert exclaims with mock earnestness that an advertising experiment exploiting the crass animal instincts of monkeys will teach us nothing about ourselves. Meanwhile, images of female lady parts pop up on a screen alongside a Diet Pepsi as Colbert ponders his "urgent reasons" for wanting the drink. To make sure that his human audience doesn't miss the punch line, a final image of Colbert appears with his own monkey grin gobbling down Jell-O as the all-revealing monkey vagina flashes in the background leaving us wondering who the real monkeys are.

When it comes to monkey see and monkey do, we turn to our own comic mix of philosophical reflection, animal studies of emotions, and histories of solidarities that cross species divides. Nonhuman animals are assumed not only in Western myth but also in our science and philosophy to be above all else inferior to humans, having been constructed as passive, ahistorical, unfeeling, or unthinking, but inevitably lacking Western, colonial, or, more recently, neoliberal virtues.[4] Throughout this post-Paleolithic history, social stratification and cultural exclusion have often entailed projecting demeaning or monstrous animal imagery onto the subaltern. Rituals of humiliation that ridicule the other as subhuman animal are primary devices for enforcing outsider or subordinate status.[5] Clearly humans have mastered the art of ridicule, and at nonhuman animal expense. But what would it mean if those very animals assumed to be the most proper vehicles of ridicule have the capacity to laugh? The association of animality with the subaltern provokes the thought that, perhaps like their human counterparts, animal subalterns might on occasion laugh back.[6]

Subaltern studies have established that ridicule and other forms of humor serve not only as accessories of cruelty and props of power but also provide discourses and technologies of reversal, leveling hierarchies by turning stratified structures upside down.[7] At the same time, animal studies have begun to document the capacity for laughter in primates, dogs, and even in the chirping of mice.⁸ Far from the uniquely human characteristic laughter has long been thought to be, primate mockery along with common forms of animal play reveal the means for an infrapolitics of cross-species outrage and solidarity. This cross-species defiance not only unsettles alpha male status but also provides spaces for egalitarian ecologies of belonging beyond our market-driven neoliberal consciousness.⁹

MESSING WITH THE MISSING LINK

Philosophers and scientists for too long have failed to question the question of what makes us uniquely and superiorly human. A popular scientific and philosophical approach is to insist on the superior cognitive or linguistic capacities of humans. An ironically illuminating variation of this kind of a claim is offered by Svante Pääbo, the world-renown head of the Max Planck Institute for Evolutionary Anthropology in Leipzig. Pääbo reflects upon the magnitude of his current projects in evolutionary genetics, including the sequencing of the genome of Neanderthal and engineering human protein in mice. These epoch-making exercises in what Foucauldian cynics call biopower have such imaginable sci-fi outcomes as making pets out of Neanderthals rescued from indenture as lab animals for Big Pharma (Hollywood-style *Rise of the Planet of the Apes* redux).¹⁰ In the eyes of Big Science, these biolicious projects are no less than "attempts to solve a single problem in evolutionary genetics, which might, rather dizzyingly, be posed as: What made us the sort of animal that could create a transgenic mouse?" This is how *New Yorker* author Elizabeth Kolbert's essay on Pääbo's ambitions restates the philosophical question about self-knowledge that has "been kicking around since Socrates and probably a lot longer."¹¹ Kolbert adds, "If it has yet to be satisfactorily resolved, then this, Pääbo suspects, is because it has never been properly framed. 'The challenge is to address the questions that are answerable,'" he informs Kolbert.

If only Socrates had thought of reframing his questions to his pumped-up interlocutors so that those Socratic questions could be answered! But then he was a pretty clever philosopher: asking only the questions that are answerable sounds like a good strategy for the scientist, but it could put the philosopher out of business. And, anyway, that so-called stingray Socrates, master of nothing except perhaps the unanswerable question, may well have been more of a ridiculing ironist than an earnest knower—the philosopher as stand-up comedian, debunking pretensions rather than proclaiming them. Such serious debunking is not, however, where Pääbo's admittedly astounding research aims to take us. If the philosophical question of what makes us human is to be framed around our allegedly unique or superior capacities—such as language, technology, or, for that matter, humor— Pääbo's restatement of the question seems in keeping with what serious-minded philosophers (Plato, Aristotle, Aquinas, Kant, and Hegel) and other straight-shooting seekers of knowledge have always sought to do—provide answers. And yet, as we shall see, Socrates's ironic style of questioning may spur a more stimulating approach to the age-old question "what is man?" This alternative approach leads not to ever more marks of distinction on behalf of man-the-alpha-ape but to a leveling of them.

The promise of Pääbo's work owes much to the continued successes of evolutionary genetics. Neanderthals—as our closest not-quite-human relative—share most of our genetic material with a significant exception, he explains, as he offers his own semitestable hypothesis as to what future investigations might find this exception to be: "By about forty-five thousand years ago, modern humans had already reached Australia, a journey that, even mid-ice age, meant crossing open water. Archaic humans like Homo erectus 'spread like many other mammals in the Old World,' Pääbo told me [Kolbert]. 'They never came to Madagascar, never to Australia. Neither did Neanderthals. It's only fully modern humans who start this thing of venturing out on the ocean where you don't see land." Of course, this adventure requires social collaboration in order to solve the problem of building the boat, Pääbo notes, all too briefly. But, then, collaboration may not, after all, provide the allusive answer to the question of what makes the human unique and superior. Pääbo continues: "'there is also, I like to think or say, some madness there. How many people must have sailed out and vanished. . . . Is it for the glory? for immortality? for curiosity? And now we go to Mars. We never stop.'" If the defining characteristic of modern humans is this sort of Faustian restlessness, then, by Pääbo's account, there must be some sort of Faustian gene. In short, for this geneticist the missing link between the human and nonhuman turns on madness.

ON TRAGIC OVERSTEP, ANIMAL SUFFERING, AND A TURN TOWARD SOCIAL COLLABORATION ACROSS SPECIES

That mythical gene—marking the human defiance of any limit and the definitive demise of rivals for planetary domination—sounds a note of tragic overstep. A nod toward anarchic merrymaking that mocks overreach instead of indulging in it could make for a more happy turn. The tragic tone, however, certainly rings through any range of possible scenarios for our planet's immanent future as one shifts from the perspective of the human to the nonhuman animal upon whom the overstepping human steps. A heartrending glimpse from the empirical sciences is found in psychologist Gay Bradshaw's research on the changing relationships between humans and elephants in Africa and Asia (see introduction).[12] Recalling that these species once lived peacefully side by side, Bradshaw and others have begun giving serious study to reports of elephants in the forests of Uganda attacking human villages. These studies portray a species immersed in tight social webs of family and tribal communities that have been frayed by our own species' hubris.[13] Orphaned adolescent males stripped of boundary-setting social regulation developed through the collaborative ties of elephant communities are left to run rogue, and, with intentional brutality, they express their trauma and outrage by violating and killing members of their own or other species.

Most of the current work in animal ethics aims to generate sympathy for the undeniable and often monstrous suffering of vulnerable creatures and for the demise of entire species threatened with mass extinction.[14] The range of ethical approaches is diverse, but two of the most influential stem broadly from 1) the poststructuralist approaches currently at the core of continental response ethics and significantly advanced by Jacques Derrida's reflections on animal alterity and 2) the reformist Anglophone literature that has philosophical roots dating back to Jeremy Bentham's late-eighteenth-century utilitarianism and to mid-eighteenth-century sentimental moral traditions associated with David Hume, Adam Smith, and the Scottish Enlightenment. We will not take either of these kinds of approaches although both have much to offer and we borrow from aspects of them throughout this study.

The moral challenge of utilitarian and sentimental traditions to the "heartlessness" of scientific rationalism and the classical liberal state is illustrated by Susan Pearson's study of the rise of "sentimental liberalism" in nineteenth-century America.[15] Enlightenment rationalism and classic liberalism, under the influence of thinkers such as René Descartes and John Locke, displaced older conceptions of animals and humans as part of the warp and woof of communal life. Recall ancient Greek festivals, where the sacrifice of a pig would invoke the ritual of dripping water on the pig's head to solicit a nod of consent.[16] The forced consent was symbolic, of course, but nonetheless offers a glimpse into a fading pre-Neolithic interspecies culture and life that lingered in pockets of Europe until the seventeenth century.

In medieval Europe, wild as well as domesticated animals were treated by legal and ecclesiastical authorities as members of the parish community. That the rights of animals paralleled those of humans was demonstrated in numerous instances of court trials across every region of Europe. Humans and animals could be tried together for such criminal violations as bestiality, with animals having their own legal representatives at public expense.[17] In one case, a donkey was defended as innocent of illicit sexual acts and hence a victim of rape based on an "honorable character."[18] Even animals that were accused of murder could be successfully defended when they were known to have suffered considerable abuse.[19] Invasive pests were not exterminated but guaranteed parcels of land in court decisions based on a theological argument of original ownership and prior claim.[20] Then, half a century after Montaigne wrote against the cruelty of animals, and of the joys of shared human and animal friendships despite chronic failures of miscommunication,

Descartes prepared for their use as resource material in the industrial revolution by pronouncing them machines.[21] As subrational creatures, classical liberalism stripped animals of the rights and fellowship they had once enjoyed in mixed species communities.

Pearson's research demonstrates how a moral discourse of sentiment and sympathy won out over the short-lived radical egalitarian ideals of the Reconstruction era. This sentimental discourse was used to challenge modernity's harshest abuses through the rhetoric of care and protection for dependents. An appeal to the shared capacities for suffering rather than agency and communal membership prepared the public to reconcile the dependency of nonrational animals and children with the claim that they were rights-bearing individuals deserving of legal or moral protection from harm despite their subrational status. Previously, the classic liberal doctrine of rights to property and the pursuit of liberty for rational and self-sufficient citizens had deemed children and animals as nonrational and unworthy of rights of their own. The promulgation of stories documenting the abuse of children and animal cruelty prompted a multitude of humane societies to agitate for the reinvention of the modern state from minimalist to interventionist. From the abolitionist through the Progressive eras, the state in alliance with private agencies was reconceived as a proper vehicle of protection rights for "beasts and babes."[22] These protection rights were granted based on the ability to feel and to suffer, not to reason, and on claims of a dependency status, not on claims for liberty or equality. While the reformist movements did not overturn the well-entrenched social hierarchies of the patriarchal family and the human/animal distinction, they did successfully appeal to public virtue and advocate for social policies that would ameliorate the abuses suffered within these vertical social structures.

The nineteenth-century utilitarian thinkers who came to the fore during this reformist time did not themselves appeal directly to sentiments nor believe that moral sentiments were the significant basis for moral appeal, as did the eighteenth-century thinkers Hume and Smith. Earlier modern philosophers of sentiment had challenged philosophical rationalism by arguing that the natural basis for moral judgments and action resided in subjective feelings or in impartial, moral sympathy alone. Utilitarian thinkers from Jeremy Bentham and John Stuart Mill to Peter Singer draw on rational principles (aka "cold" reason), not subjective feelings, in order to justify our uniquely human responsibilities to vulnerable or dependent creatures. Nonetheless, even for these thinkers, emotions and desires, and not solely the rational capacities of capable human adults, provide a solid ground for moral consideration. It is this shared focus on vulnerability and sentience that is central to the social movements of "sentimental liberalism" and that prevails in reformist discourse in the United States today.

The "cult of sensibility" in Anglo-American culture from the Abolitionist to the Progressive eras prepared a context for liberal reformers to shape a public discourse that would appeal to our sentiments and valorize our common human sympathy for the general welfare in ways that a narrow appeal to Enlightenment reason could not. Sentimental liberalism arose in response not only to particular acts of cruelty but to the impersonal brutalization and increasingly visible horrors of the industrial revolution. Its relevance has returned with the neoliberal intensification of animals' technological and industrial use, extended to biogenetic engineering as seen in cloning, genetic cross-breeding, accelerated growth through hormones, and the redefinition of the human as the creature able to create the transgenic mouse. After long decades in the twentieth century when animal rights movements lay dormant, this intensification of abuse on an ever more massive scale has prompted anglophone philosophical traditions to challenge once again the biopower of the food industry and animal research through an appeal to human sympathy for animal suffering and vulnerability.

The concern for the suffering and vulnerability of dependent creatures provides the moral ground for Martha Nussbaum's reworking of modern liberalism, and, in particular, of John Rawls's *Theory of Justice* (1971), in her *Frontiers of Justice* (2006). Nussbaum retools liberalism's classic aim of protecting individual liberty by incorporating nineteenth- and twentieth-century ideas of social equality in terms of minimal *capabilities* (among a list that include life, emotions, affiliation, and play) that should be guaranteed by the state and, moreover, extended to include animals, the disabled, and noncitizens.[23] While her proposal does not address the new studies of animal sociality and agency, and stops short of any consideration for the community life and biosocial networks that exceed individual agency, it extends liberal rights to the protection of minimal capacities and agencies of animals. The argument rests on an appeal to sympathy for the suffering of nonrational dependents, rather than on traditional liberal respect for the dignity of fully autonomous creatures. This "solution . . . requires people to have very great sympathy and benevolence, and to sustain these sentiments over time," she writes.[24] The paternalism that Nussbaum defends as the basis of justice for nonhuman animals assumes that they cannot themselves participate in developing or asserting ethical and social norms, let alone engage in acts of political solidarity. Any thought that they could is dismissed out of hand as "fantastic."[25]

The Scottish Enlightenment themes of suffering and sentiment central to Nussbaum's sentimentalist revision of twentieth-century liberal rationalism have also returned in contemporary scientific research on animal and human cognition. For example, citing David Hume, psychologist Jonathan Haidt argues that there is a sound scientific basis for viewing reason as the "slave of the passions" and that moral feelings (sometimes called intuitions) and empathy play pivotal roles in understanding human morality.[26] Meanwhile, the field of cognitive ethology dropped the knowledge bomb that threatens to radically alter the parameters for animal rights discourse. Research scientists such as Frans de Waal have established capacities for sympathy and moral feelings of fairness not merely in humans but also in nonhuman animals.[27] Animals too might have feelings of compassion perhaps even for humans.

Our challenge is to take these new scientific discoveries a step beyond philosophical modernism's binaries of reason and sentiment, based as they are on modern models of atomic individualism. If animals have agency, then what kind of infrapolitics do their societies reveal? What are the substantial ethical practices, customs, and structures (or, *Sittlichkeit*, to draw from the post-Hegelian social ontology of relations) that provide the social glue for their communities and families? Beyond modernist binaries—a subjective appeal to sentiment and sympathy or an objective appeal to abstract reason—we aim to explore the ethical norms that might emerge for collaborative efforts at interspecies living. While we support liberal and reform efforts to expand rights protecting animals against abuse, our starting point is not with vulnerability, dependency, and the compassionate concern for minimal animal capabilities, but with maximum animal agency and communities. Animals are not like our children; they are like us. Our political aim is not ultimately a reform project for securing animal rights based on their protective status but to support cross-species solidarity with animal coworkers and co-inhabitants of interspecies communities. Animals are not vulnerable sites of protection and recipients of human sympathy, but kindred political agents in their own right with interlocking histories, cultures, and technologies. Given these aims and concerns, our method draws primarily from critical social theory rather than modern sentimental moral theory (see introduction). Critical theory's eros ethics aims not solely for the cultivation of individual feeling but for a social infrastructure that substantiates norms and expectations based significantly, but not exclusively nor inevitably, on cross-species codes of reciprocity.

Perhaps the strongest nineteenth-century challenge to the sentimental tradition's obscuring of the agency of those who dare to resist oppression is stated by Frederick Douglass.[28] Douglass explains to his white readership the limits of an ethical appeal to moral sentiments in the context of American slavery and abolitionism. White people could not generate sympathy for a slave unless that slave asserted some significant degree of agency and demanded, through that assertion of agency, recognition from others, he argued. For Douglass, that agency was staged as a call for solidarity and would eventually take shape as a catalyst for the abolitionist movement. A display of vulnerability and an appeal for sympathy do not suffice to generate the solidarity that an egalitarian political ethics requires.

Moreover, Douglass extended the range of his moral concern not only to the emancipation of all slaves everywhere and to nineteenth-century women's movements but also, implicitly, to nonhuman animals. Of course, any appeal to analogies across nonhuman and human species risks reinforcing the worse kind of prejudices against black identity in a white racist culture. And yet Douglass inverted conventional expectations as he proclaimed the agency of the slave in terms of his or her "animal spirits." He envisioned the free spirit of the slave symbolically as an uncaged animal and as a winged bird in flight (see chapter 4 for more on the key role of symbols in contrast with concepts for the moral sublime). Most significantly, Douglass joined his own struggle with those of the beaten-down ox or horse on the plantation, preparing the way toward a truly revolutionary form of worker solidarity. Douglass's prophetic brilliance stems from risking the very problematic association of blackness and animality to propose what may well have been this abolitionist's most radical challenge.

Through the nineteenth and twentieth centuries, abolitionist, feminist, and workers movements continued to challenge, if not entirely successfully, the classical liberal concept of rights. To varying degrees, new constitutions in Europe would recognize basic rights to social and economic equality. Then, after World War II, the struggle against European colonialism in Africa and elsewhere transformed the meaning and scope of rights, yet again, to include recognition of communal bonds (defined in part through those local languages important for a participatory democratic ethics) and environmental rights.[29] More recently, after several generations rethinking rights, there is now a growing movement to recognize the political rights of animal coworkers in interspecies communities.

VULNERABILITY AND SADNESS IN RESPONSE ETHICS

More recently, a second major ethical tradition, stemming from continental European philosophy, and associated with various approaches termed either response ethics or alterity ethics, has expanded its moral range to nonhuman animals. Like British and American sentimental liberalism, this tradition of continental European ethics draws our attention to the pathos of suffering as the source of moral concern, but in this context the brute torture and extermination occurring on a massive scale in slaughterhouses is viewed as parallel with the horrors of the Nazi camps, rendering it difficult to dismiss the relevance of the term *genocide*. Derrida asks us to ponder the grave implications of "a world without animals."[30] The tradition's predominantly tragic perspective on nature traces back to reflections of Frankfurt School critical theorist Walter Benjamin, which are central to Derrida's own influential work on animals.[31] Derrida's work in turn has inspired a plethora of more recent philosophical studies that aim to generate respect for a "strange kinship" between humans and nonhumans.[32] This post-Holocaust tradition of ethical orientation to the Other (or "alterity") is prompted by poststructuralist and psychoanalytic critiques of the self (or the "subject") and, on this basis, rejects any utilitarian or sentimental liberal assumptions regarding the transparency and universality of either emotions or reason. Rational argument, self-understanding, and empathetic rapport are viewed as entangled with unconscious desires, hegemonic discourses, or historical forces in such a way as to throw radically into question basic premises of classic liberal moral theory, which is anchored all too narrowly in individual autonomy, subject-centered agency, or subjective feelings. The poststructuralist critique is stunning and renders any attempt to return to a narrow anchor in self- or-other transparency and nonrelational human atoms naive. Yet, problematically, this post-Holocaust tradition threatens to dismiss *any* political notion of rights, even those rights that emerged after labor and anticolonial movements; and this is despite nineteenth- and twentieth-century political movements' only partly successful yet deeply important challenges to the narrow tenets of classic eighteenth-century liberalism.

The poststructuralist approaches of continental ethics join with Anglo-American traditions in their compassionate attentiveness to the pathos and suffering of creatures otherwise dismissed as of little or no moral worth, but emphasize not the shared sentience or minimal agency but the radical alterity of these creatures. Our project instead is to subvert assumptions in both traditions regarding any underlying ontological gap between the human and nonhuman species and to do so by recasting the predominately tragic frame of ethical reflection through a comic twist that features defiance and dissent. This route offers a playfully serious inversion of the tragic tone that prevails for good reason in the discussion of affects and animal ethics, but that nonetheless risks stripping nonhuman animals of their considerable agency and interconnected lives.

Consider how Derrida develops his own solemn ethical reflections on animal vulnerability by returning to Benjaminian motifs. Nature is,

Benjamin suspects, a melancholic place. Benjamin registers nature's sadness, as Derrida believes that he should, but only after inverting the more typical claim that nature is naturally mute. Benjamin speculates that nature is silent because of the cruel inflection of trauma upon it through human domination and assault. Derrida's commentary is complicated, but we quote extensively to highlight the sadness of the plant and animal world as the dominant tone that carries over into Derrida's own ethical stance: "What is already more interesting is that this putative sadness doesn't just derive from the inability to speak (*Sprachlosigkeit*) and from muteness, [but for Benjamin] from a stupefied or aphasic privation of words. If this putative sadness also gives rise to a lament, if nature laments, expressing a mute but audible lament through sensuous sighing and even the rustling of plants, it is perhaps because the terms have to be inverted. . . . nature (and animality within it) isn't sad because it is mute (*weil sie stumm ist*). On the contrary, it is nature's sadness or mourning that renders it mute."[33] In other words, for Benjamin, the nonhuman life world possesses a degree of communicative agency that has been suppressed through violence. Derrida does not question the predominantly melancholic tone; but he turns away from entertaining any hypothesis of agency in nature or among animals, preferring to draw attention to the constitutive vulnerability that we humans share with other creatures.

Derrida thereby shifts the ethical focus from any weak quivering agency overheard as a lament uttered by other creatures to the radical passivity, or incapacity, that for him is the more relevant concern for twentieth-century ethics. As a post-Holocaust thinker, he is suspicious of the search for any saving grace or redemptive meaning, in this case, from a communion with nature's creatures in the face of suffering, which he detects in Benjamin's moral reflections on nature. (Our coda returns to this theme of communion at the death of an animal to reaffirm its vital ethical significance.) Significantly, for Derrida, Benjamin wrote his essay on the origin of the human species and language in the 1920s before an awareness of the horrors of the Holocaust. After the Holocaust, for Derrida, any search for some residing good in humanity or meaning in nature would seem obtuse amidst revelations of the brutality and unrelenting horrors of the concentration camps.

Elisabeth de Fontenay elaborates upon Derrida and Benjamin's approaches to suffering. "According to Benjamin, mourning and the sadness of nature are related to this passivity, to this stupefying wound: to have received its name and thus to find itself deprived of the power to name, to name itself, and therefore to respond."[34] Benjamin views animal or even nature writ large as, once-upon-a-time, having had the capacity for communication or for generating their own sources of meaningfulness before these creatures were silenced by human technology and modern science. Derrida, in contrast, aims to stay clear of any seeming illusion of animal communication or mutual understanding, and in this sense he refrains, as he writes from "'giving speech back' to the animals."[35] Our concern is that Derrida's emphasis on the radical passivity, or constitutive incapacity, in human and nonhuman animals leaves unexplored the precious, if few, ethical possibilities for agency and communication that are reemerging in part through our science and technology.

Avoiding any element of communicative or social agency among those who have been violated, Derrida extends a poststructuralist ethics of hospitality, forgiveness, and response to the animal Other. This ethics of "response-ability" suspends any moral judgment of who owes what to whom, while thoroughly disengaging conceptions of agency (rational or otherwise) as a prerequisite for ethical status.[36] The sheer passivity, not the agency, of vulnerable creatures calls for a generous response. This ethical approach sets aside debates on the capacities (linguistic, cognitive, or otherwise) of other species as morally irrelevant. Derrida claims in this way to draw from Bentham, the patron saint of animal rights, who asked not if animals could reason or speak, but only if they could suffer.[37] While other philosophers following Bentham are attentive to the degrees and measures of (presumably inferior) capacity in other species in order to protect them from harm, the call for generosity aims paradoxically to "respond" to the ethical demands of creatures that we can never really understand.[38]

While acknowledging the surprising discontinuities among varieties of animal species, we offer yet another provocative inversion. Our inversion begins with Kelly Oliver's invitation to imagine whether or not nonhuman animals might be our kin.[39] Of course, any self-deceptive claim that we could render these animals our kin by prodding them into our all-too-human categories is likely to solicit not the love we imagine that we deserve but a fierce "biting back" against the hand that feeds them.[40] Yet, rather than listening for the sad lament of nature, we turn to the sometimes playful, sometimes subversive social exchanges within and between species that suggest a missing moral link and support a politics of solidarity.

A TIP OF THE HAT, WAG OF THE TAIL: ON HUMANS MISSING CUES FROM THEIR ANIMAL SERVANTS

So, what if the animal other can speak? Or, given that speaking seems to always involve the use of human language, let's rephrase the question in less speciesist terms: what if the nonhuman subaltern can communicate? After all, what is speech but an address to the other?[41] Recall that Gayatri Spivak's pivotal essay on the communicative capacities of the subaltern suggests that the servants of the British Empire could not speak at least in part because the colonialist frequencies were not tuned in to hear them.[42] In a similar vein, ontological gaps between the human and its others, or within the rest of the animal world, have been grossly exaggerated by a human failure to pick up on animal social cues, community formations, and possibilities of solidarity.[43] Just as historian Nancy Hewitt suggests that scholars might tune in on neglected women's movements and untold narratives by uncovering a wider band of radio waves heard at different frequencies than those familiar as first, second, and third wave feminism, we too embrace the concept of wave transmissions broadcasted beyond the range of human perceptions in Western cultures.[44] Not all cultures assume the discontinuities between human and nonhuman animals found in the mantra that man is the measure of all things.[45] Borrowing from feminism, we understand the need to make the invisible visible for our ocular species and to reexamine the sources of mixed species community building. A history that is radically inclusive can reveal a collective ethos outside of any neoliberal master narrative—say of advertising genius, alpha males, and lady monkey parts.

Keeping Colbert's spoof of monkeys and advertising in mind, we shift our ethical focus from the vulnerability of the animal other to neglected possibilities for cross-species solidarity enhanced by the communicative vibes of a collective ethos that testifies not only to various species' capacities to care for each other but also to laugh and play across enemy lines. Animals enjoy a communicative agency that enhances the possibilities for coresponsibility through what—in contrast with the call in Herbert Marcuse's 1966 preface to *Eros and Civilization* for the liberation of an admittedly narcissistic pleasure—could be understood instead as a politics of biosocial eros, and heard in emancipatory tones. Our biosocial eros ethics makes common cause with what utilitarian Peter Singer has called "animal liberation" in his 1975 manifesto, as it has been taken up in recent Occupy Wall Street and European social movements, but with a subversively comic twist.[46]

The animal subaltern's ability to "speak" is not a sci-fi moment as analogous to the moment when the human-engineered chimpanzee in *Rise of the Planet of the Apes* challenges his human captors, uttering the word *No*. Rather, this ability is documented data in animal studies.[47] Chimpanzees, elephants, and any number of species communicate—*with varying degrees of intentionality*—emotions and social cues that researchers tend to miss, much like those well-documented human cues missed by presumably oblivious chimpanzees. Such outdated experiments claim superior cooperative skills for the human species. But the question of whose cues are being missed seems far from clear.

Consider the experiments featured in the Nova National Geographic documentary *Ape Genius*.[48] While the film provides a fascinating glimpse into some of the new science on animals, the film's interpretative frame for the new discoveries is a problem. Research scientist Brian Hare demonstrates his failed attempts to teach a young bonobo to pick up a cup, without the film allowing for any larger questions regarding the relevance of how a human experimenter could be an effective teacher for bonobos, let alone for what we humans might learn not about but from other primates. For example, the experimenter attempts to teach the ape by pointing to the cup, which is a strategy known to be effective for teaching young human children. Human children attend to special features of objects after having those features pointed out with an index finger by a (human) teacher. They also exhibit a natural tendency not shared by other primates to point to objects. The experiment is part of a cluster that is used to establish that, while other primates can learn through imitation, only humans can learn by being taught. On the basis of similar evidence on the unique role of pointing for human learning, this time in contrast with chimpanzees, Michael Tomasello too hastily concludes: "Apes [i.e., all nonhuman apes] do not, in either gesture or vocalizations, intend to inform another of things helpfully."[49] His book on the capacities for social cooperation among humans dismisses significant evidence for the cooperation of animals within or across other species.

A major problem with these kinds of approaches and studies is that they assume that nonhumans are motivated to learn from someone of a different and disconnected species.[50] We know that when the teacher is of the same species animals learn quite well from each other. The elders of an elephant clan pass down crucial ecological and cultural knowledge as well as social ethics to the youth. A loss of an elder member through poaching or other disasters is experienced traumatically by other members and threatens the survival of the clan. It also threatens the general peace. The trauma of this loss, and the absence of the educative wisdom of elders, leads to adolescent rampages (as discussed in the introduction). Orphans who are raised outside their group by humans may be rejected when reintroduced to established elephant communities as they "commit unwitting trespass because they have not learned social etiquette."[51] The elephant "possesses an extremely large and convoluted hippocampus, the brain structures most responsible for mediating long-term social memory," Bradshaw explains.[52] In an interspecies community, elephants with their memories and attentiveness to oral cultures could serve as social historians.

Hasty claims for human superiority in cooperative capacities are made without any clear evidence that finger-pointing is the most significant way in which social learning occurs for nonhuman animals or, for that matter, for humans. (Chapters 2 and 3 examine the pedagogical function of tail-wagging and other features of play behavior.) From the fact that nonhuman animals do not use pointing, it is deduced that they do not engage in genuine social learning. However, as is noted, while apes do not ordinarily use pointing to communicate among themselves, in a pinch they can learn to point to make requests to humans. These requests exemplify cross-species social learning, pointing so to speak to the potential for a cooperative ethics crossing species lines—if oblivious humans would just tune in.

Tomasello claims that nonhuman apes are not generally helpful to others and thus are not socially cooperative, and thus unlike humans. He argues that nonhuman primates are like wolves and lions and are lacking social cooperation, understood as the capacity to share goals and form a "we" identity.[53] But, in fact, bonobos display strongly "altruistic" acts, including rich capacities to console others and indeed may be, as they are called, the "most empathetic ape."[54] We shall turn to the role of social play and the capacity for inter- and intraspecies friendships and political alliances among lions, wolves, and other social carnivores shortly. The problem is that too many experiments are designed to contrast human and *nonhuman* responses with *human* styles of teaching and *human* teachers. Yet, epistemologically stubborn humans are proving to be as unlikely to learn from bonobo teachers as these primates are to learn from humans. In all probability, social animals are adept at pedagogical techniques for teaching others in their societies.

The unsurprising bias that we humans have toward our own species appears elsewhere in the Nova documentary as well. In an interesting case of historical revisionism, an experiment with a multilayered box, a stick, and a piece of candy in which chimpanzees actually outperform humans is reinterpreted as evidence for greater learning "potential" in humans.[55] In the experiment, human children are shown imitating, without using any degree of critical thought or reflection, several needless steps performed by a human adult in order to retrieve the box's candy. What looks like slavish imitation is explained by human researchers as a special talent to learn from an adult authority. The chimpanzees, who figure out that they can skip those needless steps, and, "understanding cause and effect," tap right into the correct opening for the candy, are said to be missing the human capacity to learn.[56] In other words, what appears to be a straightforward cognitive advantage in chimpanzees over young humans is said to prove instead that only humans have the capacity to learn from teachers. One conclusion leads to another, and the film ends with the claim that humans are "the most social ape." Given that their competitors for this title include the "make-love-not-war" bonobos, one has to wonder just what all these humans might be missing.

The documentary's conclusions flow from a weak philosophical frame. Many of the actual experiments in the film in fact suggest surprising parallels between humans and other primates, not metaphysical differences. The capacity for culture, for example, is no longer believed to separate humans from the realm of nature. As the documentary observes, apes can be found "generating ideas and sharing technologies—that's one scientific definition of culture." The discovery of animal cultures and technologies throws a monkey wrench into any easy formulation of what makes us humans special. Yet, despite the vast similarities, and the lack of any definitive evidence for an alterity abyss between humans and all other species, the documentary evidence in the film is set up to display "how big is the gap between them and us!" The film acknowledges that "one by one the skills and emotions we once thought were uniquely human are being found in apes." And yet it insists: "Still certain specific mental gaps, the little differences that make the big differences will ultimately explain why we study them and not the other way around." Experiment after experiment establishes that other animals are more like us than we ever imagined. There are differences in styles of communication and cognition to be sure, but these differences do not establish in any philosophically unproblematic way human superiority. After all, *superiority* is a value term. No one can *prove* a superiority claim or, at least, not through any value-free posture in what is in the end our all-too-human-centered science. Even more so, as primatologist Malini Suchak remarks, one cannot establish human superiority through an absence of evidence, which is the reoccurring fallback argument for human exceptionalism.[57] Every time a particular human skill cannot be found in nonhumans, it gets used to assert human superiority.

Do nonhuman animals have language? Linguistic along with cognitive capacities are among the most frequent approaches to tracking animal inferiority. Yet, if we listen to nature's rustling, we hear not just the mute animal's silent complaint, not even an animal that on occasion says "No" with a nod of a head or an assertion of a tusk, but a creature who can laugh and play. The shift in attention from a predominantly somber tone to an animal that can find laughter even in oppressive circumstances invokes what in a Nietzschean vein we might call a "gay science" of nature or of a science that has learned how to laugh.[58]

We do not make this shift in order to raise the question of who (or which species) will have the last laugh. For many species, playful laughter is part of a process of social bonding distinct from serious games of competition for rank and status.[59] This evidence is well established. Moreover, some evidence suggests that nonhuman animals may mix the serious and the humorous and use laughter to subvert or assert hierarchies. If so, perhaps human and nonhuman species are not that different after all: "Even the most complex mutualistic relationships in nature reflect a tug-of-war between collaboration and exploitation," as primate behavioral ecologist Joan Silk writes.[60] Our aim is to find in that mesh those social cues that we oblivious humans have too often missed—cues that allow us to avoid repeating histories of rogue warfare and rejoin with other species in an unexpected, life-affirming solidarity. History plays out not just as tragedy but also at times as a comedy of manners or farce.

ANIMAL SLAPSTICK AND SOCIAL BONDING THROUGH PLAY

Scientists, notably including Robert Provine, the author of *Laughter: A Scientific Investigation*, have studied chimpanzees and found a link between their laughterlike noises and human laughter, which might point to a common origin for animal and human communication in play. "Laughter is literally the sound of play, with the primal 'pant-pant'—the labored breathing of physical play—becoming the human 'ha-ha,'" Provine observes, establishing an evolutionary continuity between the tickling and the rough-and-tumble play that stimulates chirping in mice and laughter in other species.[61] Similarly, Jaak Panksepp's research suggests "the possibility that our most commonly used animal subjects, laboratory rodents, may have social-joy type experiences during their playful activities and that an important communicative-affective component of that process, which invigorates social engagement, is a primordial form of laughter."[62] Moreover, these waves of joy, and the styles of mutual bonding or social cooperation that they promote, transmit across species, as Panksepp discovered when he found that "inducing laughter in young rats promoted bonding: tickled rats would actively seek out specific human hands that had made them laugh."[63]

Even more astounding, Bekoff notes that "though it's rarely the focus of scientific research we observe animals making jokes or displaying a sense of humor,"[64] providing an example of a scarlet macaw who "roars with laughter; he teases all who come near, . . . and even plays 'magic carpet'—wherein his human slaves race down hallways dragging large towels with the macaw riding aboard."[65] Vicki Hearne observes that when her playful dog finds a dumbbell set on its end instead of its usual position, that he "enjoyed the play on form . . . [and would] toss it in the air a few times on his way back with it, to show his appreciation for the joke."[66] Again quoting Provine: "Most candidates for simian humor involve cases of intentional misusing of objects and misnaming of people and things. For example, researcher Roger Fouts observed the signing chimpanzee Washoe using a toothbrush as if it was a hairbrush. Moja, another of Fouts's signing chimpanzees, called a purse a "shoe," put the purse on her foot, and wore it as a shoe. Francine "Penny" Patterson observed the signing gorilla Koko treating rocks and other inedible substances as if they were foods, offering them as 'food' to people. . . . The above cases of presumed intentional 'misnaming' and 'misusing' are potential jokes." Provine proceeds to draw an analogy between adult chimpanzees and human children, but this is a type of analogy that problematically blurs significant differences and overlapping similarities between species, and so we set this analogy and related comments aside and focus on actual observations. After all, human adults often are childlike when they are laughing or playful. He continues: "Reports that apes appeared to be in a playful mood, or glanced at the caregiver for evidence of the effect of their errant actions, suggests . . . a joking intent. Another widely noted class of misnaming involves 'name calling.' . . . When upset with her caregiver, gorilla Koko referred to her as 'dirty toilet.' . . . In another possible instance of simian humor, Roger Fouts reported that while riding on his shoulders the chimpanzee Washoe urinated on him, signing 'funny' (touching her nose) and snorting."[67]

Much of laughter stems from play behavior, as Provine establishes. The implications of play behavior for ethics are intriguing. Bekoff's research on social carnivores supports a particularly fascinating claim. Bekoff believes that play may provide a training ground for learning an egalitarian formulation of social norms and expectations for reciprocity—what we humans call the "Golden Rule—do unto others as you would have them do unto you"—among such normally hierarchal species as "wolves, coyotes, red foxes, and domestic dogs."[68] We return to these studies in chapter 2 as we examine anarchic communitarianism, but here note that key features of play provide the material grounding for an egalitarian ethos by functioning to level playing fields and to build camaraderie. Bekoff explains that "for the time [social carnivores] are playing, they put aside or neutralize any inequalities in physical size and social rank."[69] A playful exchange exercises capacities for friendships through gestures generated by the sharing of joy as sometimes expressed in laughter. If playful comic routines can function as a social leveler, then a politics of solidarity might well develop from the experiences and norms acquired during social play.

Mixing species and disciplines, we turn again to de Waal. "Of the three ideals of the French Revolution [which finds its philosophical formulation in Jean-Jacques Rousseau's 1762 *The Social Contract*]—liberty, equality, and fraternity—fraternity is probably. . . . the easiest to understand from a primate perspective with survival relying so heavily on attachment, bonding, and group cohesion," he observes. "Primates evolved to be community builders."[70] Some species such as bonobos exhibit more egalitarian tendencies, others like chimpanzees are more hierarchical, with humans, he speculates, somewhere in the middle. Malini Suchak, de Waal's coworker, clarifies that although chimpanzees are more hierarchical than bonobos, on the scale of primates they are fairly egalitarian. Their hierarchies are not typically linear; they engage in victim support; they have strong ownership norms regardless of rank; and lower-ranking chimpanzees form coalitions to outcompete alphas.[71] In this context it is interesting to recall that social equality is thought to be more prevalent among humans living in the small-scale societies prior to the social upheavals that began in the Neolithic era and that sharp social hierarchies and urban centers developed very late in our evolutionary history, with the agricultural and industrial revolutions.[72] Perhaps social movements with an anarchic bent are tapping into this ancient egalitarian strain in our species. Above all else, we take our social cues from the primatologist's observation that to laugh together is to "broadcast solidarity and togetherness."[73]

HISTORIES OF TRICKSTERS, SUBVERSIVES, AND WORKER-COMPANION SOLIDARITY

To build social bonds, nonhumans may make use of more than just friendly laughter and entertaining slapstick routines. They often have an egalitarian streak of their own. De Waal reports on a raven playing deceptive tricks on high-ranking males: "The low-ranking male learned to distract his competitor [from food] by enthusiastically opening empty containers and acting as if he were eating from them."[74] Similar evidence suggests that animals can be tricksters and mockers of authority, challenging assumptions that only humans can deceive, protest, or collaborate against oppressive conditions and establishing elements of an agency that is strategic and even collective. For animals, as for humans, laughter creates a space beyond surveillance, creating a site for self-assertion and a freedom that cannot be controlled by laboratory norms. In general, humor can function to downgrade the frightening into the risible and convert negative emotions into empowering ones, staging a "minirevolution" aimed against those who may not get that they are the butt of a joke.[75] Of course, laughter may or may not successfully transform an entrenched social system, but it does lift the spirit and reclaim agency.

It is not surprising that humor might play a part in animal solidarity and political trickery, given evidence for an ethics of fairness in a number of animal species. Darwin hypothesized that ethics is continuous with animal sociality.[76] We have already noted G. A. Bradshaw's observations on elephants: "In zoos and circuses, elephants are known for what has been called 'retaliatory cunning,' a calculated, directed attack on the someone who has turned on them in the past."[77] When not excessively traumatized, elephants are normally careful to direct outrage against the perpetrators of injustice and refrain from retaliating against unintentional crimes or innocent bystanders. De Waal reports on a sense of fairness among various species, defined as "[a] set of expectations about the way in which oneself (or others) should be treated and how resources should be divided. Whenever reality deviates from these expectations to one's (or the other's) disadvantage, a negative reaction ensues, most commonly protest by subordinate individuals and punishment by dominant individuals."[78] Even monkeys, who are considered to be less "intelligent" than apes, display acts of defiance at conditions that they understand as unfair. (Note though too that the relevance of the word *intelligence* for cross-species comparisons has been questioned, given that the complexity of cognitive skills across species is easily missed through the use of a single ambiguous and politically fraught term.)[79] De Waal discovered, in an experiment with his student Sarah Brosnan, that offering a monkey a lesser reward than that received by his peer (a cucumber instead of a grape) provokes anger in the disadvantaged monkey, who "hurl[s] . . . pebbles out of the test chamber, sometimes even throwing those paltry cucumber slices. A food normally devoured with gusto had become distasteful."[80] Even a simple affect-based response to food takes on a political aftertaste, and the monkeys respond to the inequity with Occupy-style outrage. While monkey outrage sends a serious message to the experimenter—"no more monkeying around"—protest can also take a subversively comic tone.

A joke is not always a joke. Sometimes a joke can offer a subtle glimpse into an interspecies political ethics. De Waal again provides rich anecdotes. A wily chimpanzee named Georgia engages freely in teasing and mocking human visitors to her home at the Yerkes Field Station in Atlanta. De Waal reports of occasions when Georgia "hurries to the spigot to collect a mouthful of water before they arrive. She then casually mingles with the rest of the colony behind the mesh fence of their outdoor compound, and not even the best observer will notice anything unusual about her. If necessary, Georgia will wait minutes with closed lips until the visitors come near. Then there will be shrieks, laughs, jumps, and sometimes falls, when she suddenly sprays them."[81] Georgia's "spontaneous ambush tactics" can make a monkey out of any of her would-be human superiors as she turns the research station into a carnival.[82] In this context, political jokes are every bit the "the oral equivalent of guerrilla warfare," a sign less of resignation than rebellion.[83]

Apes can also turn these tactics around and use them against their own in-group superiors, which suggests that laughing in the animal kingdom can function on occasion as a comic means for defrocking the local tyrants. De Waal reports an incident—what to us humans appears as the equivalent of the slip on the banana peel—at the San Diego zoo, where apes are enclosed in an area surrounded by a dry moat with a chain for access. Apparently, when an alpha male bonobo named Vernon would visit the moat, a younger male named Kalind would pull away the chain. "He would then look down at Vernon with an open-mouthed play face while slapping the side of the moat. This expression," de Waal explains, "is the equivalent of human laughter: Kalind was making fun of the boss."[84] Like his monkey cousin, Kalind expresses outrage over injustice; but this ape enjoys as well an egalitarian sense of what counts as fair play that may not be as pronounced in more hierarchal animal societies. For Kalind, any ape positioning himself as a superior may count as fair game.

Moving out of the lab and onto the farm, it is difficult to be unaware of the range of moods and dispositions of animals within the same species and their modes of making things right. Those who have worked with or live in close proximity with animals are less likely to be surprised by stories of either species differences or distinct personalities. To be sure, not all animals are particularly savvy or capable of social camaraderie. Barbara Kingsolver, in her agrarian experiment detailed in *Animal, Vegetable, Miracle*, remarks that some animals are stupid, but they tend to be man-made—for example, turkeys genetically engineered for food production.[85] At the same, she tells of one member of the flock chosen for Thanksgiving dinner based on an unpleasant nature.[86] Her point is that singular personalities permeate animal communities.

Coming of age on a Missouri farm, we too have seen not only animal personalities but also animal politics. Some horses, for example, are much more patient and nurturing, while others have less tolerance for human mistakes. An obstinate pony would frequently sit down on the job or even roll in the dirt to get rid of an unskilled rider. Horses would also rub their unwanted rider too close to a fence or thorny bush to get pests off their back. Other horses would show much more sympathy with any human rider regardless of skill. Some would even walk gingerly knowing that their fragile and unbalanced cargo could slip off easily. Like other animals, horses have best friends who they trust to stand guard as well as swat flies away but from their face and they too have those frenemies that they will never see eye-to-eye with.[87] There is also a fair share of practical jokers, like an Arabian gelding showing off his ability to unlock not only his stall door, but those of his mates. Collectively, these horses also knew when something was awry, running deep into the woods when they heard the unmistakable sound of the veterinarian's truck coming down the gravel driveway. Observing that farmers know to be wary around their donkeys and their tricks, biologist Bekoff does not hesitate to draw the conclusion that creatures that thrive on creating mischief for a laugh can demonstrate real wit as well, posing on occasion as regular "stand-up comedians."[88]

But can the study of history offer us similar kinds of stories that may complicate this renegade science but by no means dismiss it? To be sure, science has often ignored historical context and taken its own slip on the banana peel. Bekoff's rich account of the emotional lives of animals, for example, reports as straight science an amazing horse named Jim Key. This animal wasn't just horsing around when he feigned lameness to prevent his owner from selling him off to a stranger. He even seemed to communicate through spelling out the letters of (English) words to his owner and a team of Harvard scientists. For these scientists, ex-slave and self-taught veterinarian Dr. William Key's horse companion was their sole focus of study, neglecting a complicated history of race and resistance. In *Beautiful Jim Key: The Lost History of a Man and Horse Who Changed the World*, Mim Eichler Rivas, however, tells not only the story of a remarkable horse but also the turn-of-the-twentieth-century story that shows a black professional negotiating Jim Key—"the world's smartest horse"—with Jim Crow. Stories of this horse—such as when a stranger offered to buy Jim Key away from his owner and the healthy horse pretends to be lame—continue to reverberate through our contemporary mainstream media. The story takes on a life of its own through the horse's array of unusual feats and a team of Harvard researchers' verification. We are sure that Harvard scientists are not easy to deceive, and yet African American trickster humor also reveals subtle inflections that may make it difficult for those outside the local community to catch on to subplots. Dr. William Key was no doubt clever at creating the circus drama that would keep him laughing all the way to the bank. Yet we don't want to dismiss his animal collaborator. Instead, we can imagine future alternative histories in which the human trickster does not get all the credit and there is a privileging of a *longue durée* (i.e., the big picture that a historical perspective can give us) that centers on animal agency—their tricks, pranks, and infrapolitics—as a means to reveal the workings of authority and power.

Unofficial histories that study challenges to power and authority and paradigm-altering scientific data on animal emotions and behavior afford new understandings and possibilities for collective political change. Jason Hrbal's *Fear of the Animal Planet: The Hidden History of Animal Resistance* presents an agency-oriented theory of animal oppression and collects numerous accounts of animal resistance, solidarity, and revenge against targeted abusers. Jeffrey St. Clair's introduction to the book reports the case of baboons who raid train cars to free captive friends.[89] African lore similarly reports the case of a political alliance between two male lions, who notoriously resisted British colonialism in Tsavo, Kenya. In 1889 the lions worked together to disrupt labor on a railway through their territory. This native uprising was not put down before the rebel lions had killed over one hundred British railway workers.[90] Hribal's argument that these various acts of resistance demonstrate agency turns on evidence that spirited animals willingly undertake acts of rebellion despite the fact that they know that if found out they will be subject to severe punishment including death.[91]

Labor historians, among others, should be intrigued by the language of "solidarity and togetherness," but also by the desire of animal theorists to pull histories from below. Although a call to listen to voices unheard may seem like old school social history, the problem of human exceptionalism gives it unexpected relevance. The centrality of social history—its aim to find agency where official histories were blind—is well understood, yet histories outside traditional archives still uncover tropes that have wrongly deemed groups of historical actors passive. Recall Vicki Ruiz's classic work bringing voices and experiences of Mexican American women "Out of the Shadows" and, more recently, Annelise Orleck's oral histories and subsequent monograph exposing the agency of African American welfare recipients and how they "fought their own war on poverty."[92] Can we push social history to another frontier, one in which animality is no longer the last acceptable figure of mute passivity?

Animal subjectivities challenge narrow assumptions in traditional Marxist histories that assume that only man labors and only men's labor can be alienating or world making. Feminists argue that child care, service occupations, and the labor of intimacy are also skilled and creative labor and can be done under oppressive or world-making conditions.[93] Similarly, histories of animal labor practices should expand beyond accounts of animal suffering to explore the ways in which diverse animals give meaning to our overlapping worlds. Animal subjectivities breathe new life into social history by not only bringing more actors to the stage but also unearthing new energies and visions of collective action.

Tragically, oppressed social groups are not exempt from the general rule that the history of triumph turns on the power of exclusion and not on the ability to hear the subaltern speak. Indeed, great labor historians have found not so much moments of distinct discourses in unison but, in the words of Alexander Saxton, an "indispensable enemy," which, in his study, turns on anti-Chinese sentiment bolstered by subhuman imagery to prop up caste and class unionism.[94] David Roediger has traced the tragic appeal of whiteness in which racial and gender tropes reemerge in spaces that range from nineteenth-century worker protests and union halls to turn-of-the-millennium sporting events, prisons, and, of course, presidential elections.[95] Vijay Prashad has also described the problems of seeking bread-and-butter multiculturalism that too easily makes its move up the neoliberal ladder in search of bright whiteness.[96] Yet social historians, like social activists searching for an elusive global link or for the intricacies of intimate labor, celebrate when the desire for change engenders, however unexpectedly, a shared consciousness.

Animal tropes that have passed under the radar as second nature in so many histories of solidarity make us wonder if we should not reconsider these tropes as pointing to some literal basis for human-nonhuman solidarity. Thus far, natural history (including the intersections of human and nonhuman species) has been inextricably bound to studies of indigenous people.[97] For working-class and labor studies, the history of the worker (long assumed white and male) finds the only sympathetic animal trope to turn on mute passivity. Popularly imagined in Upton Sinclair's *The Jungle* or Charlie Chaplin's *Modern Times*, capitalism dupes rational workingmen, turning them into little more than a mindless herd of cattle or sheep or a machine.[98] Yet labor historians are also finding emerging patterns of what Donna Haraway understands as worker–companion species solidarities that defy these animal tropes.[99] In Thomas Andrews's recent groundbreaking study of human, animal, and natural history—what he defines as a "workscape" of Colorado's turn-of-the-twentieth-century mines—workers witnessed the power of collective animal resistance. "Mules, claimed one driver Victor Bazanele, 'had sense like a human.'" Andrews notes, "Drivers even likened the mules' resistance to their own struggles. Victor Bazanele joked that mules 'knew when starting time was and quitting time was.' When 'quitting time came around,' he declared, 'you couldn't make those mules do nothing.' [Alex] Bisculco concurred; the animal workforce, he claimed 'was unionized before some of us.'"[100]

Andrews discusses miners' relationships to mice that went beyond the role of the canary in the coal mine. To be sure, mice hearing and sensitivity to vibrations caused them to scatter when there were underground dangers such as a cracking wall and, like their better-known counterparts, they died from even small amounts of exposure to carbon monoxide. Andrews sees more than practicality as the source of interspecies solidarity. Mice shared lunchtime food scraps with the miners, who found them amusing, but also learned to differentiate between their lunch companions on the basis of marking and behavior; some even began to name the mice. "'Oh yeah,' Dan DeSantis recalled with a smile, 'the little buggers they knew their name, yeah Pete this and that, boy they come out of the crack and they get that close with you.'" Insightfully, Andrews argues that "in the camps above, the act of breaking bread together often cemented communal bonds across deep cultural divides; in the mines below, sharing food across the boundary between species helped colliers turn rodent fellow travelers into friends."[101]

Similar stories of solidarity occur between soldiers and dogs on the World War I battlefields in Susan Orlean's *Rin Tin Tin: The Life and the Legend*. Rin Tin Tin's owner and trainer, Lee Duncan, created film scripts illustrating heroic action for the world-famous canine orphan he had brought back from Europe. The dog's heroism grows out of an empathy that, as Orlean explains, "is broader and deeper and more pure than what an ordinary human would be capable of." The silent films of the 1920s were the perfect medium to showcase the virtues of animals who couldn't speak in words, but who could express a range of emotions and real personality: "A dog was at no disadvantage to a human in a silent film: both species had the same set of tools for telling a story—action, expression, gesture. In fact, an animal acting without words looked natural and didn't fall into pantomime and exaggeration the way human actors in silent film often did."[102]

Here our social history joins with Donna Haraway, who wonders why scholars and philosophers such as Derrida, sensitive to the fact that animals may experience life's maddening chain of events through their own singular personalities and points of view, return to engage in scholarly reading and writing practices rather than take the chance to respond to the "lure" of "deconstructive communication." Engaging the call-and-response of the life world in which we are immersed, Haraway leaves a question for the social historian as well as the philosopher: "What if not all such Western human workers with animals have refused the risk of an intersecting gaze?"[103]

We need to move beyond witnessing vulnerable animal others and allow for the study of and engagement with animal discourse and society. Animals not only suffer from acts of cruelty and structures of domination but also assert an agency that at times takes a turn toward the comic. Our critique of long-standing Western assumptions of the passivity of animals learns from feminist critiques of traditional, patriarchal histories that have rendered invisible not only the work of caregiving but also the importance of laughter. The idea that women, let alone feminists, could be funny once seemed as far-fetched as a mule that knew the meaning of a fair day's work. Like feminist humor, an animal's work is never done—especially when it comes to invoking signs of visibility that deconstruct the all-too-serious binaries that have left the subaltern animal anything but a laughing matter. Yet it is laughter and joy that render topsy turvy the very notion of a missing link—now a neoliberal link that purports ontological gaps and other monkey business. Perhaps if we disrupt old school assumptions that animals can only be funny when they perform human tricks we might also be able to tackle other oppressive norms collectively. The alternative is the reassertion of neoliberal fears and fantasies imagined in sci-fi as the uprisings of the "planet of the apes." Our own comic version would feature a mischievous Stephen Colbertian twist in which instead of enjoying our bread and roses we must pay monkeys for our jello and porn.

2

PALEOLITHIC ETHICS

Ethics' Evolution from Play, the Interspecies Community Selection Hypothesis, and Anarchic Communitarianism

> *The best indicator of a peaceful, relaxed atmosphere is play.*
>
> —FRANS DE WAAL, CHIMPANZEE POLITICS

> *A map of the world that does not include Utopia is not worth even glancing at.*
>
> —OSCAR WILDE, THE SOUL OF MAN UNDER SOCIALISM

> *There is a promising autre-mondialisation to be learned in retying some of the knots of ordinary multispecies living on earth.*
>
> —DONNA HARAWAY, WHEN SPECIES MEET

> *KillCap is the transformation of everyday life into a revolutionary game... a kind of radical play that re-enchants the world and in the process sparks a people's insurrection against corporate rule.*
>
> —FOR THE WILD, CULTURE JAMMER'S HQ, ADBUSTERS AMERICA

After the *New York Post* ran a front page headline "Occupy Wall Street Animals Go Wild ... ZOO-COTTI,"[1] the instinct of those connected to the facts on the ground may well have been to charge the newspaper with wild misrepresentation.[2] The manners if not the aims of the protesters camping in Zuccotti Park, in contrast with the high-stakes gambling of finance capital, were comparatively moderate. One would be tempted to say that the "animals" out of control were those positioned well inside of Wall Street. But perhaps this defensive response in support of the Occupy movement does not capture the anarchists' deeper political aim of challenging power's hubris wherever it may be. The loss of livelihood and shelter among the impoverished is a serious Occupy concern that readily expands to question the ways in which nonhuman animals along with humans have been stripped of their habitats by unchecked economic growth. Ordinarily we do not take nonhuman animals to be of primary concern for understanding either the principles or implications of human ethics; yet what if those very creatures most readily dismissed as less than legal or moral persons—those residing below the 99 percent of Occupy's populist refrain—hold the key to any visionary project of social and political ethics? Perhaps the alleged resemblance of the so-called animals on Wall Street (the anarchists) and those in the wild might be more telling than we initially think. Why not interpret the tabloid's misrepresentation of the communitarian anarchists as animals less as an occasion for derogatory name-calling than as a most provocative vision of what our ethical instincts might sometimes be (and become)?

Indeed, an earnest pairing of animals and anarchists may well allow us to spot a wildly utopian moment—what biologist Donna Haraway proposes as an *autre-mondialisation*—in an otherwise dystopic world.[3] Ever more research from "renegade" ecologists and biologists (a bit wild themselves!) challenges the nature-as-red-in-tooth-and-claw model of capitalism at its roots, calling into question both capitalist assumptions regarding the nature of the economy and the nature of nature itself. These left-leaning Darwinians are producing a growing body of evidence that evolution and cultural change does not inevitably turn on struggle and competition but on affective networks and social affinities as well. Indeed one of the earliest theorists of the anarchy movement, the Russian scientist Peter Kropotkin, not only produced the classic statement on the meaning of anarchy as friendship; he rebalanced the overemphasis on competition in the original Darwinian paradigm (1859) by drawing out and stressing the cooperatist aspects of evolution based on mutual aid.[4] Rather than defend the manners or aims of the anarchists against charges of their *wild animality*, we shall turn to aspects of a profound ethical sensibility found both in ourselves and animals in the wild. The anarchists at Occupy organized communities based on a horizontal principle of mutual aid with an egalitarian ethos that crosses rank, class, and species barriers.

Of course, anarchists seem to lack any rule-bound governing apparatus, and in this respect they may resemble animals in the wild as well as the "animals" of our tabloid imagination. I restrain myself from noting the lack of a governing apparatus on Wall Street itself and turn instead to the central point here: If prosocial anarchists aim to cultivate a natural sense of justice rather than either top-down apparatuses of governmentality and bureaucratic management (laws and institutions) or abstract theoretical apparatuses of right and wrong (systematic philosophy), they may in this very respect resemble "other" animals.[5] For, as it turns out, Hobbes's depiction of the state of nature as a place where "man is wolf to man" is hardly more than tabloid philosophy. On the contrary, as biologist Marc Bekoff explains, wolves may offer a glimpse into a radical origin of ethics as they suspend normal social hierarchies and competitive predatory and mating behaviors.[6] These wolves do not suspend the normal rules to lay bare some primal chaos of the natural world. On the contrary, this suspension of norms opens a space to cultivate friendly bonds in joyful play, providing a dynamic training ground for developing a cooperation-based ethos.[7]

What then if we were to replace the classic liberal hypothesis of an original state of nature where "man is wolf to man" with an alternative political imaginary where social carnivores are friends? In post-Marcusean critical theory, this alternative ethos would cultivate *biosocial eros* while artfully dodging the demands of hyperproductive, predatory economies and exhausted, inauthentic lives. Its playfully erotic ethos maps onto what Henri Bergson took to be laughter's most serious aim—the mockery of rigid habits of character or thought for the sake of an élan vital that laughter frees. Of this "delicate adjustment of wills" necessary for community life, Bergson explains, "a cut-and-dried agreement among persons will not satisfy it, it insists on a constant striving after reciprocal adaptation."[8] Play exercises social desires and generalized reciprocity suppressed by social contract theory's egoistic individual and "tit-for-a-tat"-style bargaining. The egalitarian practices at "Zoo-Cotti" may well translate into an anarchic ethos associated with animal life, but only because these anarchists have tapped into ethics' revitalizing animal core.

The legacy of philosophical anarchy, from the ancient Cynics (anarchists and formidable stand-up comedians *avant la lettre*) to Kropotkin's evolutionary-based argument for mutual aid and Haraway's retrieval of the feminist anarchism associated with Emma Goldman ("If I can't dance, I don't want to be part of your revolution") for her companion species manifesto, serves as a backdrop for our investigation of trans-species ethical practices in the context of contemporary social movements. Among the lessons of the ancient Cynic Diogenes of Sinope is the insight that the "plainness of living" required to become a "citizen of the world [*kosmopolitês*]" could be learned from other animal species.[9] What we discover along with this plainness, however, is not the philosopher's single-minded search for self-sufficiency, but a light carbon footprint and a daring social life. A natural culture of play and mutual aid overturns classic liberalism's state of nature hypothesis to acknowledge solidarity among animals as coworkers and friends (chapter 1).

THE LEFT DARWINIANS

Not since Kropotkin have evolutionary biology and political theories of anarchic freedom appeared as such close friends. Yet, over the past couple of decades, these two strands of Kropotkin's research have reemerged in even more favorable terms. New evolution theories are fusing epigenetic, behavioral, and symbolic dimensions to the nineteenth century's standard one-dimensional model of natural selection.[10] Attention to collaboration, affinity groups, and play in ethology and evolutionary theory parallel speculative thought's traversal of post-Foucauldian, neocynical critiques of neoliberalism toward political "heterotopias."[11] One prominent activist theorist who has not ignored the radical implications of the science-politics fusion, David Graeber, refers back to Kropotkin for a link between evolution and anarchy's emancipatory ethics in his book *Debt: The First 5,000 Years*.[12] This

PALEOLITHIC ETHICS

chapter takes up Graeber's insights and pursues two strands of his project—scientific theories of evolution and neoliberal political critique—as contributions toward the project that Kropotkin inaugurated over a century ago. We begin by turning to some of the key contributions of contemporary left-leaning Darwinians in the natural sciences. The assumption is that there is no scientific theory of evolution whose philosophical frame and basic concepts are not inflected by politics. After all, nature is political. Scientific theories of evolution are therefore susceptible to political critique. Like chimpanzees and other seekers of knowledge, we humans, as scientists and philosophers are political animals.

The left Darwinians are critical of what they see as a political bias built into Darwin's first formulations of evolutionary theory and offer an alternative developed from later insights into animal affect and sociality. Citing Douglass Caldwell, biologists Lynn Margulis and Dorion Sagan note the unfortunate frequent use of such terms as *individual, perfect* or *perfection, race, kill, exterminate, death*, etc. in Darwin's most cited work; "by contrast, the following terms are absent from *The Origin of the Species:* 'association, affiliation, cooperate, cooperation, collaborate, collaboration, community, intervention, symbiosis.'"[13] While these biologists intend to avoid any essential use of metaphor, they offer in place of struggling individuals and competing social groups images of biosocial associations tying together members (their lighthearted term is *committee members*) who are now viewed as woven into an integrated living system that they dare call "Gaia."[14] Cooperative and symbiotic processes complicate any simple picture of life as the struggle of a self-determining and self-organizing or otherwise bound biological units, regardless of whether these units are thought to function in competition or in sympathy with others. Organisms do not have clear and distinct boundaries that separate them from other living things. They survive cooperatively and symbiotically or in struggle, but not alone.

The biosocial processes of living matter challenge the atomistic individualism in classic liberal state of nature theories more radically than one may first think. Frans de Waal proposes to understand the evolution of morality through the Scottish Enlightenment claims on behalf of natural sympathy, but the philosophical notion of sympathy does not capture the complex dynamic of symbiotic and cooperative processes that he and other scientists have discovered. De Waal remarks in *Primates and Philosophers* that liberal economists have neglected the fact that such key figures as Adam Smith believe that natural sympathy is just as important as self-interest in explaining human motivation. Note that Darwin's evolving theory has similarly been read too one-sidedly due to its first unfortunate formulation. Darwin was eventually influenced by the philosophical theories of natural sympathy to look for instances of altruism among nonhuman species and to hypothesize that sympathy rooted in the family provides a basis for understanding altruism among larger nonrelated social groups. Darwin even believed that sympathy among group members would provide the grounds for "group evolution." The natural sympathy of a group was thought to sustain a degree of group loyalty that would account for how groups and not just individuals or kin could form a unit for natural selection and evolutionary survival.

De Waal himself steps back from any strong theory of group selection, arguing that theories of kin selection and reciprocal altruism account for much prosocial behavior in primates. Of course, other social mechanisms may also play a role, including the use of revenge as payback inflicted on "cheaters" and gratitude for those who cooperate over time.[15] But important here for de Waal is the fact that primates learn to do favors for others in their group because their generosity to others in the group will be remembered, and they will over time also become beneficiaries. He explains how social mechanisms such as reciprocal altruism that originally functioned to strengthen a group could even account for those rare acts of compassion directed toward strangers. This happens, he writes, when "the impulse became divorced from the consequences that shaped its evolution. This permitted its expression even when payoffs were unlikely, such as when strangers were beneficiaries" (15). He counters Darwin's hypothesis of group selection by citing the problem of intergroup migration (hence gene flow) across groups or tribes (16). Finally, he develops an account of natural ethics with a layered system of empathy, beginning with the contagion of emotions and, at its most complex development, the ability to adopt another's perspective (39). (We return to aspects of this layered system in chapters 4 and 5). The failure among philosophers to understand this natural basis for ethics provokes de Waal, somewhat playfully yet seriously enough, to cite sociobiologist E. O. Wilson's "call for the temporary removal of ethics from the hands of philosophers" (15).

Of course, de Waal along with the sociobiolgist are fully engaged in quite a round of speculative philosophy themselves. As a philosopher, I would like to see sociobiology's challenge and raise it by drawing on the research of those biologists and ethologists who are shaking up the world of philosophy and its modernist legacies. With de Waal, I am setting aside any problematic appeal to a rigidly defined and readily identifiable group as a basis for natural selection and also Gaia (although for an enlarged sense of home in meditation and wonder see chapter 5); however, my focus will be on the ethical relevance of biosocial webs and interspecies communities. The symbiotic and parasitic processes exposed powerfully by Margulis and Haraway, among others, suggest that we are not naturally frozen into genetically defined groups with clear and distinct boundaries, but, for the same reasons, we are not individual atoms either. Rather than individuals or groups, we function at times like nodes in multispecies networks and selves-in-multispecies-communities.

In fact, some evidence suggests that clusters of interdependent animal species seem to coevolve as interlinked groups, in a process that I would formulate as "the interspecies community selection hypothesis." Neurologist Katherine Bryant points out that biologists study co-evolution, but not multispecies groups as units of selection, yet this hypothesis is not without some plausibility.[16] Alternative evolutionary theories characterize coevolution as a network array where mineral, vegetable, and animal are negotiated as a hybrid unity, but these approaches detour too far afield from a political ethics centered on communicative sociality.[17] Multiple layers of species interaction, culminating in intersubjective signaling, weave meaningful patterns in biosocial lives. To support an interspecies community selection hypothesis, we would have to test whether ecotypes measurably compete with one another, and there doesn't seem to be any reason why they would not. In terms of coevolutionary patterns, one of the classic examples draws attention to trees and tree squirrels. Squirrels have evolved the teeth and guts for breaking down acorns, but also behaviors for dispersing the seeds (which aid in seedling recruitment). In turn, nut production by trees can strongly influence squirrel survival and reproduction. There's also quite a bit of mysterious fungal symbiotic interactions that appear to be crucial for supporting forest species. We basically barely know anything about subterranean fungal diversity and its role in community ecology. If evolution can coordinate between two or three different species (for example, squirrel-tree-fungus), it would be possible for more successful co-evolutionary relationships to be favored over less successful ones.

The interspecies community selection hypothesis takes up and expands upon coevolutionary processes through an elusive fifth dimension in Jablonka and Lamb's theory of evolution's four dimensions: genetic, epigenetic, behavioral, and symbolic variation. Each of these dimensions suggests multispecies coevolutionary processes, and especially rich in this regard is symbolic variation and the resulting increase in social learning. These theorists explain that "with variation transmitted by the symbolic system, there is a quantum leap in social complexity, with families, professional groups, communities, states and other groupings all influencing what is produced in art, commerce, religion, and so on. Construction plays an enormous role in the production of variants, yet because symbolic systems are self-referential, the rules of the systems are powerful filters. The ability to use symbols also gives humans the important and unique ability to construct and transmit variants with the future in mind."[18] Now we know that other species too construct cultural and social codes for the transmission of information within and even across species boundaries. These symbolic codes, along with the other three dimensions, forge communicative routes for trans-species interdependence. In effect, multiple species function as part of the "environmental niche" and hence in interconnected or multispecies communities for potential evolutionary benefit.[19]

Perhaps there is no more powerful example of the complexity of these interspecies groups than the elephants of Uganda documented by G. A. Bradshaw (see introduction). These elephants not only enjoy elaborate social interactions with members of their own tribe but, as we have learned painfully through their retaliation against human villagers and tourists, are acutely aware of their relationships with other species. The vital spirit of flourishing bonds and traumatic symptoms of violation, passed down quite possibly through epigenetic, behavioral, and symbolic processes, suggest that individual and group boundaries are relatively porous, opening up these evolutionary units to the constitutive influence of other species.

The nexus that at times connects diverse species in social and political solidarity, at other times transmits the horrors of assault and retribution tearing apart a social landscape and haunting future generations. This nexus grounds a nuanced sociality, with potential for tragic pathos but also joy. As we began to investigate in chapter 1, comic dimensions of ordinary life reveal a playful eros that generates unexpected forms of alliance and solidarity. Crucially, this eros ethics does not rest on the subjective capacity for sympathy alone, but operates in part through the horizontal ethicality of collective agency and the intersubjective politics of a communal dynamic.

Much of the Western philosophical tradition does not assist as much as one might hope our understanding of the ethical implications of the biosocial networking and social clustering revealed by new biological studies or evolutionary theories.[20] Perhaps because subjective sentiment never seems adequate for explaining the complexity of ethics, philosophers inevitably resort to moral reason to do the work of this communal dynamic. Even theorists like Adam Smith, who value the role of sentiment in moral theory, claim that only humans are capable of the highest level of moral development because they alone have the ability to construct abstract and disinterested judgments: "It is in this specific area, famously symbolized by Smith's . . . 'impartial spectator,' that humans seem to go radically further than other primates."[21] On this view, humans internalize the perspective of an impartial spectator in order to construct objective moral judgments.

Yet the elephants living on the edge in Uganda, with their rich social memories, do not seem to require an impartial spectator stance to carry on a complex ethical life. Meanwhile, the impartial spectator positions appropriated by colonizing humans who receive credentials through an education in the same modern canon that has configured animals as their mute inferiors do not appear to be neutral to the objects of their study. After extensive research on baboons in the wild, Barbara Smuts is sure that these communal creatures ("selves-in-communities") read past the socially out-of-tune scientist-observer's pretense of an objective posture to search for the ulterior motives of what, in their eyes, is just another social primate.[22] For these primates, the scientist's neutral style of engagement demonstrates a distinct lack of manners. Given the history of moral failures of scientific and philosophical reason, social animals (humans and nonhuman) may well find key resources for ethical flourishing not in abstract laws constructed by intellectual or political elites but in the social intelligence of animal societies.

EROS AND THANATOS; OR, POCKETS OF LIFE AND ENTROPY

Is not nature trapped in biochemical and physical laws that deprive it of any final ethical relevance? Is that not what the science after all amounts to? Symbiotic and parasitic processes account for how living systems add complexity to physical systems and may thereby suspend but not ultimately contradict the laws of physics. As physics' laws predict, living systems succumb to the second law of classical thermodynamics concerning entropy and the dispersal of energy. These systems are indirectly and dialectically headed toward the prescriptively neutral plane of self-annihilation. The death drive rules. Yet, against creationists who insist that the scientific laws cannot explain life because "thermodynamic systems become random, disorganized, less complex over time, whereas livings systems apparently [have] increased in levels of organization and complexity," Margulis and Sagan suggest that life's origin and increasing biodiversity are entirely consistent with all the laws of physics including entropy.[23] Living matter, they argue, organizes itself into locally complex structures for the very purpose of reducing gradients of energy within the larger environment in which they function. Their example is the tropical forest, where increasing biodiversity in fact works to cool the environment. This ultimate cooling, or decrease in gradients of energy, as predicted by thermodynamics, sets the backdrop for Margulis and Sagan's otherwise astonishing conclusion, given that this same diabolical science has seemingly stripped any ultimate sense of purpose from our experience of nature: "Thus it seems to us that, without invoking any vitalism or mysticism or spiritualism, we can recognize in ourselves a 'purpose.' This purposefulness is an offshoot of the thermodynamic tendency to come to equilibrium."[24]

In short, this movement toward increasing diversity and complexity defines life, and yet living matter functions in a larger physics where the "purpose" of life is overridden by a drive toward entropy. This biological glimpse into purpose and meaning replaces but also in an uncanny way maps on to Freud's life and death drives—with the life drive aiming now for symbiotic or cooperative systems of complexity and biodiversity but ultimately toward chaos. Here is a cosmology driven by death and yet sustaining pockets of life. Life is a comic detour—a happy passage in the old Greek sense of flourishing, not the new modern sense of subjective pleasure—through the increasing complexity of matter otherwise headed toward absurd demise.

Donna Haraway steers clear of the near magical uplift of life as a single living Gaia, as well as its demise into entropic chaos, as she forcefully mobilizes this cosmology of life for a more strictly down-to-earth, left-leaning visionary political ethics. With her, we turn to pockets of life. She introduces her 2008 book *When Species Meet* with an enticing piece of data: "human genomes can be found in only about 10 percent of all the cells that occupy the mundane space I call my body; the other 90 percent of the cells are filled with the genomes of bacteria, fungi, protists, and such some of which play in the symphony necessary to my being alive at all, and some of which are hitching a ride and doing the rest of me, of us, no harm."[25] Such a deconstructed displacement of an undone subject who reappears as a knot in a weave of multispecies associations supports a novel political model of world building, which Haraway invites us to imagine as an "*alter-globalisation* and *autre-mondialisation.*"[26] Here she draws her terms from European political activists whose provocations against "militarized neoliberal models of world building are not about antiglobalization but about nurturing a more just and peaceful other globalization. There is a promising *autre-mondialisation* to be learned in retying some of the knots of ordinary multispecies living on earth."[27]

While Kropotkin primarily understood the evolutionary force of cooperative societies through the interactions internal to each species, the new animal studies in the vein of Haraway's *autre-mondialisation* offer an interspecies communicative ethics, untying and retying knots in the multilayered fabrics of an affect-laden sociality that wrap the planet. It begins as an "interdomain communication," a signaling structure that rejects the old view of "animal development as an autonomous process directed by the genome," as Margaret McFall-Ngai and her coauthors explain in research that corroborates Margulis's originally controversial and visionary work.[28] Shared ecosystems or intimate symbioses allow for mutual flourishing through "social behaviors" found all the way down to bacteria, which communicate with each other and their hosts, most likely from their home in the gut, through chemical signaling (3233). "Although animals and bacteria have different forms and lifestyles, they recognize one another and communicate in part because . . . their genomic 'dictionaries' share a common and deep evolutionary ancestry" (3233). "The ecosystem that is an individual animal and its many microbial communities . . . does not occur in isolation but is nested within communities of other organisms that, in turn, coexist in and influence successively larger neighborhoods comprising ever more complex assemblages of microbes, fungi, plants, and animals" (3234–3235). "Applying metacommunity and network analyses" suggests that "features once considered exceptional, such as symbiosis, are now recognized as likely the rule" (3235).

A living web of interspecies communities functions more or less effectively, as Margulis and Sagan suggest, by a tranquil cooling off of bioregions; it ultimately may yield to random entropic equilibrium—the end of everything. But before giving physicists and their laws the last word, and going all in with their dice-throwing god, the vital élan of life's comic detour demands more play. This force of life emerges most artfully for Haraway in ludic interactions, especially in those cross-species companionships that perhaps no one describes more intriguingly than Marc Bekoff. Bekoff is among the handful of biologists whom Haraway praises when she calls upon recent academic philosophers, including Jacques Derrida, to engage more fully with the animals they speculate about, so that they might begin their reflections from the experience of companionship. Science undertaken as a mode of companionship contrasts with the impersonal spectator stance, which when viewed through age-old comic techniques sets itself up as in the position of the imposter or tyrant (*alazon* or *hybristae*) ripe for unmasking. In the case of Derrida, his by now famous encounter with the gaze of his cat in the bathroom, stripped down to the full monty—or *au naturel* for the French—provides an occasion for him to reflect upon the shame of a human history that has figured animals as reactive machines rather than responsive creatures with their own point of view.[29] Haraway wonders if Derrida's subsequent appeal via Jeremy Bentham to the virtue of pity in the face of animal suffering misses the affective richness of a light-hearted encounter—the companionship he might have enjoyed had he not been hung up on the cat's apparent lack of "the Name." Rather than pitying animals as poor wordless creatures, "how much more promise," Haraway ponders, "is in the questions, Can animals play? Or work? And even, can I learn to play with this cat?"[30]

Whatever thoughts might cross one's mind regarding Derrida's self-exposure to his cat, Haraway's seductive attunement to the interspecies politics of camaraderie and play offers a delightful glimpse into an *autre*-ethics. Animals at play and anarchists at work (or vice versa) generate a vibe of synergy that can challenge social inequalities and hierarchies while serving to strengthen social bonds. Poststructuralist critique exposes the ruses of reason, but gives too little in its hand waving toward the vulnerability of unknowable others. Derrida's cat remains a figure and not a character in his life. Haraway's provocative critique allows us to pursue another ethics, one that enjoys glimpses of communion in play. Haraway links her own contributions to political ethics in terms of an inevitably elusive but nonetheless revitalizing ideal that she borrows from chemist and philosopher Isabelle Stengers. Stengers proposes, "in the spirit of a feminist communitarian anarchism," what Haraway describes as a "utopia of equality and spontaneous nature."[31] Haraway also alerts us that neither she nor Stengers aims to denounce life in the name of some ideal other world far removed from ordinary reality. The cosmopolitan peace that she seeks "demands work" and occurs in a "force field, not in some Eden outside it."[32] Here green-world ideals serve as guides and inspired moments of peace in the flux of ordinary life (see also chapters 4 and 5).

For Haraway, a "polite" encounter between or within species suspends the effects of otherwise inevitable force fields, detouring around the looming chaos of random fights and flights in biothermodynamic systems for the sake of the highly organized chaos found in pockets of life. This is how she understands the "cosmopolitics" of "peace"; to be sure, these polite encounters offer insight into trans-species politics. With or without what philosophers call logos, social carnivores such as wolves, humans, and other predators reveal themselves as capable of suspending aggressive sexual or predatory drives to cultivate friendly relations with creatures who otherwise might have served as prey. The social dynamic of play provides an opening into what may well be the most egalitarian origin for ethics. Long before its discovery as a central philosophical notion by the German romantics, play had entered into the social field as a transformative force.[33] While German romanticism narrows the liberating potential of the play impulse to the freedom of art and the imagination, here the locus of play is shifted resolutely from the interior psyche of the subject to a social arena that crosses species barriers. That revolutionary eros, which Marcuse recovers from German romanticism, and celebrated as a freeing of repressive sexuality, reemerges more recently as a playfully serious ethics of mutual aid in Occupy and autre-globalization social movements. Moreover, this eros ethics plays across species lines.

ROLLING OVER FOR SOFT BITES: CARNIVORES AT PLAY

That revitalizing moment of what Judith Butler, in "Bodies in Alliance and the Politics of the Street" (2011), characterizes as European social movements' "passage through anarchy" unleashes a subversive politics of eros that has attracted social theorists at least since Kropotkin.[34] This eros politics may resist systematic articulation, and in fact the missing link to any system may be just the point. However, anarchy's resistance to normal, normative aims displays an unexpected resemblance to what biologists observe among wolves and other animals in the wild. Egalitarian social gestures among animals cavorting across lines of rank and species reveal capacities for suspending predator-prey relations and violent drives for sexual release and for earnestly mocking those baroque social hierarchies that repress the élan vital.

Anecdotes of cross-species communion abound. At another zoo, this time in Tokyo rather than on Wall Street and featuring nonhuman animals rather than our tabloid fantasies about them, "a rat snake named Aochan befriended a dwarf hamster named Gohan. The hamster was originally offered as a meal; Oachan refused to eat the animal and seemed to prefer sharing a cage with her; now Gohan even naps on Aochan's back."[35] Such pleasure-driven social capacities that "our old Paleolithic brains" share with other species can, as Bekoff speculates, reengage humans in the "close interrelationships with other beings that help us figure out who we are in the grand scheme of things."[36] These delightful capacities for enjoyment certainly give a wholesome new meaning to playing with one's food. "Some ecologists take this even further," Bekoff continues, "to wonder if, when studying 'ecological interactions'—that is, encounters among different species of animals and interactions between animals and trees and plants—it makes more sense to concentrate on positive ecological interactions rather than on competition and predations."[37]

This Paleolithic-era ethics has cosmopolitical consequences. Those occasional egalitarian interspecies relationships may have preceded the rise of highly stratified urban and cultural centers and the inflexible abstractions these centers produce.[38] Hunting and gathering societies from the Paleolithic era had mild social hierarchies compared to those that developed along with large-scale agriculture. These hunter-gatherer societies are now thought to have cultivated alliances and communal practices with other species with whom they shared a home or a habitat. While these Paleolithic societies may seem far removed from urban lifestyles, a small-scale society ethos may continue to shape social expectations in large-scale societies. Toni Morrison writes of the ancient communal ethos of African and Greek cultures surviving in African American cultures (see introduction). Capacities for cooperation and prosocial behavior may have developed in hunter-gatherer societies a long time ago and even then may have extended, if tenuously and uncertainly, beyond intimate communities to communities of strangers.

The endless modern quests for meaning undertaken by those outsiders within and strangers among us—including renegade scientists, feminist anarchists, and subversive philosophers rematerialize, I am arguing, in this Paleolithic ethos. "Darwin [in his later and previously neglected work] argued that emotions evolved in both animals and humans for the purpose of furthering social bonds in group-living animals."[39] Social bonds, and not just emotions or reasoning capacities per se, are key. Research on the evolution of human morality typically focuses on primates and looks for signs of the moral reason presumed to occur uniquely or superiorly among modern humans. But Bekoff's studies of play behavior in social carnivores alters this evolutionary trajectory.[40] If play behavior, as he suggests, provides a training ground for learning the "Golden Rule—do until other as you would have them do unto you" in "wolves, coyotes, red foxes, and domestic dogs," then the very meaning of "rule" changes.[41] Philosophers might think of a moral equivalent to Wittgenstein's game-changing discussion of rule following for linguistics in *Philosophical Investigations*. In contrast with the abstract equality of atomized individuals before modern laws, friendly play provides a training ground for a concretely situated reciprocity that binds selves-in-communities.[42] Moreover, unlike modern moral laws whose core concept of fairness abstracts from concrete situations and inevitable power differentials, codes of play have built-in rites and rules about self-handicapping that do more than ignore social hierarchies. These codes protect the vulnerable by enforcing the requirement that the powerful set aside their power. These are the codes of anarchic communitarianism.

The development of social codes for fair play among wolves and other social carnivores establishes the basis for a radically egalitarian solidarity across an indefinite range of species. The two key features of play praxis—role reversal and self-handicapping—exercise social equality by leveling playing fields and building camaraderie. Role reversal functions as an ethical gesture when a dominant carnivore rolls over on her back exposing her vulnerable belly to a trusted playmate. Self-handicapping occurs in the soft bites of play-fighting. In the context of the normal operations of hierarchal societies and predatory hunts, both these behavioral gestures would compromise status or safety and fail to serve aggressive or sexual desires. "For the time they [these carnivores] are playing, they put aside or neutralize any inequalities in physical size and social rank."[43]

The playful exercise of capacities for reciprocity likely establishes social codes akin to what humans conceptualize as the golden rule, as Bekoff suggests. But note that social play's purposeless purposefulness lacks the determinate character assumed by deontological (Kantian) interpretations of the golden rule. In playful exchanges, wolves and other carnivores appear to break out of normal roles and social expectations, allowing creative and spontaneous responses to fellow creatures. The carnivore's rule is felt and formative, not formulaic. Self-handicapping fosters creative encounters where playmates differ significantly in capacities or desires and thus cannot be treated exactly like, or strictly analogous to how, one would want to be treated oneself. Determinate moral laws fail to account for this kind of flexibility because of their abstract formulation. Play's tacit social knowledge is gestural and affect-based and through its conceptual indeterminacy tuned to concrete situations. Moreover, social play exhibits an egalitarian element that goes beyond law's abstract equality. Participants in play treat each other as more than abstract equals. Through self-handicapping and role reversal, the dominant participant actually yields real and symbolic power to the playmate. This yielding of social and political capital grounds horizontal reciprocity and contrasts with the charitable giving of resources, which might display the character virtue of benevolence, but does not alter the social field.

Carnivores who fail to play well are expected to signal an apology and to attempt to reestablish bonds of trust. In dogs and wolves, this apology is signaled with a bow, the same gesture that also indicates a voluntary intent to play.[44] Similarly, humans seek to rectify transgressions through symbolic gestures or words and deeds of repentance. Those playground bullies and political tyrants who persist in breaking the social codes for selves-in-communities are isolated or ostracized.[45] As warned of in ancient tragedies, the *hybristai* are not the harmless parasites; like those financial wizards of Wall Street, their acts of arrogance unravel the basis of trust in communities.

This lawless lawfulness of the anarchic encounter is not wild rage and unorganized chaos. Playful engagements allow animals to suspend the normal rules of hierarchical societies and cultivate *autre* codes, aspects of which appear in what may well be among the most complex of our arts, those of satire and comedy. These arts of life and laughter are those as well of anarchic communitarianism.

CARNIVORES AT THE CARNIVAL

The egalitarian gestures of carnivore social life take center stage in human cultures as various techniques of comedy. These comic techniques are found, for example, in what Russian literary theorist Mikhail Bakhtin describes as ancient rituals of the carnival and have since reappeared, for instance, during the time of American slavery in New Orleans's Congo Square. These folk festivals unleash biting satire to mock the elites, signal common vulnerability to lower everyone's psychological defenses, and celebrate a "utopian realm of community, freedom, equality and abundance."[46] Too often overlooked by political and moral theorists, carnival techniques subvert norms, disrupt authoritarian discourse, and release a contagious and revitalizing energy across lines of rank and privilege. Without the carnivalesque, social movements may turn puritanical and lose their communitarian spirit.

Marcuse falls just short of the carnival vision when he declares to the protesting youth in his 1966 preface to *Eros and Civilization* that their sexual liberation operates according to a biological necessity rooted in animal instincts. These youth were said to be at the "forefront of those who live and fight for Eros against Death, and against a civilization which strives to shorten the 'detour to death.'"[47] Sexual drives, he thought, offered a detour (in Butler's terms, an anarchic passage) against the inevitable regression to the inorganic. But Marcuse narrowed life-affirming eros to sexual eros and play to the highly cultivated art of the individual and human imagination. The carnival transposes what Marcuse identifies as the "political fight . . . the fight for life, the fight for Eros" into a comic key where multiple species might play along, too.

"Carnival was the true feast of time, the feast of becoming, change, and renewal."[48] Variations of medieval marketplace carnivals, including religious travesties and parodies known as the "feast of fools" and the "feast of the ass," would feature processions of dancing animals mixed in with grotesquely copulating, growing, aging, and decomposing average folk. Amidst this spectacle, destabilizing, regenerative laughter refused to respect social distinctions, and the fool was expected to speak truth to power.[49] Think of what modern liberal political philosophy—whether based on deontological respect or that utilitarian preference for Socratic dissatisfaction over a fool or pig's pleasure—is missing!

Central features of the carnival—playful contests, the mockery and inversion of arbitrary social ranks, and the refusal to allow any single voice to dominate—repeat in human and animal vernacular the core gestures of carnivore play. The playful coupling of generating and degenerating bodies that is erotic but not narrowly sexual explodes in carnival as life's central force. Satiric attacks on imperial Rome, the modern State, and the medieval Church denounce false idols and proclaim from more ancient times "a bodily democracy."[50] Carnival "play, like Christian grace, can allow the last to become first, with joyful results," as Haraway finds with her companion animals.[51] Here, in the green world of comedy, death is deferred and degeneration redeemed. "Time plays and laughs!"[52]

The carnivalesque draws from yet other aspects of carnivore play. In addition to role reversal and self-handicapping, recall that Bekoff mentions a third gesture that keeps the play in carnivore play. "Play frequently begins with a bow . . . [in dogs and canids], and bowing is repeated during play sequences so as to insure that play doesn't turn into something else, like fighting or mating."[53] Through the use of this signal, the ludic mood can prevail despite temptations to reassert the privileges of rank or status. The joy of play (akin to opiates in the brain) can overwhelm and suspend negative emotions, including fear of play's risks. The suspension of fear and aggression determines when play can occur across vertical social hierarchies, even for species that normally relate as predator and prey. Bekoff explains the significance of the bow in terms of a humility that reassures the other one intends no harm. This play bow, I suspect, may also translate into what we humans call self-irony, or the humor that includes oneself among the vulnerable targets of the joke. In this case the carnivore's bow, like self-irony, would signal that one does not exempt oneself from laughter's leveling field.

What Bekoff enlists as a fourth feature of carnivore play—the social contagion of a shared mood—illustrates play's emancipatory reach beyond individuals to a group or community. The play spirit of carnivores can generate through contagion a field of affect larger than the individuals engaged. Along these same lines, Malini Suchak has found that playful moods are among the most contagious in chimpanzees, fully capable of defining that larger social field.[54] There are days, she observes, when first two individuals are playing and then others join and then still others. Finally, most individuals are playing, even those who are not particularly playful. She believes that this happens far more often than the spread of a negative mood (such as an aggressive mood). The playful mood is stimulated in part through contagious laughter, which various animal species exhibit in diverse ways. Dogs, for instance, laugh through a dry panting noise.

Waves of laughter lower defenses and mock the borders of subjects and groups, exposing these borders as more porous than might have been thought.[55] Of course, not all laughter works this way. Sometimes it reinforces social boundaries; other times it serves as mere entertainment and a safety valve for life as usual. But laughter can also open pathways for unexpected alliances and for the purposeless purpose of those social and political arts though which the rules of justice are learned as the rules of fair play. A statement appearing in Occupy's *Adbusters America* calls for a "kind of radical play that re-enchants the world" and is signed "for the wild, Culture Jammers HQ."[56] Perhaps a glimpse into the wild at "ZOO-cotti" can recapture for a moment the emancipatory vision of a profoundly social eros: this time one that reties knots for interspecies living, Paleolithic style.

3

AFFECT ATTUNEMENT

Discourse Ethics Across Species

The first language of mankind, the most universal and vivid, in a word the only language man needed . . . was the simple cry of nature.

—JEAN-JACQUES ROUSSEAU, *DISCOURSE ON THE ORIGIN OF INEQUALITY*

Compelling glimpses into the striking communicative capacities of our animal kin reveal elements of coevolving biosocial norms. The potential for cross-species norms of social interaction broadens what Habermasians (and other second-generation critical theorists) define too narrowly as "communicative," or "discourse," ethics.[1] Habermasian discourse ethics counters classic liberalism's atomic individualism by insisting that rational discussion in a public sphere, rather than rational arguments constructed solely by a lone individual, generates an appropriately communitarian basis for moral norms. Feminist critique has prompted recent critical theorists to acknowledge more inclusive discursive styles. The concern is that old school discourse ethics, by privileging elite, formal styles of communication based on rational debate, dismisses gestures, narratives, and other affect-based modes of public persuasion together with broader conceptions of what counts as political space (Iris Young, Noëlle McAfee).[2] Advancing critical theory further yet, we ask: Are there not multiple channels for biosocial exchange across diverse species? Do not communicative lines through visual, aural, gestural, olfactory, pheromonal, and neurochemical transfers of social signals and crisscrossed modes of social contest open networks of discourse in mix-species public spaces? In this quasi-naturalized cosmopolitical setting, the sexually charged eros/

affectless logos binary of first and second generations of critical theory (Marcuse and Habermas) morphs into a biosocial ethos that forges a political ethics of connections and communities within and across species. Central to this dynamic process of contestation and ethical engagement is not formal debate in human-only societies but a multimodal flow of affect attunement in mixed species societies.

ANIMAL ATTUNEMENTS AS ELEMENTARY ETHICS

Consider the remarkable report of a female bonobo confined in a British zoo who assists a bird found in her cage by spreading its wings so that this fellow creature might fly away to freedom (chapter 4).[3] Or the report of a cat in a nursing home who curls up around dying elderly patients and remains steadily by their side as they, unbeknownst to the medical personnel, pass away.[4] Or a sacred moment of shared silence by a stream for baboons in East Africa (chapter 4).[5] Recall as well the ethical practices that spontaneously emerge among wolves at play (chapter 2).[6] On the basis of extensive new work in the field of animal studies, Frans de Waal argues that such anecdotes are far from rare and that the core elements of ethics appear across a number of species. Perhaps nonhuman animals fail to have a capacity for abstract moral reasoning.[7] Yet, as psychologists point out, even in humans, ethical concern for others transpires primarily through the affect-laden images, gestures, and symbols that guide judgment and action.[8] Think of the symbolic force of a bird in flight for human, and, perhaps too, bonobo, ideals of freedom! Our hairy and feathery kin without a doubt demonstrate elements of ethical response, and they have been known on occasion to extend their concern to creatures beyond their own species. Of course, they will also bite each other's heads off or eat their young as well. But this is just to say that animals are neither natural innocents nor savage brutes in some mythic state of nature. Like us, they are citizens and coworkers armed with various ethical capacities and communicative technologies in a postlapsarian world of good and evil.[9]

What kind of philosophical approach could account for psychologically and politically savvy, post-Nietzschean genealogies of cross-species ethics? Biologists, primatologists, and anthropologists are redrawing the lines for what Isabelle Stengers refers to as cosmopolitical ecology.[10] This worldly biopolitics aims to locate relevant social norms and expectations encompassing diverse species in contested but overlapping habitats. In search of tacit communicative channels across species, this chapter examines well-established research on the responsive, preverbal connection of the human infant and adult caregiver.[11] Affect attunement articulates a preverbal social bond between infant and adult based on a predominantly nonconscious immersion in the rhythms and tones of ordinary life.[12] We then trace how emerging research in animal studies mobilizes nonrationalistic eros ethics beyond its human exceptionalist and occasionally sexualized roots in Luce Irigaray, Enrique Dussel, Africana feminism, Freudo-Marxist critical theory, and Plato to an ethics of affiliation and cohabitation across multiple species.[13] This *biosocial eros* ethics does not consign nonspeaking subjects or preconscious agents to a mute or melancholic ethical and political status. On the contrary, as we shall see, affect-laden protoconversations weave substantial threads of a communicative ethics across regions of the biosphere.[14] Due no doubt to overlapping, coevolving, or parallel evolutionary processes, communicative channels within and across species provide pathways for a postmoral critical theory of interspecies ethics.

This postmoral ethics recontextualizes the standard philosophical tools of moral reason and abstract thought within a larger range of sense-giving experiences relevant for meaningful animal (and human) life.[15] A meaningful animal life is not one of struggle, self-preservation, or adaptation, as postulated by some evolutionary theories, but of exploited labor and transgressive challenge, intimate friendships and contested terrains, and micro- and macro-communities and biosocial clustering. Life's ethicality—its meaningfulness—primarily grows out of this breathing tapestry rather than from moral capacities for self-organization, self-legislation, or self-cultivation per se. The latter formulas for personality grooming may unwittingly weaken life of its prime virtue—resilience—and empty existence of meaning by unloosening threads and untying knots of local biosocial and worldly webs.

A tentative glance at the extensive animal and childhood research supports the relevance of several key layers for a multispecies ethics including: 1) attunement through rhythms, smells, affect-laden tones or other often preconscious channels of biosocial signaling; 2) face-to-face, nose-to-crotch, or alternative modes of intersubjectivity;[16] and 3) community or cohabitation that may conjure a felt sense of place or home through social expectations. In our earlier chapters, we examined everyday norm formation, through solidarity, play, and reciprocity as layers of engagement constituting the second and third layers of eros ethics. There we discovered that with "prolonged exposure, members of two different species can co-create shared conventions that help to regulate interspecies encounters," as Barbara Smuts concludes from her friendships with nonhuman primates and dogs.[17] A sense of belonging as home emerges for some species through the felt and formative rules of play rather than determinate moral law or the abstraction formulations and calculations of liberalism's social contract. A playful encounter is the best indicator not only of peace in primate societies but also of friendly belonging. This ethos of peaceful cohabitation is far from the border patrol of any homeland security apparatus in part because its sense of home is not insulated from struggle and contest. On the contrary, its golden rule sizes up power differentials and subverts them, reconfiguring politics' groundless ground through Jean-Jacques Rousseau's emancipatory call for fraternity as solidarity and mutual aid. To Rousseau and other modern thinkers of the Enlgithenment, we have posed the question: Are not perhaps animals too born free and yet everywhere in chains? This chapter explores ethical comportment through affect attunement occurring at a more elementary level of social engagement, often emerging below the level of conscious awareness and extending to micro-organisms. Aspects of this phenomena constitute biosocial eros ethics' first layer, composing the dense texture of mixed species societies. Later chapters turn to an ever more speculative, vertical axis of experience to expose a possible fourth dimension of interspecies life.

A PRELIMINARY STAGE: BIOSOCIAL NETWORKS OF MICRO- AND SUPERORGANISMS

This chapter's primary focus is on communicative awareness of ethical claims and social expectations through affect attunement. However, social animal politics reverberates with the imperceptible transmissions of energy of often very simple organisms. Scientific research tracks biosocial forces of meaningful attunement, or "structural coupling" (to borrow a suggestive term from Humberto Maturana and Gerda Verden-Zoller), that can cross natural and built environments apart from any actual or possible subjective attention or conscious awareness.[18]

Consider the partly measurable impact of minuscule organisms on human affects. A team of neuroscientists theorizes that those of us living in a "cleaner, modern society" suffer from a greater risk of depression due to modern practices that fail to expose us to some of the smallest animals.[19] According to these neuroscientists, there is "mounting evidence that disruptions in ancient relationships with microorganisms in soil, food and the gut" strip us "superorganisms" (including those of us previously known as individuals) of little creatures, or "parasites," who might better be called old friends. This research raises the question of how we might relearn to accommodate these "'old friends,' [who] have taught our immune systems how to tolerate harmless microorganisms."[20] Given new research on the "gut brain," one could hypothesize that exposure to these networks of germs would make us more resilient and, to draw upon a colloquial expression, that virtue that now turns out to have some science behind it, downright gutsy.[21] This gutsy resilience (recall, from chapter 1, Douglass on "animal spirits") may well be thought of as the primary virtue cultivated in living creatures and their social networks.

Indeed, not just microorganisms, but massive superorganisms, as described by various social network theories, can likewise regulate the affect and physical function of nodes—aka people—through a process generally mysterious and yet statistically measurable. It is as though we humans not only have a multiply inhabited gut brain, but belong to a larger one.

Consider studies suggesting that one's friends and even one's friends' friends—including people we do not know—can affect any number of dimensions of our lives, including obesity patterns as well as levels of happiness. Researchers have found that if a person's friend, a friend's friend, or a friend's friend's friend loses weight, then that person is also likely to lose weight.[22] A happy association of friends is more likely to make for individual human happiness than lots of money, but also more than sad friends and sad friends of friends and so on to what scientists postulate as typically three degrees of separation.[23]

Affects can spread like a physical contagion across thousands of miles via waves of energy transmission. Whole epidemics of panic, fear, and even laughter spread through these imperceptible waves in diverse and crisscrossing social media. One creature may smell another's fear or disgust. This happens without any personal acquaintance with other nodes (people) in the network and without what we could call personal agency or responsibility for the norms or behavior that people imitate and spread to others. In seasonal depression, the biosphere itself changes the mood of entire populations, as energies flow from node to node in the network without conscious intentionality. Nicholas Christakis and James Fowler portray these ripple effects as "a kind of synchrony in time and space . . . that resembles the flocking of birds or schooling of fish. Whole interconnected groups of smokers, who may not even know one another, quit together at roughly the same time, as if a wave of opposition to smoking were spreading through the population."[24] Psychological states and physical diseases ranging from depression and anxiety to cancer develop regardless of individual exertion because we inhabit a social milieu that broadcasts them.[25]

Needless to say, these researchers are as perplexed as any of us would be with what becomes of that modern concept of moral responsibility. Modern moral theory (Kant's ethics of duty and Mill's utilitarianism) attributes the primary responsibility for moral acts to those relatively bound creatures called individuals. Indeed, the metaphysics for bound substances, in contrast with erotically charged, ecstatic ones, goes back at least as far as Aristotle. These modern and classical traditions leave us wondering: How can we interpret responsibility in relation to those nodes of networks for cascades of agential affect that occur at this level of the superorganism? Might we reinvoke the tragic ethos of primitive societies, those for whom a foul air and a symbolic scapegoat carry the toxins of damage or harm? Or do we shift away from a moral discourse of blame to a therapeutic discourse of adaptation and normality and recommend, as do the investigators, that social policy "target [for treatment] the hubs of the network, namely those at the center of the network or those with the most contact"?[26] Perhaps neither scapegoating rituals nor disciplining therapeutic models rest easily among those who are wary of the cruel rites and arbitrary techniques of communal exclusion and bureaucratic surveillance. In the next chapters, we examine cathartic dimensions of community building and spiritual rituals within and across species. But here one thing is for sure: just the attempt to draw clean modernesque lines around the problem of agency can be an angst-ridden if not a downright depressing undertaking.

Cycles of energy circulate through superorganisms and microorganisms to produce good and bad climates of affect and biological well-being. Patterns of affect may crystallize into cultural norms or social expectations and further shape individual behavior. In turn, waves of resilience and resistance (certainly from the hubs of networks, but perhaps, more subversively, from alliances at the margins as well) may loop around and undermine norms or precipitate large-scale climate changes in the collective mood. The absence of capacities for self-management among nodes may be, as these theorists suggest, unsettling. However, network models that call into question the bound self do not entail that subjectivity and agency are vacuous notions.

THE WAVE-AND-PARTICLE MODEL OF ETHICS

Let's take one lesson by way of an analogy drawn from the epistemological reflections of physicist philosopher Karen Barad.[27] The discovery of light diffraction prompted physicists to model elementary matter as both a particle and a wave depending upon the measuring apparatus, rendering reality fundamentally indeterminate prior to technological intervention. Similarly, new research on biosocial networks and affect prompts us to propose that while social phenomena on occasion take the shape of bound and discrete moral subjects (particles), we particles also can function as ecstatic nodes within clouds of collective affect (waves). Semimeasurable waves of kinetic and hedonic affect suspend or otherwise play with our bounded identities and relocate us through connections that zigzag unexpectedly—comically, tragically, mysteriously—through regions of the biosphere. Eros ethics aims to capture the impact of this zigzag through the biosphere in search of possibilities for coflourishing. In the meantime, a counterintuitive dual model of ethics shatters the metaphysics that reifies substances as the sole unit of the real. Perhaps the fluidity of waves escapes conventional metaphysics due to our cognitive and linguistic limits, given that the human species often learns by pointing and communicates through words that are names for things. (Recall distinct primate learning styles from chapter 1). Other communicative modes, patterned after the dual model of energy transmission, map routes for broadening biosocial ethics.

Given our wave-and-particle model of ethics, all is not lost for those erotically charged creatures all-too-narrowly conceived as bound individuals. The wavelike circulation of energy and affect from microorganism to superorganism *seems* to render those of us formerly known as sovereign subjects or autonomous agents as impersonal nodes, mere theoretical entities, playthings for scientists and policy makers or primitive sacrifices, but otherwise unreal. However, in this new world where science and paradox are good friends, these waves of affect can accentuate rather than diminish singular personalities even as they fray edges and traverse individual and group identities. Through their zigzag action, these waves expand the self from an inner psyche to relational webs with and within other organisms that hover together in affect clouds. The unfurled "I" with its wings spread wide does indeed, as Walt Whitman proclaims in *Leaves of Grass*'s central poem, "Song of Myself," "contain multitudes."[28]

The beauty of these atmospheric attunements is that they need not erase our unique singularity even as we lose ourselves in the transpersonal and presubjective experience that interlocks any number of living creatures. As every caregiver at some level knows, newborns manifest distinct temperaments before they develop a sense of self. Similarly, schools of fish caught in algorithms of wavelike motion may be subjectless (who knows?), but nonetheless feature the antics of singular creatures with their distinct styles of response. In short, waves of energy reveal singular creatures who coexist as nodes of biosocial networks.

CROSS-MODAL CORRESPONDENCE IN THE BIOSPHERE'S MIDDLE ZONE: THE CASE OF HUMANS AND THEIR INFANTS

Attentive parents experience to varying degrees preverbal modes of communication with their infants through the nerve-racking anxieties and novel pleasures of attempts at affect attunement. At early stages of infancy, we interact in improvisational modes of affect exchange. These modes of interaction trace at an elementary level the social dynamic of a call-and-response eros ethics. The locution from Africana culture not only suits parenting well but also jazzes up what has been misperceived, along with other invisible "women's work," as unadventurous and repetitive routines of nurture and care. This charged dynamic between infants and caregivers occurs before a sense of self emerges in the infant. The unique patterns of affect give the neonate a special feel of its own prior to more complex aspects of personality, including emotions, motives, intentions, and intersubjective play. During this early period, social interaction through crying, touching, rocking, and, after the first couple of months, cooing and eye-to-eye contact establishes a nuanced basis for the expression and communication of affects. The warm smile of an affable infant may beget a smile back from a responsive caregiver, or, as a variation, a hug. This communication of affects either within or across sensory modalities (visual, tactile, olfactory, etc.) is the basis for "affect attunement."

The significance of attunement for the development of the emerging self has been explained in detail by Daniel Stern.[29] Theories of affect attunement explore how we share but also, crucially, how we challenge and alter moods, affects, and desires. Attunement is not a simple imitation or mirroring process by any means. An adult may respond to the irritated cry of an infant by intoning a light and soothing "there there there," and the very young infant, who can already recognize the mother's voice from before birth, may respond by calming down. The infant's irritated cry may be soothed just as readily through a reassuring touch as by an adult's modulated voice—that is, adult and infant may vary the sensory modes they use to respond to each other. The older infant may respond to the enthusiastic shimmy of a playful adult with a quasi-musical cooing that matches in hedonic tone and kinetic energy. This communication of affects across sensory modes is called "cross-modal correspondence." Unlike simple mimicry, this crossing of modes in call-and-response fashion communicates that someone is "home."[30] As we shall see, these proto-conversations can transmit that ineffable feeling that someone is at home all the way across species barriers.

Affects flow back and forth between infant and adult, establishing routes of communication without determinate concepts that the child, parent, or scientific bystander could draw upon to explain the correspondence. The significance of this point can be understood in the context of art and poetry. Consider the correspondences between alternative choreographies and the same musical piece. There are a multitude of seemingly right dance steps as well as wrong ones. The potential for reinterpreting the musical piece is part of the fascination of art. Just as there is no real accounting for tastes, so too there is no fixed rule or determinate concept or judgment for why one "response" works and another does not to any particular "call." Variation in styles of call and response makes these patterns meaningful expressions of singular creatures in particular cultures, and accounts in part for the variability of ethical life. Postmoral ethics is aesthetics.

What Mary Bateson explains as turn taking in these proto-conversations gives them ethical relevance, suggesting an original site for learning the norm of norms, reciprocity.[31] These playful patterns of call and response exemplify a rapport between infants and adults far from a flat-footed, nonludic utilitarian exchange or market-based calculation of equivalence. This spontaneous, creative turn taking in face-to-face play is an early step toward full-scale social play. As we discovered among social carnivores (chapter 2), human and nonhuman animals acquire a sense of fairness based on such egalitarian gestures as self-handicapping and role reversal as well as the turn taking of play-based reciprocity.

Through proto-conversations, creatures without adult human logos communicate a significant range of affects. Influenced by the work of Silvan S. Tomkins, Stern distinguishes affects into two types: (1) *categorical affects*, such as happiness, sadness, fear, anger, disgust, surprise, interest, shame, which exhibit both *hedonic* qualities of pleasure and pain and *rates of arousal* and activation (this last could have perhaps better constituted a third type); (2) *vitality affects and contours* (easily confused with arousal and activation rates), which express dynamic, *kinetic* patterns such as surging, crescendo, decrescendo, or explosiveness. Vitality is felt profoundly, for example, when one is energized and elevated in mood. Categorical affects, on the other hand, introduce the ethical qualities of good and bad to experience. Stern explains these affects in terms that, in retrospect hint at their vast relevance across the animal kingdom: "One can readily imagine, in fact, that the infant does not initially perceive overt acts as such, as do adults. (This act is a reach for the bottle . . .) Rather, the infant is far more likely to perceive directly . . . [the] vitality affects they express. Like dance for the adult, the social world experienced by the infant is primarily one of vitality affects before it is a world of formal acts."[32] As Stern elsewhere indicates, hedonic tone likewise enters into communicative exchanges with infants, as, for example, when infants seek the pleasant touch or the sweet milky fluid from another warm body, and, again, like vitality affects, without necessarily any grasp of an intentional act.[33] How networks of hedonic and vitality affect produce meaningful patterns of experience is a matter of speculation for psychologists. Yet these well-observed patterns do establish a basis for communication without requiring the presence of what we would ordinarily call a self or subject and intentionality. The "subjectless sociality" of early infancy becomes more complicated with the emergence of a self, but affects constitute an elementary ground for communicative ethics from infancy through adulthood.[34]

A genealogy of subjectivity, as explored in the waves that penetrate through the membranes of the atomistic self and compose affect-laden proto-conversations, aims to do justice to the felt relationships of unbound social creatures in ways that Enlightenment-era moral theories cannot. Physics' post-Newtonian shift in explanatory models inspires counterintuitive insights into relational subjectivity beyond the grasp of a finger-pointing, substance-oriented metaphysics. Like the phenomenon of light, ethical agency fluctuates between particle and wave models. This dual model of subjectivity unsettles the old metaphysical models and generates channels for ethical rapport and norm agreement across species.

At the same time, research on affect attunement in the caregiver relationship challenges rational autonomy and the possession of a coherent life plan as the most relevant ethical goals for maturity in humans. As Anna Gibbs observes, affects in adults "are not rudimentary, infantile, or so-called primitive modes of communication: rather, they are the essential prerequisites for, and working collaborators with, verbal communication."[35] The transmission of affects, however, is not, as affect theorists sometimes suggest, primarily a mirroring phenomenon. Affect exchange makes critical use of variations in sensory modes (vocal, facial expression, visual image, gestural, even olfactory) to communicate a significant range of corresponding meanings. Even the very young infant is capable of a cross-modal exchange that composes preverbal dialogue. The use of an alternative but matching mode of expression—say the adult's rhythmic moves and gestures back to the infant's preverbal cooing or vice versa—constitutes the surest way to acknowledge the other and respond in one's own singular signature style. Without such variation in modalities between infant and adult, either party might mistake the other's response as a mechanical reaction and lose interest in the exchange. For this reason, straight imitation or mirroring mimicry is not as central to social bonds as cross-modal response. Infants and parents are as ethical agents veritable artists, cocreating musical dialogues by varying the themes and the format for calls and responses.[36] The play is improvisational, not planned. Affect attunement across sensory modalities constitutes the basis for a call-and-response exchange at a level that may be preverbal, nonrational, and mysterious and yet vital for the ethicality of biosocial bonds.

This artistry signals the biosocial eros of creatures driven by something more than nutritive, sexual, or survival needs. Humans, their infants, and, as we shall see, other social creatures populate musicals of song and dance or other creative modes of attunement. Their affect-based exchanges may not exhibit the rational self-direction that defines autonomous individuals. In their proto-conversations, however, creatures display the willful character that testifies to desire and agency. A sensitive, mild-mannered creature may turn away from a loud or rough encounter. An adult might respond to a phlegmatic infant by jazzing up the encounter. Affect attunement is the primary bio-discourse of social creatures.

CROSS-MODAL CORRESPONDENCES ACROSS SPECIES: NONHUMAN PRIMATES AND THEIR INFANTS

Ever more evidence suggests that communication occurs within and across a wide range of animal species. Research on nonhuman primates alone renders clear the significance of affect-laden communication, beyond any formal discourse ethics, as the material stuff of social bonds. Without the social grooming relayed through affect attunement of mammals there is no basis for the social bond (aka the social contract) and thus no basis for a political community. Rational principle, bureaucratic rules, and institutionalized procedures cannot substitute formal agreement for the social materiality and existential depth of this felt bond and its social climate.

Steven Mithen, author of *The Singing Neanderthals* (2006), traces back our human capacity for multimodal communication through our evolutionary history, accounting for cross-cultural human responses to music and the prosody of our language. Analogous communication systems evolved independently in other primates. He cites Bruce Richman's study of "a profusion of rhythmic and melodic forms" in the movements and vocalizations among gelada monkeys: "As they approach one another, walk past one another or take leave of one another, as they start or stop social grooming, as they threaten someone because he is too close to a partner, solicit someone's support or reassurance, in fact as they do the infinite variety of different social actions that make up the minute-to-minute substance of their social lives they always accompany these actions with vocalizing."[37] Geladas are known as the "humming baboons," Malini Suchak explains further.[38] Unlike other baboon species, they eat grass, which means that, like cows, they are pretty much constantly pulling their nourishment from the ground and munching. That keeps their hands busy, which is a problem for a primate since the primary method of social bonding is grooming. Hence their constant vocalizations, mostly humming, may function as a sort of "vocal grooming." They use it to maintain social bonds when their hands are otherwise engaged. These vocalizations also fall into a pattern of call and response. Close social partners will hum back and forth to each other much as close social partners of other primates reciprocally groom each other. Crossing species lines, psychologist Lea Leinonen adds that even apart from social context humans can understand the emotional content of monkey calls.[39] In short, the capacity for multimodal communication, rooted in evolutionary history and based on social grooming, may account for coevolving, corresponding animal languages and ground peaceful coexisting communities.

Not all primates or even other baboons express themselves through vocalizing. While gibbons perform duets, and monkeys vocalize, the great apes employ multimodal communication by augmenting gestures with grunts and barks.[40] As Robert Provine reports, chimpanzees use these alternative means to develop as humans do, through creative attunements and misattunements. The playful dimension of these attunements may be the original instigator for play-based laughter, which, Provine argues, is one important element of the social glue that bonds friendships and communities. As he reports,

> In a rare field study of the interactions between chimpanzee mothers and infants, Frans Plooij made an important discovery about the roots of laughter. Baby chimps control the behavior of their mothers, with tickle and laughter playing significant roles in a nurturant *pas de deux*. . . . The chimp baby initiates mother-infant play by biting the mother, who then looks at and tickles the baby, triggering cycles of biting/tickling interplay that continue until the baby signals "too much" by "defending," fussing or crying. The baby signals the "just about right" amount of stimulation with a "play face" and laughter. In these duets the baby, not [or at least, not necessarily, I would add] the mother, initiates and regulates the interaction.[41]

If even baby chimps can assert claims in the social world, then so too might any number of creatures from other species.

BECOMING ANIMAL AND POSTMORAL ETHICS

The mounting evidence for animal communication moves us, with Donna Haraway, off poststructuralist tracks of repetitive critique and onward to visions of a communitarianism and cosmopolitanism across animal species.[42] The deconstruction of metaphysical notions of the subject along with those of substance leaves poststructuralism and its heirs without sufficient means of accounting for the multispecies eros of companionship or cohabitation.[43] Gilles Deleuze and Felix Guattari, for example, champion a process that they term "becoming-animal." In the chapter "Becoming-Intense, Becoming-Animal, Becoming-Imperceptible" from *A Thousand Plateaus: Capitalism and Schizophrenia*, they trace "a circulation of impersonal affects, an alternate current that disrupts signifying projects as well as subjective feelings, and constitutes a non-human sexuality."[44] This current is said to break up capitalist rhythms of repetitive dronelike work and mechanical expression to release vital forms of energy. Strangely, animals are recognized as having affects, but so are crystals: "it is the effectuation of the power of the pack that throws the self into upheaval and makes it reel," they write.[45] This release of erotic energy does not register the flows of affect that Haraway finds compelling in the "sentimental relationships" she enjoys with domestic companion animals.[46] Her concern is that the "pure affect animals" that Deleuze and Guattari admire, which they describe as "intensive, not extensive . . . sublime wolf packs," owe their sensibility to the perhaps sublime, but politically problematic, 1909 Futurist Manifesto, which glorified violence and war.[47] According to Haraway, the aesthetic interest in the intensive energy of animal packs, rather than of individual creatures, lends itself to disdain for domestic pets and presumably also for sentient, vulnerable creatures in the wild.[48]

Stern's distinction between the two kinds of affect (vitality and categorical) sheds light on Haraway's concern, offering one way to account for those cherished pleasures of companionship that she misses in Deleuze and Guattari's aggregate of "man-becoming-dog."[49] Through the Deleuzian aggregate a creature may transmit intensity (or what Stern terms vitality affects), but not the full range of hedonic social emotions and affective cognitions that account for affiliative and conflictual relationships. Moreover, the vitality affects lived in becoming-dog do not seem to express any particular subjectivity or singularity, but only the impersonal waves that flow through a pack. Vitality affects alone—no doubt richly used in such artistic enterprises as abstract expressionist painting and modern dance[50]—flatten the multiple dimensions of biosocial encounters. Unleashed vitality affects as expressed in man-becoming-dog might reinvigorate that death-driven, chaotic type of anticapitalist, antioedipal anarchism that Deleuze and Guattari celebrate. But this brand of anarchism neglects the playful, prosocial affects circulating among individuals and groups in those pockets of life sought by Haraway's feminist anarchic communitarianism (chapter 2). These social and cognitive affects compose much of the basis for the "proto-dialogues" between mutually grooming, companion species such as humans and dogs. Hedonic affects such as tenderness and warmth account for important features of intimacy and friendship. The impersonal sexual charge of man-becoming-dog contributes toward, but falls far short of, a full-fledged post-Marcusean critical theory of biosocial eros. The aim is to recognize animal agency and build intimate and political solidarities across species lines, suggesting an affirmative answer to Haraway's questions: "Can animals play? Or work? And even, can I learn to play with this cat? . . . What if work and play . . . open up the possibility of a mutual response?"[51]

While philosophers of eros (from Plato to Deleuze and Guattari) trace its origin to the electricity of sex, Haraway's attention to the tender pleasures broadens the valences of eros ethics from sexual libido toward social companionship. The early and foundational phase of sociality that prompts an affective exchange between infant and adult mammals orchestrates complex nonindividualistic identities: "Psychoanalytic observations suggest that pregnancy is a period of profound physiological and psychological change that culminates in a reconfiguration of the self as forever a part of a mother-child dyad," Bruce Wexler observes.[52] Haraway's reflections on dog-human companionship expose similar dyads for that significantly high percentage of the human population that challenge classical and modern philosophies of friendship by proclaiming their dog as their best friend. The pleasure induced by nonsexual, bonding hormones such as oxytocin, or, in male animals, vasopressin, may well serve to sweeten the deal. Such hormonally charged encounters are not necessarily sexual and yet, like sexual ones, morph ethical subjectivity beyond an atomistic identity.

Not all animals solicit a sentimental response from humans, and in this respect of course there are some limits to Haraway's communitarian approach.[53] Bunnies are cute and cuddly, but tender young chickens end up more readily as fryers. Still, even humans who are sensitive to the big-eyed, round-faced infants can also engage in discourse via touch, bodily movement, gaze, or voice with beady-eyed chickens or, for Barbara Kingsolver, apparently mean turkeys (chapter 1). Humans along with other species can express and recognize distinct personalities, and they can ride those waves of affect that flow back and forth across personal boundaries. Affect attunement and misattunement, perhaps unlike impartial sympathy or mirroring empathy, and to be sure any flat sentimental ethics based on these mimetic capacities, expands ethics beyond liberal sentiment to the biosocial materiality in those pockets of life where we humans are thrown together with other species.

The Deleuzian spin down below the level of hedonic affects and individual or social agencies to the level of "becoming-molecule," that is, to flows of energy and connection that occur at the impersonal level of microorganisms, risks obscuring that ethical encounter and evacuating the social bond. Still, the molecular level of energy exchange plays in to the composition of creaturely encounters.[54] As we have seen, impersonal micro- and superorganisms mess with biosocial networks and impact moods.[55] They do not, however, constitute all that is relevant in the contestations and affiliations at the center of eros ethics.

EVOLUTIONARY BASIS FOR CROSS-MODAL COMMUNICATION

One may wonder, how could affect attunement offer any realistic alternative to moral reasoning and universal rules for a cosmopolitical ecology? We humans may show an interest in other creatures who remind us of our own infants, but what becomes of unattractive or disgusting creatures? The indifference or disgust toward many species does not bode well for an affect-oriented, discourse ethics. Species are tuned to modalities of experience and expression inaccessible to humans. Bats detect other creatures through sonar, a capacity that humans lack without assistance of sonar-detecting devices. The smile in rhesus monkeys does not indicate delight, as it might for humans, but subordination. In chimpanzees the smile indicates stress.[56] Elephants may express a complex range of social emotion beyond human comprehension.[57] The human penchant for misinterpreting other animals leads some to wonder if the interspecies realm could yield only moral skepticism. Moral skepticism in turn prompts others to return to practices of self-cultivation as explored, for example, in Hellenistic and post-Foucauldian philosophies.[58]

Yet, despite the variations in modes of expression, humans and other animals do learn to communicate to varying degrees. Theories of coevolution[59] and parallel evolution[60] suggest that synchronization between species is an ongoing occurrence. The coevolution of dogs with humans over the past thousands of years is now believed to account for their enhanced communicative capacities. Wolves, unlike dogs, do not bark because they do not have the same urgent need to communicate with humans. Capacities for some degree of mutual understanding may also be accounted for through "parallel evolution" (or "convergent evolution") as, for example, between birds and mammals. Neuroscientist Todd Preuss explains that "the expansion of the dorsal ventricular ridge in corvids (a family of birds that includes magpies, crows, and ravens) and the expansion of the neocortex in primates, both of which support derived cognitive functions, represent the parallel evolution of non-homologous forebrain structures."[61] Based on recognizable similarities between corvids and mammals, including grieving for the dead and a sense of humor,[62] parallel evolution together with coevolution may establish a range of social signaling and affective cognitive capacities across disparate species.[63]

TOWARD A POST NEOLITHIC DISCOURSE ETHICS

The capacity for communication across coevolved and parallel species is not always based on mutual flourishing and sometimes requires advanced sonar or other technology for humans to detect. The attunement of predator and prey may be the most dramatic example of synchronization. Butterflies detect bat sonar to escape capture. Nonetheless, human and nonhuman communicative technologies expand the range of critical ethics beyond what philosophers have previously imagined. Barbara Smuts suggests, "Until recent times, all humans possessed profound familiarity with other creatures. Paleolithic hunters learned about the giant bear the same way the bear learned about them: through the intense concentration and fully aroused senses of a wild animal whose life hangs in the balance. Our ancestors' survival depended on exquisite sensitivity to the subtle movements and nuanced communication of predators, prey, competitors, and all the animals whose keener sense of vision, smell, or hearing enhanced human apprehension of the world."[64]

We modern humans might relearn this older knowledge with the assistance of post-positivist sciences and technologies that recover otherwise imperceptible communicative channels. Enhanced apprehension has enabled Barbara Smuts, after extensive fieldwork, to learn how to live with baboon communities. Smuts explains that while she did not "literally [move] like a baboon—my very different morphology prevented that . . . —I was responding to the cues that baboons use to indicate their emotions, motivation, and intentions to one another, and I was gradually learning to send such signals back to them."[65] The exchange of gestures between baboons and their human guest was able to relay a range of meanings from polite acknowledgment to the need for privacy and respect, lending evidence for a human capacity to engage other species not as objects or dependents but as fellow travelers and citizens of the world.

Animals synchronize affects through multiple sensory modalities to forge fields of value. Within the alternating currents of these fields of value hedonic tones and vital rhythms express multiple dimensions of lived meaning. Felt relationships across species can be pleasant or painful, intense or mild, joyful or outrageous, or of little consequence. For the most part, we humans will probably never know. Still, the range of value and meaning in fields of affect points toward a wider scope for a discourse ethics.[66] Animals, long ago vanquished from human society and consigned to the status of mute nature, may once again participate as more than innocent objects of our pity or tropes of return to Edenic life. To varying degrees, they join in a multispecies social dynamic of call and response and, through their appeals, they may express, as de Waal suggests, "a natural sense of injustice."[67] Affect attunement opens pathways across coevolved or parallel creatures inhabiting together pockets of life in a postlapsarian world of good and evil.

4

WATER AND WING GIVE WONDER

Meditations on Cosmopolitan Peace

Of the first philosophers, then, most thought that the principles which were the nature of matter were the only principles of all things. . . . Thales, the founder of this type of philosophy, says the principle is water.

—ARISTOTLE ON COSMOLOGY

Is it not possible that these performances are stimulated by feelings akin to wonder and awe? . . . What is it, this water?

—JANE GOODALL ON CHIMPANZEE WATERFALL DANCES

PHILOSOPHY BEGINS IN WONDER

Wandering along a stream in Gombe National Park in Tanzania, anthropologist Barbara Smuts was following the usual path to the sleeping trees.[1] Smuts has often made sojourns to study primate social behavior, and she had already documented the social manners encountered among her baboon friends in the African parks. On this particular occasion, however, something strange happened. The wild troupe of baboons did not proceed forward at their typical pace, but instead paused and sat motionless by the stream's still pools for moments of "silent contemplation." "Without any signal perceptible to me, each baboon sat at the edge of a pool on one of the many smooth rocks that lined the edges of the stream. They sat alone or in small clusters, completely quiet, gazing at the water. Even the perpetually noisy juveniles fell into silent contemplation. I joined with them. Half an hour later, again with no perceptible signal, they resumed their journey in what felt like an almost sacramental procession," she narrates.[2] Searching for some word to give to the astonishing posture of reverence among the monkeys, Smuts settles on a Buddhist term for a spiritual community: "I was stunned by this mysterious expression of what I have come to think of as baboon *sangha*."[3]

Any interspecies ethics could do well to flip the claim of human exceptionalism several times on its head.[4] Before entertaining a claim to naturalize human beings (with the risk of a reductive model of biology), an enchanted nature merits some degree of speculation. The usual lineup of metaphysical suspects for shoring up human superiority—impartial reason, moral or spiritual freedom, and self-awareness—have been used to gravely overstate our human capacities while obscuring genuinely mind-bending powers that cross species barriers. If there is a common path for ethical and spiritual enlightenment,[5] as an alternative to humanism's rational enlightenment, it does not seem to originate in any cross-species capacity for high-level reason but in an affect-laden intelligence instead.

Humans and other animals have a range of capacities for ordinary ethical engagements with fellow creatures. This engagement occurs typically in everyday interactions not through the conscious application of abstract moral principles or rational rules but as an ongoing tacit negotiation of the modes of reciprocity and of the social norms that are required to maintain groups and communities. Hence ordinary communication-based ethics does not rely on the normative features (abstract rules) of modern institutions and states as defended in the moral traditions of Kant or J. S. Mill (even if large-scale societies have come to depend in part upon abstract rules).[6] While humans are armed with a range of rational ("rational") laws, not just democratic but also fascist or capitalist and neoliberal, it is not clear if these laws have raised us above other social animals with regard to fairness and the treatment of others. Our lauded reason has been viewed as our great hope against evil. However, consider for a moment how this reason is manifested in actual laws or moral judgments, shaped as they are by special interests, perfected in the training of wealthy elites, and enforced through corporate or state bureaucracies. How would we know whether the very confidence that assures us that our own reasoning rises above its instrumental uses is not, in fact, from an outsider perspective, hubris? Or, if our sophisticated cognition functions among technologies of power that blindly but profitably structure domination and exploitation? For thousands of years, one man's reasoning—whether Plato's or Marx's or some other's—strikes his rivals as a ruse of power, and once again reason falls short of bringing any real peace to the world.

Yet we humans have more than one trick up our ethical sleeves, and, as it turns out, so do other animal species. Social carnivores, corvids, dolphins, elephants, the great apes, and even monkeys display expectations, desires, intentions, and, apparently, as we shall see later in the chapter, perhaps also some funny fetishes, that not only sustain the groups they depend on to survive but generate some surprisingly expansive social interactions as well. Consider the sexual politics of bonobos. The bonobo policy of substituting sex for aggression renders them, in Frans de Waal's phrase, "the hippie apes" that "make love, not war."[7] This sexy social policy may not serve as a cosmopolitical formula for trans-species peace, but it does not hurt to wonder what other worldly practices for peacemaking might be cultivated between us and other species. We humans have been quick to point out the cognitive limitations of nonhuman creatures in view of our own big-brain achievements. We have insisted that other animals' cognitive processes lack the advantages of linguistic signs (words and propositions) and are restricted to a loose stream of affect. We forget, however, that as a species we humans, at least since the time of Aristophanes' *Lysistrata*, may be lagging somewhat behind on playful peacemaking skills, at least by bonobo standards.[8]

The peaceful reflections of the baboons at the African stream's still pools offer intriguing hints of what may be a more widely shared experience of enlightened repose. The still waters seem to unlock for these primates a sacred experience of unity with nature not unlike what may be found in the meditative practices of Buddhists and other spiritual communities. Of course, these spiritual experiences are rarely an everyday practice for any group of animals, human or not; but they do suggest animal capacities for transposing ordinary life into a dream of cosmic peace.

Such a dream of peace would be fragile at best and by ordinary standards would strike anyone as a bit mad, and it should. Animal species cannot survive without preying on other living species and will resort to murderous territorial rages even against their own kin. But what if such madness (the cosmic dream, not the territorial rages) is a more common experience than one would first think? Of course, it is also true that madness has many manifestations—some admirable in their own way, some more ambiguous. Recall that Svante Pääbo, the world-renown head of the Max Planck Institute for Evolutionary Anthropology, suspects that a certain kind of "madness" is a uniquely human trait that accounts for extraordinary feats of technological and planetary domination (chapter 1). Pääbo has speculated that, some forty-five thousand years ago, propelled by a "Faustian" madness, modern hominids became the only primate who dared to cross open water.[9] Could the serene reflections by the African pools open a path for another kind of madness, this time one that is neither exceptionally human nor bent on domination? Countering that Promethean impulse that may well be caused, as Pääbo hypothesizes, by a devilish Faustian gene, this peace by the water echoes the contemplative features of a madness once upon a time called divine.

DIVINE MADNESS AND THE MONKEY NARCISSUS GENE

Plato's *Symposium* and *Phaedrus* are among ancient philosophical dialogues devoted to the role of madness in ethical and spiritual vision. Asking the question "What is love?" (eros), the *Symposium* offers not final answers but seductive fragments of a myth that Socrates learns from a priestess and mystic named Diotima. In the *Phaedrus*, Socrates and an interlocutor sit by a stream to ponder the nature of the soul inspired by their "divine madness." Divine madness is said by Plato to compel the seeker of wisdom to suspend ordinary passions, which are portrayed for his students as sexual, erratic, and debasing: "the slavish love of isolated cases of youthful or human beauty." In Plato's divine madness the seeker finds instead a spiritualization of erotic passion, a tranquil counterpart to Dionysian frenzy and Buddhist Tantra. This higher love (eros) takes one by surprise as an experience of overpowering, not through the sexual allure of another body, but through the deep stillness of "the vast sea of beauty . . . that every other beautiful object somehow partakes of," as the mystic priestess reveals to an unknowing Socrates.[10]

Philosophical reflection transcending ordinary passions can occur in a restful pose by a stream or a sea, as Plato teaches us, where near magical glimpses into cosmic tranquillity are found. Could the pause of the baboons by the running waters of the African stream offer for these primates some similar vision of cosmic peace? And, if so, wouldn't this heightened ethical vision be grounded not in any cognitive or linguistic skill peculiar to the superior primates (subset of the ones without tails) but on a common plane of an elevated affect—a plane that monkeys and humans might share with a range of other creatures? And what if this spiritualization of affect grows out of not what Plato, Nietzsche, Freud, and Marcuse supposed to be eros's wild sexual energy but a sublimated biosocial eros instead?

Impartial reason is the uniquely human capacity proposed to account for how ethics might be extended beyond friends, kinship groups, and others with whom we share interests and attachments and embrace, through cold moral logic, the stranger. Kantians require rational duty to provide the moral ground for a cosmopolitan peace, which, Tom Regan argues, may include those less advanced species if they are the "subject-of-a-life" and thus likewise deserve some human respect.[11] Peter Singer calculates that a rational concern based on abstract utilitarian rules could be expanded to include the interests of subhuman animals as well as outsiders and strangers.[12] The underlying hypothesis among these modern moral theorists is that humans are unique among animals in the capacity to make decisions apart from the biases of ordinary sentiments, fantasies, images, and desires. Only through this unique capacity for cold reason can the human, as the unique animal among animals, cultivate a calm regard for strangers.

WATER AND WING GIVE WONDER

Yet recent science and critical theory cast doubt on any moral capacity for decision making that is metaphysically free from affects, cultural wisdom, and social beliefs. Critical theory raises suspicion against any claim to an objective moral stance that would be unburdened by the nonrational politics of cultural, racial, historical, or socioeconomic (and species) identities. In a similar vein, psychologists have established through studies of brain injury that an affectless creature relying on reason alone lacks the capacity to make any ethical decision at all.[13] Affects, including those nasty biases born of in-group/out-group social dynamics, shape moral decisions and judgments of the moral worth of others. Warped social fields, for good and for bad, curve the waves of affect upon which our individual selves, with our powers of reason, speech, and imagination, swim.[14] Even Plato, who may aim to usher in a "logocentric" moral system, can only manage to cast his obscure vision through puzzling fragments of arguments mixed with images, myths, and often even logical fallacies! In fact, a definitive account of reason never appears anywhere in the history of Western philosophy—what reason means remains open to debate, disagreement, and speculation. Rival schools of thought (ranging from dialectical Hegelian or Marxist philosophies to Kantian or utilitarian traditions, among others) continue to diverge wildly from one another. In these contexts, reason functions as a tribal marker. Ordinarily, like other social animals, we help our own, harm our enemies, and ignore others.

Still, our common animal status is nothing to be ignored, not if it holds open paths to enlightenment. Barbara Smuts's discovery of sangha among her baboon friends conjures an enchanted world where fellow creatures might cross over species lines to ponder together. Imagine a monkey narcissus gene countering Pääbo's Faustian one.[15] Monkey brains might not be capable of grasping an abstract concept of the sacred, let alone of elaborating any philosophical system of moral or theological thought; the capacity for highly abstract and systematic thinking may indeed be unique to modern technologically-driven humans.[16] But a phenomenological approach suggests that the tranquil or ecstatic heights of spiritual states and enlightenment are not experienced as conceptual anyway.[17] In fact, as practitioners of yoga, meditation, or simple prayer know, too much thinking can block the practitioner from the experience of a spiritual core. A sacred place or practice frees the mind of moral judgments, weighty abstractions, and everyday beliefs, opening the psyche to elevated feelings of wonder or awe. The boundless uplift of these feelings may be prompted by witnessing natural wonders from "the starry sky above," as Kant attests, or, as for Thoreau, the uncertain depths of Walden Pond.

"People often refer to viewing great art, hearing a symphony, or listening to an inspiring speaker as (crypto) religious experiences," Jonathan Haidt observes. He distinguishes these spiritual experiences from symptoms associated with mental disorders: "When the hallucinogenic drugs LSD and psilocybin became widely known in the West, medical researchers called these drugs 'psychoto-mimetic' because they mimicked some of the symptoms of psychotic disorders such as schizophrenia. But those who tried the drugs generally rejected that label and made up terms such as 'psychedelic' (manifesting the mind) and 'entheogen' (generating God from within)."[18] The use of animal tropes as abject figures of wild savagery and exotic limit experiences is sheer projection. No doubt these images are fostered in part by a misunderstanding of the traumatized animals in the psycho wards that we call factory farms, research labs, circuses, and some zoos. Yet a number of species seem to partake naturally in "psychedelic" and "entheogen" drugs. Could they experience variations of what the mystic or shaman calls divine madness?[19]

"Verticality is the vector of mystery and reverence," Anthony Steinbock explains in his phenomenological study of religious epiphanies and mysticism.[20] This vector of transport enables "in each of us . . . something like a conversion experience," writes novelist J. M. Coetzee, who firmly believes that conversion is the only likely path for human enlightenment regarding our treatment of other animals.[21] Our question here is whether these mystical heights of ethical and spiritual enlightenment could be attained not just by humans but also by some significant range of other species. If the upper dimension of the vertical vector includes the experiences of the divine, then the bottom end of the vector includes the obverse of the divine, the disgusting and the ridiculous. Some tentative field research suggests that animals experience the upper level—as in the spiritual immersion evoked by the stream's still pools. Even more so, it is clear that animals partake in the lower aspect of the vector.

A SECOND VERTICAL VECTOR: INTERSPECIES STRUGGLES FOR RECOGNITION

Before we pursue the question of whether other species might share a purifying drive for an enlightened sense of life (and its obverse), the verticality of the sacred should be distinguished from another prominent vertical dimension of social life, the organization of society along hierarchical lines of rank and status.[22] This second vertical vector can impact our understanding of moral and spiritual transcendence.

Jockeying for position in social hierarchies is typically battled out in "struggles for recognition" (to borrow Hegel's well-cited phrase) and is found among any number of social species. Hegel himself thought that only humans were capable of risking their lives in a struggle for prestige and social standing, but on this matter he was dead wrong. Hegel's mistake is common, of course. Humans often represent the willingness to risk one's life (think of the James Dean character and his challenger racing their cars toward the edge of a cliff in the 1955 film *Rebel Without a Cause*) as what establishes the basis for our ontological difference from the rest of the pack. The problem with the usual interpretation of this common scenario is that even roosters play "games of chicken."[23] Quite conceivably some of these games for honor and status or dignity are played across species: Think of the playful bites of a social carnivore with a donkey suddenly shifting from a ludic game of friendship to one of deadly rivalry. Here we might imagine the political "underdog" aiming through aggressive self-assertion to regain the dignity originally granted and respected in play. Significantly, this struggle for dignity is moral, social, and political. Under conditions of domination or exploitation, self-assertion is an act of resistance, as we saw with the pair of lions who mastermind counterterrorist activities against the invasive Uganda railway in British Kenya (chapter 1). If the willingness to risk one's life is really the key to understanding our moral freedom, as Hegel thought, then humans do not transcend the rest of the animal kingdom, certainly not in this respect. On the contrary, the drive to be free interlocks humans with other animals that may compete with each other for status and dominance within but also across species.

Clearly, it is not easy to keep the transcendent and the secular kinds of verticality distinct, and indeed lived experience folds these distinctions back into life's dense weave. Consider the nasty representations of those who occupy the lowest rung of social hierarchies. When the two kinds of verticality are combined, and the order of the pure and the elevated adds its emotive force to the social lines of rank and status, lower social classes or undervalued social groups may be marked as among the truly despicable and, in a double insult—an insult both to their human targets and to nonhuman species—viewed as "animals."[24] Here lies a true capacity for evil. Genocides may be an outcome of this double vertical force bearing downward. There is discussion as to whether genocides are the one kind of evil found only among humans, and in particular modern humans.[25] Perhaps our ultrasocial species is uniquely positioned to carry out evil on a grand scale though bureaucratic apparatuses, cold-blooded technological efficiency, and systematic determination. Certainly, different degrees and variations of social violence and social shunning—from playground cooties to out-groups and outcastes—is chronic among social groups, human and nonhuman.[26]

Moreover, some degree of social hierarchy may not inevitability be a problem for various species, but bullies and tyrants are. Malini Suchak has observed primate groups that for a variety of reasons have had no clear alpha individual emerge and end up with the wrong kind of anarchy.[27] Some degree of leadership can be important for reenforcing the social norms of a primate group, but high-ranking individuals who obtain their power by force are shunned. Low-ranking individuals can be among the most socially connected. These individuals have a lot of friends and also generally have some protectors, who may well form alliances to oust the dreaded tyrant.[28]

In near magical breaks from these vertical social hierarchies, some nonhumans as well as humans may, on occasion, experience modes of transcendent spirituality or ethical compassion. Before approaching further the fragile possibilities for trans-species cosmopolitical peace, the next sections shift focus down the vertical vector from the sublime to the disgusting and ridiculous. Our hypothesis is that just as others can be morally shunned or shamed within and across a range of species, trans-species relationships can take an ethical turn toward peace and love.

VERTICALITY FROM THE BOTTOM UP: HUMAN DISGUST WITH ANIMALITY AND ANIMAL DISGUST . . . WITH HUMANS?

Disgust is a potent emotion with some redeeming moral and political value within and across species. Note its general characteristics with their inevitable social connotations: Disgust (unlike fear and other negative emotions) typically evokes a visceral response of nausea. It may be directed against vomit, parasites, necrophilia, and whatever (or whoever) else is indigestible, untouchable, or otherwise unpalatable. It provokes expulsion of the irritant or withdrawal from it. The social representation of others as not just a class below but as lower than the low triggers the dangerous and often frightening politics of disgust. But the target of disgust can also be enjoyed as oddly amusing and comical, as occurs with a dirty joke or the comically grotesque. In this context, laughter at the disgusting target may promote the social body just as it bolsters individual immune systems. Laughter or other signs of revulsion do not always aim to expel undesirables. A community can celebrate social parasites as wise fools and as necessary irritants for social renewal or tolerate them as amusing pests. Or a community might decide, as Athens did when it offered Socrates the hemlock, that enough is enough. The disgusting or ridiculous can trigger a carnivalesque culture of rebellion against elites or fraudulent leaders. The down-and-out outcast may be the obvious target of insider jokes, but social movements can turn laughter around to expose what is disgusting in social codes and their enforcers. Politics is a dirty business, and, as suggested in chapters 1 and 2, it is one we share with other animals.

The deadly politics of disgust can be found everywhere—from the ordinary neglect of the "unworthy" poor to social bullying on playgrounds to genocides, and not only against ethnic communities but also in the treatment of other animals. In the United States, as elsewhere in the modern world, humans live in denial of the horrors of factory farms, and yet we are collectively responsible for tormenting other species on a massive scale and as part of a calculated, rationally planned and technologically advanced system of food production. Consuming pork or beef from an industrial mode of production tacitly supports a genocidal system both for pigs who show every sign of surpassing dogs by human standards of intelligence and for cows who enjoy rich capacities for friendship; the peace-loving cow may well be among those who merit what in Hinduism is a sacred status if any creature does.[29] Animal torture in factory farm's concentration camps is not in the end different from any other banal evil that so-called good people carry out through a toxic brew of ignorance, self-interest, denial, and misplaced disgust—disgust not for the cruelty of torture, which would put to good use this morally and politically charged emotion—but for torture's victims.

This spiraling downward dynamic illustrates, I suspect, a common outcome of what psychologist Paul Rozen describes more broadly as the slippery logic of disgust.[30] It seems to be psychologically difficult to escape this downward sweep—displacing disgust from a heinous practice to its victims. But, as Rozen argues, the social target of the emotion is not at all fixed. It can change across individuals and groups, both due to our own individual efforts as well as social movements (here is a political rendition of the Baradian wave/particle model from chapter 2). Disgust's slippery logic is not hard to explain in scientific terms. What we call *disgust* operates as a "primary" or even perhaps a "secondary" emotion with social and ethical implications, perhaps in contrast with *distaste,* which is tentatively understood by some psychologists as a reflexive sensory affect. The primary emotions are understood to have a cognitive component that renders them more than an immediate reaction to a present external stimulus and subject to some degree of learning and cultural modification.[31] Primary emotions are those that are thought to be primarily genetically determined or hardwired, but distinguishing between these emotions and secondary emotions, which are shaped more readily by learning processes, the social environment and perhaps some degree of reflection, is not easy. Given the need for animals to adapt to local dietary niches and cultures, it makes sense to assume that their disgust responses would be triggered by their culture's norms and adaptive taboos. To be sure, scientists are discovering a surprising number of secondary emotions in other animal species.

Indeed, those domestic animals, including chickens, pigs, and cows, maintained and slaughtered under disgusting conditions, show every sign of possessing capacities to struggle for their freedom, to think intelligently, to enjoy interspecies companionship—and also for some feelings of disgust of their own. Darwin classified disgust as one of the six basic human emotions expressed across cultures through facial interactions.[32] More recently, researchers have found disgust in a number of species (including not only primates but also lowly rats, as we shall soon see). Yet, while disgust is displayed across some parts of the animal kingdom, only one species—the human—is said to experience this emotion common to animals as revulsion toward a common animality.

The representation of human disgust (or the abject) as naturally targeted toward animality is the prevailing view of modern psychology—from the psychoanalytic school (Freud through Kristeva) to Rozen's empirical science-based theory. This bias against animals is so strong that even Martha Nussbaum, who appeals to human compassion in advocating for laws against animal abuse, reasserts without critical examination the claims (1) that disgust is all about "animals and animal products" and (2) that "the motivating idea [for this most common animal emotion] has to do with our interest in policing the boundary between ourselves and nonhuman animals, or our own animality."[33] One has to wonder, do nonhuman animals experience disgust as a compulsion to police some similar boundary of animality? Surely it couldn't be that the disgust experienced by other animals is directed on occasion toward the human—or could it be?

In addressing these questions, we might consider whether even the best of us could at times be a bit confused. It is true that the metaphoric use of the term *animal* is relevant for analyzing modern human triggers of disgust.

But perhaps disgust's real target is not animality per se, but whatever our biopolitics and life experiences lead us to perceive as nasty stuff. Purifying rituals such as washing and grooming or separation function to stave off sources of contagion and to protect life against harmful germs, parasites, and toxins.[34] These purifying or grooming practices, as anthropologists suggest, also function to provide a sense of shared identity and to cement in-group bonds, often through separation from or the exile of an outcaste. That diverse biosocial functions grow together and interpenetrate in statistically inseparable strands of social life is fairly well established for humans.[35] But now there is an emerging body of research on the emotion of disgust and separation rituals in other animals. Recall that unpopular leaders viewed as bullies or tyrants are shunned in primate societies, suggesting the political relevance of disgust. Indeed, it makes sense that the dethroning of unpopular leaders in primate societies would originate in disgust when one thinks of how social grooming works among many species. Grooming functions simultaneously for cleaning and as a social ritual signaling attachment and belonging. The failure to groom is a telltale sign of social rejection. We could imagine that dethroned tyrants (*hybristai*) in primate societies might not be physically unkempt, but their rejection would render them appropriate targets of militant ridicule and popular uprisings fueled by a politics of disgust. Here politics and laughter function as symbolic equivalents of the refusal to groom, creating for some, justly or unjustly, a cold social climate.

Disgust, perhaps unlike a sensation or sensory affect, unfolds in many modes, and sometimes takes on some pretty fascinating social functions.[36] Consider how plastic disgust is even for rats. J. Pfaus explores one seemingly natural target of disgust in the scent of death, which rats share with humans, and uncovers the malleability of a richly complex social emotion. Typically, rats exhibit the expected disgust response of withdrawal from any whiff of mortality. However, the target of rat disgust is not fixed, as Pfaus discovered when he painted estrous females with a synthetic form of the death smell. Virgin males exposed to the nauseating chemical mix eventually learned to get used to it and bed these females. The real surprise, however, came in the second stage of the experiment with these same rats. Males who were exposed to this cocktail of sex and death later expressed a preference for death-scented mates over "normal" ones. So much for any assumption that death or at least death's effects of decay and degeneration are the unalterable roots of disgust. Given the biosocial eccentricities of cultures—here the culture of modern laboratory rats and perhaps their human handlers—one has to wonder, what is desire without a fetish?[37] Remember Freud's famous case of the obsessional fantasies of the "rat man"? Even man rats are polymorphously perverse!

In general, the functions of social and cultural practices are multivalent and ambiguous and their biosocial meanings can vary widely across individuals and groups. Jonathan Haidt underscores what he believes to be the unique significance of cleanliness for human culture when he invites us to "imagine visiting a town where people wear no clothes, never bathe, have sex 'doggie-style' in public, and eat meat by biting off pieces directly from the carcass. . . . In this imaginary town . . . the temples have gone to the dogs."[38] A problem with this picture is not only that there are humans for whom this hypothetical is more utopian than dystopian (the ancient Cynics—a more or less human group—seemed to be happy living the imagined life of the dog, dirt and all). (Recall the etymology of the term *cynic* in the Greek term *kynicos*, or doglike.) However, the average dog seems to have a sense of disgust of her own. Doggie-style sex apparently is not a problem for dogs, but cold, wet human hands on doggie fur is reportedly (at least by one anecdote) a real turnoff.[39] The disgust expressed by other species may be directed, at least on occasion, not at animality per se, but at the cold, wet human. There goes not only any smug assumption regarding universal human disgust with animality but also, recalling the dog's perspective on wet hands, any abstract generalization about the sacred properties of water.

VISCERAL CONSCIENCE AND THE GUT BRAIN

As a social emotion, disgust can take on useful ethical overtones despite its lowly origins, forming what we might call the visceral conscience, and relate to explicitly moral phenomena such as shame.[40] In the context of weighing the pros and cons of vegan and vegetarian lifestyles, Donna Haraway suggests, intriguingly, that some degree of indigestion after eating meat might well tap into a gut-level register of disgust; this visceral register might serve well to prompt carnivores to question whether their dietary habits can ever be unambiguously right and morally "clean."[41] "Dyspepsia," she adds, might appropriately accompany other morally problematic behaviors, including laboratory research practiced on nonhuman animals. If so, then perhaps the thick neuron concentration around the digestive tract, comprising what psychologists term the "gut brain," might account for a role for dyspepsia in ethics.[42]

This second brain, largely independent of immediate voluntary control, can trigger anxiety in the head brain in response to infections and other disturbances of the body and alter mood and individual behavior. But as Elizabeth Wilson explains in her study of depression, the gut can also respond directly to social encounters, registering the ups and downs of social relationships or prompting responses to social situations. Citing new research on the enteric nervous system, she suggests that the gut brain "is a vital organ in the maintenance of relations with others. . . . Maybe ingestion and digestion aren't just metaphors for internalization; perhaps they are 'actual' mechanisms for relating to others. That is, perhaps gut pathology . . . is another form of perturbed relations to others."[43] Here I take this speculation on psychosomatic malaise a step further. Consider the gut-wrenching feeling of not being able to stomach some act or event, such as harming another animal. Visceral responses to complex social situations seem to register ethical reactions. Indeed, in situations where our head brain may press us to action, our gut brain may register deep-down moral reservations.

Some of the resulting ambiguities are tragic, and may be interpreted in terms of the gut-wrenching phenomenon of shame. Recall the function of shame in ancient literary representations: Greek tragedies and epic accounts of social crimes portray tragic acts (hubris) primarily in terms of violating social bonds, not property rights important in modern legal contexts. In the modern context, an assault on a person is conceived as lack of respect for self-ownership. Boundaries are regulated by abstract and rational principles. Once a cognitively mature individual has internalized rational moral principles, he is said to be responsible for his own actions and decisions and to be capable of experiencing guilt for infractions. In contrast, the experience of shame as incurred through the violation of social bonds draws attention to ways in which social creatures are touched to their visceral core by others. Sometimes these responsibilities conflict, leading to dizzying, often tragic, ambiguities. Crucially, other species including chimpanzees, dogs, and other mammals in addition to humans seem to display shame and embarrassment in relation to social norms.[44] And, like disgust, these moral or social emotions register down deep as queasiness in the gut. As such, shame or disgust may circuit through the visceral conscience.

Modern moral theory asserts sharp distinctions between so-called primitive shame cultures and modern guilt cultures. But these distinctions may break down when moral phenomena are reinterpreted in terms of their biosocial significance for social animals. Modern moral theory aims to distinguish guilt from shame through the former's focus on action and internalized laws rather than on social identity and social norms. A person is said by moral theorists to feel guilt for what he does, but not for who one is or what role one plays in a social network. The modern individual is said to exercise a capacity for autonomous decision making that should be immune from social influence. But what becomes of the distinction between who one is and what one does if individual identities are not exclusively private and inner but gut-wrenchingly social? What if humans, like other social animals, are not autonomous, but down deep heteronomous from the inside out?

Shame may be more telling than modern theories of individual guilt for understanding the symbolic impact and social relevance of crimes and moral violations. The inner self is highly vulnerable to feelings of having been dirtied or tainted by external social processes. Transgressors may feel shame for having shamed another, in which case there is a visceral feeling of "not having clean hands." In other words, shame lends itself to social meanings and functions that broaden identities and responsibilities beyond personal choices and private lives. The inappropriate shaming of another through hubristic assault ricochets back to stain the actor, indicating an entanglement of both agent and victim in a biosocial web of corresponding affect. As relayed in ancient drama, this affect can spread as a communal malaise or pathos. In this nonmodern context, repentance for social violations aims finally not for punishment and individual reform but for restoring communal relationships through cathartic practices. Given the importance of the group for individual survival, communal justice is not just retributive but also restorative and socially transformative.

De Waal leaves open the question of whether our closest cousins, the chimpanzees, can experience shame as self-failure, rather than as disrespect for lines of rank and authority, while nonetheless beautifully highlighting its central visceral and ancient ethical significance: "Shame reflects awareness that one has upset others, who need to be appeased. Whatever self-conscious feelings go with it, they are secondary to the much older hierarchical template."[45] The criminal repents through gestures of submission. Transgressions in primate societies can have "the worst imaginable consequences, including expulsion from the pack," a punishment that reverberates with tragic justice.[46] The judgment of misdeeds is guided by communal outrage, which for chimpanzees can swell "into a deafening chorus."[47] As in ancient drama, choruses of the demos solicit the norms of primate communities.

Shame crimes (hubris) can be as minor as a causal insult that backfires to embarrass the insulter or as grotesque as genocide or holocaust passing down trauma to generations. The tragic scenario of the Nazi SS officer (and, incidentally, unsuccessful poultry farmer) Heinrich Himmler, sick to his stomach in the face of his "rational duty" to exterminate the Jews may be a case in point.[48] A visceral conscience may on occasion offer the moral guide missing in the impersonal abstractions and rules of modern bureaucracies.

Modern moral theorists assert that the achievement of a moral conscience, as the capacity to feel guilt for personal failures before abstract moral laws, is the culminating achievement of modern society. The queasiness that accompanies shame, however, may indicate a viscerally rooted conscience based on norms and ideals that are significantly shared with other social animals.[49] "Nothing is more telling than how we react after a transgression," de Waal writes, as he explains that chimpanzees express the prototype for shamelike behavior as do human primates: they lower the face and clearly "want to sink into the ground"; for chimpanzees this may mean literally crawling in the dirt.[50] When an individual chimpanzee violates a social norm, we often see her make vigorous attempts to reconcile—holding out hands, approaching the other individual, grooming, etc.[51] Meanwhile, even the decisions grounded abstractly in reason, if not always producing the horrendous actions of the Himmlers, may produce significant harm, as our species' pervasive meat-eating habits admittedly do, and yet at an emotional distance that makes the harm more difficult to acknowledge and rectify. The moral register of indigestion reminds us, down deep, that even the most systematic cases of rational justification by creatures who are, as psychoanalysts and empirical psychologists agree, "constitutionally ignorant" of themselves and awesome "confabulators," can hardly guarantee the moral purity of a "rational" decision.[52] Shame and moral disgust share a visceral component that could well function in trans-species ethics. Could pigs, every bit as smart as dogs, be morally disgusted with the shameful hands they have encountered at the slaughter? It doesn't seem all that far-fetched to assume that any number of social animals might share with humans the ethical capacities of the second brain.

Thus far I've aimed to establish that humans share some common ground with other species on the vertical vector, at least at the bottom end. In the next section, we take one last spin around the bottom pole before we ascend (with Diotima) to the vertical heights, but this time alongside other animal species.

ANOTHER VIEW FROM THE BOTTOM: A DIGRESSION ON THE DISGUSTING AS THE RIDICULOUS

The morally disgusting and shameful at the bottom pole on the vertical vector can generate a sense of the ridiculous rather than of the tragic if the situation is relatively harmless. Policing our boundaries with animals has long been thought to be the primary source both of disgust and laughter. In conventional humor, animals are viewed as the ultimate outsiders, incapable of community membership (or of responding to its norms) or of possessing self-awareness, which are the capacities required in order to appreciate the comic. We humans use animals as vehicles for laughter and, compounding the insult, we rank ourselves above nonhuman animals through this very same capacity to mock them.

There are at least three ways in which humor has been used to affirm speciesism. In his book *On Humour*, Simon Critchley identifies the first two as the "reduction of the human to the animal or the elevation of the animal to the human," or what he names as ridicule and comic laughter, and then offers a third, existential variation.[53] In all three cases, the joke teller signals her own superior status as human. We can use examples from the comic skit "Whales Aren't People," performed by Stephen Colbert on *The Colbert Report* (2011) to explain the standard accounts of ridicule and comic laughter. However, this skit exhibits humor's truly awesome transformative power for dissolving species barriers by demonstrating just how ridiculous speciesism can be, suggesting yet a fourth form of humor. Colbert's skit begins as a satiric response to People for the Ethical Treatment of Animals, which had filed a lawsuit challenging SeaWorld Parks and Entertainment Corporation to free their orcas (a type of whale) under the Thirteenth Amendment antislavery laws. Colbert mocks PETA by insinuating that animals are in a moral outrage over a human organization that would dare speak for them: "They can speak for themselves," he retorts, exposing PETA to ready ridicule.[54] Moral self-righteousness is one of satire's favorite targets, and, in this instance, Colbert's wit seems to set up PETA for an easy fall. The target (PETA) is viewed as even dumber than dumb animals and hence lower than the subaltern that they would claim to represent. Colbert also invokes an apparently innocent pleasure that is found in animals imitating the human when he reports that SeaWorld entertains its customers by dressing dolphins in hats and training sea lions to dance to Michael Jackson's "Thriller." Both formulas for laughter serve to mock any claim that animals could be people.

Colbert's satiric wit takes a sly turn, however, as he deconstructs those standard humor formulas where all the fun comes at the expense of (other) animals. Before turning to his final inversion, it is important to see how easy it is to cast SeaWorld-style entertainment and standard joke formulas into serious metaphysics. The phenomenologist Helmuth Plessner's view of man as uniquely aware of his own mortality sets up for Critchley a third and highest form of humor. Plessner is not the first to prop up that mythic wall between the human and the animal in terms of what he sees as the incapacity of the dull animal to experience morality and life's dark humor. However, Critchley's appeal to his definition of dark humor as the tentative troubling, and then resolute reassertion, of an alterity abyss separating the human from the animal gives this old-school phenomenology renewed relevance.[55] This "laughter confirms the eccentric . . . position of the human being in the world of nature. . . . The animal simply lives and experiences. . . . By contrast, the human being has a reflective attitude towards its experiences and towards itself."[56] Critchley finds this uniquely human eccentricity in the mirthless resignation of gallows humor. His example comes from Freud: "Freud speaks of a criminal who, on the morning of this execution, is being led out to the gallows to be hanged, and who remarks, looking up at the sky, . . . 'Well, the week's beginning nicely.'"[57]

The bottom-up laughter of subaltern subversion (chapters 1 and 2) suggests still other sources for humor. Colbert unexpectedly opens wide the cage door to alternative humor in the final inversion of his PETA segment. After he has mocked animal lovers (he loves his "beef, pork, poultry and even fish") and the arrogance of animal rights moralists (those who would "speak for others"), he quips: "Whales aren't people—no court will say otherwise. However, corporations like SeaWorld *are* people. The Supreme Court says so, and as people we have to treat corporations with care and respect and not cage them with ethical treatment of animals."

Recall once again the metaphysical definition of the person as the animal burdened with an awareness of death. Are corporations like SeaWorld aware of their mortality? What about those that are "too big to fail"? To be sure, we humans may find higher meaning through an acute awareness of our own mortality. But consider Jane Goodall's account of the chimpanzee mother who cannot abandon her dead infant and who carries the body for days.[58] Could chimpanzees and whales be people, too?

The social animal, as Henri Bergson argued, employs comedic techniques to attune the individual to the community.[59] Any person who is out of joint with his companions might be mocked gently or militantly to bring him back into the fold. Of course, satiric laughter can be used to police hierarchies and serve as a savage technology of social control. Like all party politics, it has a left and a right wing. Still, humor can strengthen a cooperative society by nudging the self-righteous and the bully. Through reconciling enemies, humor, like a kiss, can bring violence to a halt.

Of course, there are as many philosophies of humor as there are of life. Sometimes lonely resignation is all that we can muster before the absurdities of the world. But the humor of attunement through playful camaraderie and the salutary mockery of alpha hubris can elevate the spirit of the subaltern while regenerating solidarity and mutual aid across social barriers. Here the disgusting and the ridiculous, located on the bottom pole of the vertical vector, mock not those at the bottom end of the social ladder, but the ladder itself.[60] A good belly laugh not only strengthens the body's immune system but also protects the community (the social body) against toxic environments and nasty pests.[61]

MIRROR, MIRROR ON THE WALL, WHO'S THE FAIREST . . . TOWARD AN INTERSPECIES MODEL OF ENLIGHTENMENT

The central Darwinian insight that ethics evolves out of the needs, desires, and relationships between social animals is by now fairly well established. Frans de Waal foregrounds dimensions of primate social infrastructure such as forgiveness and reconciliation, those communal drives relegated by modern moral philosophy to Hollywood comedy's happy endings or Hegelian metaphysics. Philosophers, however, continue to ignore the communitarian implications of de Waal's research and focus narrowly on his analysis of empathy for locating the social glue of societies. This analysis lays out various stages of empathy in terms of social capacities that are theorized as "mirror neurons" or individuation as measured through the "mirror recognition test." Mirror neurons are said to explain how mimicry of affect occurs at the cellular level, allowing the viewer to literally feel another's pain. Self-recognition is measured through the capacity of an animal to recognize itself in a mirror; it is said to underlie a self-other distinction required for the capacity to understand another creature's perspective. This capacity for understanding another is elaborated further in terms of possessing a "theory of mind," which is in turn thought of as largely a cognitive achievement. Ironically, this particular arsenal of morality's building blocks—empathy through mirror neurons, the mirror recognition test, and a cognitive theory of mind—all reflect a distinctly modern human conception of the self as asocial atom.

The modern model of the self culminates in a bound individual separate from others and ruled by reason. Chapter 3 proposes instead a rich social interplay through affect attunement occluded in theories of mirroring empathy or sheer imitation. The modern model insists that the capacity for understanding the perspective of others hinges on a capacity for self-recognition, which may well be. Yet self-awareness is measured, way too narrowly through the mirror recognition test. In this test, scientists seek to observe whether animals with, say, an orange mark on their face indicate awareness of this mark when peering into a mirror by attempting to touch the spot. Great apes, dolphins, and occasionally elephants (who lack good vision) do pass this mirror test. However, other species, including the dog, fail this particular test, despite significant ethical sensibilities and alternative modes of self-and-other awareness. Something is wrong with this test.

Marc Bekoff remarks that dogs have a special ability to distinguish the unique qualities of their own individual urine from that of other dogs, suggesting that, at least for some species, encounters happen not necessarily face-to-face but snout-to-crotch.[62] The fact that dogs are capable of using their signature product as a prop for self-awareness—much as humans (or at least us good-looking ones) delight in using a mirror for our self-image—challenges the relevance of this or any other human device for measuring self-identity. The canine capacity for self-reflection also gives new meaning to the old proverb that every dog smells its own self first. This uncanny means for canine self-recognition has some pungent implications for human theorizing on the intrinsically abject as a boundary for the self—dogs clearly don't think that their own urine stinks. They also express strong interest in that of others, apparently identifying others through their distinct waft.[63] The fact that the abject or disgusting can vary across species, cultures, and individuals misleads us into thinking that others lack a sense for it at all. The same variation in recognition of self-and-other boundaries can also mislead us regarding tests for self-awareness. The dog's capacity for self-recognition through the smell test might strike some of us as disgusting, but then the overemphasis on self-images gleaned from reflective surfaces can strike others as a narcissistic or even ethnocentric. As Malini Suchak observes, "There are a lot of problems with this test including the fact that Kenyan children upwards of age 6 do not pass it. No one would suggest they do not have a sense of self."[64] The mirror recognition test as a cultural gauge of selfhood may serve to reinforce, rather than question, metaphysical dogmas of the self as inherently bound, atomistic, asocial, and split off from nature and others.

The variation in modes of self-awareness is important to catch because selfhood has long been thought to be crucial for any significant capacity to engage social norms that ground genuine ethical behavior. Any purported criterion would have to acknowledge divergences across species and cultures. By the canine standards of self-awareness, humans fail the test. Note though that a dog can be a human's best friend, indicating that social norms can be shared despite diverging modes of self-awareness and self-constitution.

Along with the mirror test for self-recognition, I question the moral relevance of a cognitive theory of mind. Consider what it might mean if the other whom one understands via a theory of mind is (no insult intended) a veritable birdbrain? De Waal presents as a striking example of empathy a captive bonobo named Kuni in a British zoo who attempts to assist a fallen bird to freedom by spreading its wings and tossing it in the air for flight.[65] We will return to this example in the next section. The question is whether the targeted help of strangers—indeed, in this case, across species lines—might require an alternative model to one that culminates in the "high-stakes testing" of other animals, first, for a sense of self through the mirror recognition test and, second, for any concept-based theory of mind. In assisting an unfamiliar starling—the proverbial bird of a different feather—Kuni indicates that she understands the bird's intentions and conscious emotions and demonstrates a concern for a stranger without close evolutionary ancestors. Again, dogs too are impressive creatures in this regard. They are known to rescue strangers and not just to bark at them. These and similar examples of a targeted helping suggest that, at least on occasion, something other than theory-and-concept-guided cognition or mirrored selves may explain an ethical concern for strangers.

A highest stage of morality, if I understand de Waal correctly, is said to be evident only in humans. In this instance, de Waal argues that only humans demonstrate a capacity both to internalize the perspectives and needs of others or of their society and to reflect rationally upon these internalized perspectives in determining their own goals. "We, humans, follow an internal compass, judging ourselves (and others) by evaluating the intentions and beliefs that underlie our own (and their) actions. We also look for logic. . . . The desire for an internally consistent moral framework is uniquely human. . . . I consider this level of morality, with its desire for consistency and 'distinterestedness,' and its careful weighing of what one did against what one could or should have done, uniquely human. . . . Our internal dialogue . . . lifts moral behavior to a level of abstraction and self-reflection unheard of before our species entered the evolutionary scene."[66] At this stage, moral judgment is self-reflective and often logically reasoned, presumably, from internalized principles or abstract ideals.[67]

An important implication seems to be that other species could not experience the emotions of shame, guilt, or pride because these states internalize perspectives of the community. Only humans internalize social norms or expectations and construct rational rules based on them. However, consider the pride that the famous bonobo Kanzi displays when he refuses to apologize until months after an act of retribution against a perceived violation. Kanzi lives in the Great Apes Trust in Iowa with his human mother, Sue Savage-Rumbaugh, who taught him written (via a keyboard) and oral human language.[68] This male bonobo once overheard a verbal attack on Sue by a visiting investigator and commanded his human friend and researcher, William Fields, to punish the visitor. When the friend refused, he bit off part of his friend's finger and did eventually apologize, but only after months of attempting to renew the friendship. He signaled his shame by keeping his head and his gaze down and even "elected to punish himself" by separating himself from the group.[69] These examples suggest that the two capacities—one for internalization of social norms and the other for systematic, abstract reasoning (as displayed supremely by Kant, Hegel, and Mill, and none of them, incidentally, managed to reason themselves out of rising tides of racist or imperialist ideologies)—might be kept distinct.

While insisting that science does not support a metaphysical break between humans and animals that would undermine the genuine ethical capacities of other species, de Waal yields to the claim of his Kantian and utilitarian critics that there may be "no parallels in animals for moral reasoning."[70] He observes that this moral reasoning includes a "desire for an internally coherent moral framework" and a concern for "why we think what we think."[71] Yet the solidarity of mutual aid and egalitarian social norms do not require an abstract statement, as expressed in the propositional form of the golden rule, and defended in systematic treatises of academic philosophy produced in modern bureaucracies. Social carnivores enact the golden rule through styles of social cooperation and in playful interactions, sometimes across rank and species lines.[72]

IMMANENT TRANSCENDENCE AND MORAL SYMBOL

How does an enlightened attitude toward the stranger enter into our shared animal lives? No doubt some kind of ontological break is required from everyday pursuits of food, sex, and alliance; however, the meaning of this break is not at all clear. Recall that Coetzee believes that only through a conversion might we humans find compassion for the suffering of other species. Compassion, or *agape*, understood as an unbound and universal love, carries an element of transcendence missing from ordinary community-bound sentiments and rituals. Do animals exhibit anything like agape in their approach to others?

With the completion of his magisterial *Phenomenology of Spirit* (1807), Hegel believed that he had culled from the entire tradition of Western philosophy the steps on the ladder for access to the real. Among the steps he included the limit experience of moral transcendence. As we have seen in our discussion of "games of chicken," this dialectical thinker misunderstood transcendence as originating in a distinctly human capacity to conquer our fear of death. The fear of death was thought to be the ultimate marker of an animal nature, and by overcoming this fear humans display an ability to rise above all other animalistic desires as well. This presumed difference with regard to transcendence experiences between humans and animals recurs in Western philosophical traditions. Kant offers, in an oft-quoted reflection from his *Critique of Practical Reason* (1788), another version: "Two things fill the mind with ever new and increasing admiration and awe, the more often and steadily we reflect upon them: the starry heavens above me and the moral law within me."[73] Given the legacies of Kant and Hegel, we are not surprised to find the problematic metaphysics of a gap between the free and rational mind of men ("the world of reason") and deterministic animal life ("the sensuous realm") recur in twentieth-century phenomenology (as in Plessner's theory of humor).

What if we returned to the notion of transcendence without the anti-animal metaphysics? As has been suggested, it would seem that any purported animal-human gap has less to do with unique human capacities than with the rise of urban centers and the loss of contact with other species and their habitats (introduction). Hunter-gatherer societies from the past lived amidst a variety of animal species, and most likely had skills of communion and communication with other species that have faded from modern cultures. The revolutionary thinker Herbert Marcuse, who artfully combines Hegelian dialectic and Kantian ethics, questions the anti-animal metaphysics (as John Sanbonmatsu has argued).[74] Like Kant and Hegel, he characterizes human history in terms of a growing estrangement of the spiritual from the sensuous realms of experience. But unlike most of the Western tradition, he finds redeeming value in an ancient spirituality experienced "erotically" and rooted in the sensuous passions: "The notion that Eros and Agape may after all be one and the same—not that Eros is Agape but that Agape is Eros—may sound strange after almost two thousand years of theology."[75] Liberated from metaphysical distortions, transcendence has profound implications for interspecies living.

Scientific studies provide some evidence for this nonmetaphysical transcendence. Meditation or repetitive movement and chanting, especially when performed as part of a collective ritual, have been observed to deactivate certain "orientation association areas" in the brain's parietal lobes, resulting in the oceanic experience reported by shamans and mystics.[76] Moreover, the studies point out, these related states of unbound immersion (sometimes induced by naturally occurring "drugs") may be experienced by species with brain structures parallel to those of humans that seem to respond similarly to hypnotic rhythms.

If this brain science is right, the streams in the African forests may be among those sites that can conjure what we humans through our myths and romances portray romantically as the mystical repose and wild transformations of "green worlds beyond city walls" (remember Plato's so-called erotic dialogues)—for us and for other species.[77] Jane Goodall suspects that the ecstatic dances of African chimpanzees occasioned by waterfalls and violent gusts of wind "may be stimulated by feelings akin to wonder and awe."[78] Michael Tobias witnesses immanent spirituality swimming in the ocean among whale sharks: "These sharks exhibit bliss, the ultimate state of meditation and indwelling referred to by such diverse luminaries as Buddha and Thoreau."[79] Katy Payne has discovered meditative moments among elephants.[80] The baboons in Gombe National Park display signs of reverence and awe in their communion at the still pools along the path to the sleeping trees, as Smuts discovered. Smuts also finds a spiritual connection similar to baboon sangha with her dog, Safi, in a respite from a game of fetch played, yes, by a stream, where Safi caught Smuts's gaze and elevated her melancholic mood: "She held her position and my gaze for about twenty minutes and then quietly approached and lay down next to me. My dark mood vanished. This was my first lesson in meditation."[81] These spiritual experiences may partake not only of nature's beauty but also of the sublime mystery of its incomprehensible force. Whether an experience of the sublime or the beautiful can achieve an ethical character for these nonhuman species requires yet more speculation.

Yet, this speculation is also not without some basis. Consider the acts of compassion witnessed in other species. The alpha male chimpanzee named Freddy in Disneynature's 2012 documentary film *Chimpanzee* adopts a starving orphan named Oscar who has been rejected by the rest of the community—surely an act of moral beauty. Even more of a wonder is Kuni, the bonobo who assists the feathered stranger who lands in her cage, whom she is destined never to see again, to a freedom that she will never know: "Kuni picked up the starling with one hand and climbed to the highest point of the highest tree where she wrapped her legs around the trunk so that she had both hands free to hold the bird. She then carefully unfolded its wings and spread them open, one wing in each hand, before throwing the bird as hard as she could."[82]

For de Waal, Kuni's act seems to display the highest type of empathy, indicating that she possesses a theory of mind. But, perhaps rather than an abstract concept of the bird's mental thoughts, the drive for freedom as expressed symbolically in the unfolded wings of the bird in flight spurs Kuni's compassion.[83] More than a cold exercise in abstraction or theory-and-concept-guided empathy, this compassion may be symbol driven and truly sublime. Recall that symbols operate between the sensory and conceptual realms, offering intelligible meaning that is not fixed by well-defined concepts. In a symbol, the material element presents itself as the incarnation of meaning, in contrast with an arbitrary word or sign, where meaning occurs in an unrelated signifier; only in conceptual knowledge are representational object and knowledge distinct.[84] Here we have a symbol-guided compassion, perhaps the basis for a highest stage of morality without need for determinate (concept- or law-based) judgments. Vivid symbol, not dry concept, may guide an unexpected and elevated response to the stranger.

Jonathan Haidt explains the psychological basis for moral beauty in terms of heightened sentiments experienced upon witnessing an act of kindness.[85] This experience of moral beauty results from an activated vagus nerve in the parasympathetic nervous system, which calms and undoes the arousal activated by the sympathetic (fight-or-flight) system. The "vagus nerve works with the hormone oxytocin to create feelings of calmness, love, and desire for contact that encourage bonding and attachment," which is understood as significant for mothers and children.[86] Freddy's adoption of young Oscar seems to engage generous impulses that promote attachment.

The bonobo's concern for the bird, however, does not rest on any expectation for intimate attachment or friendship's eventual reciprocities. This act of compassion suggests a capacity for generosity that is unbound by any normal interest or attachment desire of any kind. It may overcome a feeling of disgust for the repulsive or fear for the threatening through the calming of the sympathetic nervous system. Modern moral theory treats this capacity as a pure form of altruism, but more can be said. The self-sacrifice for a stranger bears the spiritual overtones of Christian agape or Buddhist *karuna*.[87] This sublimation of biosocial eros is sublime.

Moral disgust functions to establish firm commitments to personal and social boundaries; the ethical sublime breaks these boundaries down. From the sublime's elevated stance, the self and its concerns appear small or insignificant.[88] Spiritual rituals may attempt to develop this capacity, or "desubjectifying incapacity" (as theorized in alterity ethics), through cathartic practices that undo the ordinary boundaries of the self, allowing for participation in a reality beyond narrow needs and normal social desires. This experience diminishes the ego, yet it also channels agencies beyond individual powers that elude verbal expression or conceptual understanding.[89] Here is an unbound connectivity that is receptive and nonjudgmental.[90] Ethical comportment no longer depends on membership in a particular community or society and on expectations for social reciprocity.[91] The alterity ethics that we earlier set aside (see introduction) to give prominence to ethical agency and community in social animals now reappears not just in our human compassion toward animal others but as a distinct possibility in those other animals as well.[92] Is this what the baboons find reflected back at them from the still pool? For these baboons, chimpanzees, orcas, elephants, and dogs, is water an ethical symbol?

Science resonates with reports from African societies on surviving practices of interspecies fellowship. In a comparative study of African and Western attitudes toward wild animals, Workineh Kelbessa explores Oromo attitudes through a rich anecdote:

Once upon a time, baboons had multiplied and disturbed the people in Yayo locality in Illuababorra zone. They destroyed crops and made life very difficult for the people. The people then decided to chase away the baboons from their locality. After a while the area was hit by serious famine for seven years. All crops were ruined. The people were wondering how to explain the cause of the present famine. After reading an animal's entrails, a prophet told the people how to solve this serious problem. He advised them to bring baboons back by performing traditional reconciliation ceremony. The people were advised to ask the baboons for forgiveness by splashing maraacaa and asking them to eat their crops. He also advised them to sow crops on the border of their farmland specifically for baboons. The people then did what they were told to do. The baboons returned to Yayo after one year. Since then the Yayo people have never faced serious famine.[93] This wisdom tale relates how humans and nonhumans join together in peace-making reconciliation ceremonies.

Other Oromo stories relate the significance of sacred places where wild animals run to secure a refuge that is mutually recognized by them and their human hunters. At the end of his study, Kelbessa reaches a conclusion:

> What is distinctive to the Oromo tradition is that their beliefs and practices have contributed much more to the preservation of animal species than the Western beliefs and practices. . . . In Oromo society it is not only a group of individuals who have positive attitudes toward nonhuman species but also the society at large, because there have been laws that have been shared by all members of the society. . . . But in the West, it was mostly only some individuals (for instance, writers and religious leaders) who have been concerned with the rights of animals rather than the government and all members of Western society.[94]

Perhaps it is not realistic for modern bureaucratic societies disconnected from nature's "wild justice" to have any sense for the rituals that make for a peaceful coexistence with other animal species.[95] Yet ethics need not entail an anti-animal metaphysics. Visionaries in other cultures bridge the gaps between the sensuous and invisible worlds by tapping into transcendent powers and the agencies of animals (along with the wind, plants, and water) for their healing rites and meditative practices. Those who engage in the oldest known religious complex, shamanism, have long believed that other animals have their own shamans and magical transformations.[96] Most sutras in Mahayana Buddhism teach that the seed of spiritual awakening is found in every sentient creature.[97] Couldn't we humans return from time to time to the revitalizing meaning of nonhuman agencies and the aspirational purity of compassion, even while acknowledging that, like any animal, we are ever susceptible to bouts of indigestion?

BABOONS IN A GREEN WORLD

"I felt like I was turning into a baboon. . . . I had gone from thinking about the world analytically to experiencing the world directly and intuitively. It was then that something long slumbering awoke inside me, a yearning to be in the world as my ancestors had done, as all creatures were designed to do by aeons of evolution," Barbara Smuts writes.[98] Wouldn't it be funny if the ability to immerse oneself in the flow of life, that is, to live for a moment fully in the waves of the present—a state thought to determine animal modes of awareness as inferior to human consciousness—is in fact not the lowest stage of consciousness but the highest? Narcissus looked into a pool and saw an image of the self. The baboon sitting along the stream in sangha may for a moment lose the self rather than find it. In the stillness of that moment may be found not nothing but wonders untold. "All things are full of gods," Thales is reported to have taught.[99] Perhaps the fount of time that adventurers cross open waters in search of—the source for the reenchantment of our ordinary lives—is not lost in some far distant past or impossible future, but ever recurring in the depths of the moment—not above our human animality but running through it. Like water.

5

REFLECTIONS

A Model and a Vision of Ethical Life

> How is it
> Other Species know courtesy
> And limits?
>
> —CHI YUAN, *PRELUDE*

"I felt like I was turning into a baboon. . . . It was then that something long slumbering awoke inside me, a yearning to be in the world as my ancestors had done, as all creatures were designed to do by aeons of evolution."[1] "Learning to be more of an animal came easily as I let go of layers of thinking," Barbara Smuts continues. "This shift I experienced is well described by millennia of mystics but rarely acknowledged by scientists. Increasingly, my subjective consciousness seemed to merge with the group-mind of the baboons. . . . [I had] relinquished my separate self and slid into the ancient experience of belonging to a mobile community of fellow primates."[2]

Smuts presents this experience with baboons as an example of the highest level of friendship attainable across species. In contrast, Hegel, Kant, Plato, and several thousand years of Neolithic metaphysics have proposed that accomplishments in moral reasoning or linguistic capacities raises humans (typically, in fact, some select group of them) above other animals, opening an abyss between human and nonhuman and, for many philosophers, within the human psyche as well.[3] One wonders if this metaphysics diminishes what ethics could be. In any case, metaphysical and technical achievements seem small compared to the eons of coevolution and mystical practices that have channeled the agencies of living creatures to participate in some larger sense of a shared life.[4] Extraordinary discoveries from scientists are recovering a lost wisdom of interspecies friendships and communities. Smuts's research on baboons joins with Jane Goodall's research on chimpanzees, Frans de Waal's on bonobos, and Marc Bekoff's on social carnivores to unfold a thickening plot of diverse ethical capacities across species and a renewed vision of the courtesy and limits required for common life.

With Darwin, the abiding assumption of this new research is that ethics originates in the affects, bonds, and meaningful existence of a social life. Complex biosocial attunements are lost sight of in the exclusive valorization of linguistic and cognitive skills necessary for large-scale human societies. It is not enough to renaturalize humans or to insist that nonhumans too possess technology and culture, but these are good places to start. The old binaries of human versus animal, art versus technology, nature versus culture, and, for that matter, ethics and politics versus scientific fact are no longer conceptually or statistically separable on the frontiers of epigenetic, ethological, and evolutionary-based science's evolution as part of interspecies life. The repeating binaries distract from what is at stake in the alliances and struggles of interspecies communities.

In the spirit of recovering a vibrant ground for these alliances and struggles, a model for an interspecies ethics will be presented in this chapter. This model aims not to establish a measure for ranking the moral worth of a species but to tease out layers of ethical engagement within and across animal societies. The first *three* layers expose *horizontal* capacities for cross-modal communication across differences of species and rank. Drawing upon these capacities, biosocial norms and expectations for reciprocity and distributed responsibility bind together members of more or less cooperative animal societies where conflict, dissent and the threat of predatory violence insistently erupt. Reciprocity, believed by philosophers to function as the norm of norms and as the common ground for a community, may enhance mutual attunements across species. Moreover, social rituals such as reconciliation and forgiveness may also on occasion cross a species barrier, altering the social climate and revitalizing life.[5]

The *fourth* layer presents heightened experiences of reverence and cosmic peace, and supports capacities along ethics' *vertical* axis of generosity and compassion for strangers. Around the vertical axis lurks also the potential for evil as expressed in disgust toward the outcaste or the ecstatic violence of all-out war. This model's final stage contrasts with those modern theories of moral development that are centered on unique human capacities culminating in universal moral reason (logos). Compassionate encounters are found in the response of one creature to the appeal or plight of another. A heightened vision can explain the motivational force, symbolic justification, and social understanding—where moral reason alone falls short—for assisting a distressed creature, regardless of cause or fault.[6] Here the ordinary norms of reciprocity that Peter Kropotkin observed in Siberia as mutual aid within cooperative animal societies yield to extraordinary acts of unrequited generosity or compassion displayed by elephants, dogs, bonobos, chimpanzees, and humans toward unknown members of their own or other species.

In brief, the four layers of agential ethical engagement are (1) the transfer of social affects such as laughter and fear or panic from one creature (or a node in a web) to another (as discussed primarily in chapter 3); (2) friendly relations through intersubjective attunement, including face-to-face play for visually oriented creatures or a wag of the tail for some others, and their disruption through hostility or avoidance (chapters 1, 2, and 3); (3) interspecies communities and "clustering phenomena" in biosocial networks as living landscapes that provide a sense of meaningful existence or "home" (chapter 1 and introduction); and (4) unbound experiences where ethical valences occur as acts of moral beauty in generosity toward loved ones or as sublime compassion toward an orphan or stranger (chapter 4).

These multifaceted layers root eros ethics in agential communication and biosocial signaling. In this sense, this interspecies ethics grows out of a playful reinterpretation of discourse ethics as proto-conversational play. A communicative ethics does not depend on any unique human capacities for propositional language or rational argument. The use of a rational argument or a system of rules, say to render norms consistent within or across community practices, may contribute to fairness but also risks introducing rigidity in the weave of improvised connections and cross-modal correspondences underneath abstract and otherwise decontextualized rules. These abstractions function in modern bureaucracies, but hinder flow in those friendly relations that compose life's biosocial grounding. Syncopated rhythms and tuneful correspondences—with or without abstract generalities and concept-based moral systems—provide an animating source and an epistemological basis for ethical judgments. Behind these judgments, the cadences of call and response—the social gum of the ethos—is the means but also, significantly, the end of this eros ethics.

For if one had to identify in life's phrasing some unlikely final meaning for ethical life, its principleless principle might appear less clearly in human words than in play's laughter. Across a multitude of species, laughter exposes the "mammalian triad of tickle, touch, and play . . . at the root of our social and emotional being."[7] Laughter punctuates the sense of belonging, or home, as more than merely a liveable place for the creatures of the Anthropocene's diaspora. In a sentimental modern ethics vital relationships may devolve into subjective feelings and sympathies unmoored from the convoluted matrix of biosocial life. It is difficult for a theory of sentiment or affect to capture what is at stake in the gut-wrenching meanings of grief or the compelling rituals of friendship and community.[8] Feelings may be transitory and fleeting, but grief and love have histories and futures. Real love and grief do not disappear the moment a creature does not feel them. These emotions take their shape and meaning through social rituals (among elephants, of welcoming home or of mourning but also of combat) and symbols (among some birds, the use of twigs in burial rites; for the incarcerated bonobo, a winged bird's flight to freedom). Layers of biosocial meaning and engagement establish horizontal relationships of friendship and symbiotic cooperation and concern for their violation. Gut- or brain-based affects and emotions are not solely subjective because they open creatures from the inside out to layers of sense in the world and of the world. These affects may culminate in uplifting experiences of moral beauty and sublime repose or collapse into bouts of ridicule or disgust—across a range of species.

REFLECTIONS

The Four Layers of Interspecies Ethics

> Layer 1: Subjectless Sociality
> Layer 2: Intersubjective Attunement
> Layer 3: The Biosocial Network as a Livable Place or Home
> Layer 4: Animal Spirituality and Compassion

ANALYSIS

LAYER 1: SUBJECTLESS SOCIALITY

Metaphysical traditions for the past few thousand years have alleged that animals and human infants are driven by no higher motivations than mere appetites prompted by bodily pleasure and pain. However, even the affects of creatures lacking clear boundaries for a self bear biosocial meaning. Social animals are born into biosocial networks, mixed into the musicality of the surrounding environment. Warm or cold tones and vitalizing or devitalizing rhythms can be communicated apart from any sense of self-awareness within and across species. Ethical comportment (toward an infant or another creature) does not require the presence of a self on either side of the encounter. This social origin of subjectivity, even at this early stage before any evidence of a self or a subject, challenges moral theories that assume a natural narcissism (based in appetite or instinct) that might eventually be managed by reason (philosophical rationalism) or alienated or interrupted by the radically Other (poststructuralism).[9] Subjectless creatures could be treated as worthy of ethical consideration not just with regard to their appetites but also with regard to biosocial drives, such as touching or licking in the case of a number of species, significant for meaningful living.

The sharing of affects provides a basis for biosocial attunement in two modes, as anticipated by a Baradian wave-particle biophysics (chapter 2): (A) the wavelike contagion of an "affect cloud" across a social field and

(B) a singular response of a particular, particle-like creature to the expressed affect of another:

(A) Energy waves that propagate intensities and hedonic affects compose meaningful formations, which circulate as affect clouds. Waves of fear and despair or joy can sweep within or across species lines, creating an atmosphere of shared feeling for a social group. The mimicry of micro-expressions, say of the retching expression of disgust (the gape face in the human species) or laughter (vocal panting in a range of nonhuman animals), can be transmitted apart from any conscious awareness or voluntary control from one body to another.[10] In fact, emotional contagion occurs prior to the development of the subject or self, yet sets a mood and a group pattern of response. Creatures do not function here as bound self-organized unities (autopoiesis) but as nodes in biosocial networks. These networks may transmit energy across diverse sensory and affective modalities with uncertain translation. One creature may flee regardless of its own situation because it smells another's fear. The network in which creatures are immersed can inflect affect-laden tones and rhythms or other biocommunicative technologies with specific cultural styles and group identities. Whales and birds, for example, express regional accents in their songs, as do humans.[11]

(B) The subjectless agency of simple creatures is found in the ability to express discrete and specific (particle-like) responses in interactions with others. One creature pulls toward or away from another to resist or accept the communicated affect. The attunements between singular creatures respect unique ways of being-in-the-world through a process that Daniel Stern terms *correspondence* and links to the artistry of synesthesia (chapter 3). With minimal presubjective awareness, creatures may communicate—say with an uttered sound to a physical gesture—across sensory modalities. In this way, these correspondences do not presume capacities to experience the same affects in the same mirroring way. Nor do they rely on the same brain functions or simple duplicating mimicry, but operate instead as transspecies variations of an affect-based "signaling system."[12] As correspondences between discrete creatures, this signaling broadens the notion of a primitive empathic response (contagion) beyond the misleadingly narrow assumption that one creature can experience (hypothetically, through "mirror neurons") exactly what another is experiencing. Even subjectless creatures may resonate distinctly and dissonantly with one another rather than mechanically mirror each other.

In more complex creatures, the codification and ritualization of the affect-based signaling system eventually regulates a dynamic phrasing of reciprocity. For example, the give-and-take of a tickle between human and chimpanzee mothers with their babies teaches infants styles of reciprocity at the root of their culture's social encounters.[13] These interactions establish social norms and expectations within and even across species. Communication and codification of social norms and expectations through affect attunement occurs throughout the animal kingdom. At this layer of ethical life, agency emerges prior to or apart from the development of a subject or a self not as a conscious choice, and, to be sure, not as a law-abiding rational will, but as a biosocial drive or desire that may be cultivated for some species through social expectations and tacit norms.

Social signaling is vital for a creature to develop bonds in clustered networks and to flourish. Some species thrive on tender touching or vigorous licking and suffer trauma without this felt connection.[14] Separation from basic sources of attachment (kinship, political alliances, long-term relationships, clusters in massive biosocial networks, or communities) may be a reality in modern societies, but severing elementary bonds in social primates, elephants, and an unknown range of other species can spread a malaise that may ripple through generations. Maturation for social animals is the work of sustaining and struggling through biosocial attachments and their complex histories.

LAYER 2: FACE-TO-FACE PLAY AND OTHER MODES OF INTERSUBJECTIVE ATTUNEMENT

Another creature's soul may not be seen, but is, nonetheless, "felt." For social animals, the self emerges through affect attunement. Even for modern human infants, and to be sure for a range of other animals, self-awareness develops critically, not as much in mirroring reflections and mirroring mimicry as in social interplay that may be centered on the face or, as for dogs, on wags of the tail and bows (chapter 3). Through affect attunement, creatures may learn expectations for turn taking and cooperation that may also sustain mature modes of communication and social comportment. Laughter is an ancient social signal that exhibits a pattern of turn taking and modulates social bonds according to playful norms of reciprocity against ingrained social hierarchies or predatory relations. At this level, laughter may advance beyond tickling to conversational modes of intersubjective exchange.[15] Tail-wagging dogs and tailless primates play together (for example, taking turns as to who takes the lead and thereby creating norms of fair play) despite the fact that dogs, unlike primates, fail to recognize themselves visually in mirrors and seem to experience the boundaries of their selves and others instead through bodily smell (chapters 2 and 4).

Self-awareness occurs often through face-to-face interactions for many mammals, but birds, reptiles, and fish lack much facial expression. While visually oriented animals develop through face-to-face interplay, animals with other dominant senses engage through different modes of interaction. Odors or eye movements, tails, and mobile ears or other muscular motion too can carry expressive force and hence display a diversity of sites for self-emergence and self-awareness through engagement with others. The philosophical focus on self-recognition, especially as measured through mirroring processes, obscures the critical role of social interaction in the formation of a self.

Along with self-recognition, philosophers have thought that a unified consciousness constitutes an important criterion for determining if a creature has a sense of self. However, this notion of a unified self, like that of self-recognition, is interpreted narrowly through modernist ideologies. No doubt a sense of unified consciousness emerges in part through personal memories (David Hume), but these affect-based memories can be intertwined epigenetically with intergenerational histories, including the traumas of ancestors. For elephants and humans, transpersonal affects from community experiences and social histories can infuse a subjective patch of sadness. The creaturely soul exceeds the boundaries of personal consciousness through macro- and micro-biosocial affects, epigenetic markers, and cultural inheritances.[16]

Through multimodal social signaling, intersubjective engagement can foster a range of modes and styles of ethical comportment, including the obligation to play fair together with a visceral conscience. Social carnivores can engage in play with those who might otherwise serve as a useful meal. A courteous dog may self-handicap and play-bite a human or a donkey. A trusting wolf might roll over and expose a vulnerable side in role reversal. A sense of fairness shaped through patterns of reciprocity can produce among playmates a heterotopian, egalitarian ethics that we ultrasocial humans formulate abstractly or programmatically as the golden rule (chapter 2). A narrow focus on an abstract rule and its application, however, disengages the conceptless concept of fair play and spontaneous agency that occurs not solely within the human realm but across species.

The recognition of limits on behavior in the cultivation of social cooperation occurs in some animal societies alongside rituals of repentance, forgiveness, and reconciliation. This restorative social ethics may also have evolved from play behavior. Laughter or a play face can signal an intent to play, where the contagious force of conviviality spreads to playmates.[17] Play may suspend momentarilycompetitive and sexual contests or established political alliances and open alternative pathways of alliance and companionship. Yet, through this play, not only laughter and humor but also social norms of solidarity may develop. The social carnivore who bites too hard is shamed, suggesting an origin of a situation for ridicule or "biting satire." The carnivore then may bow to ask for forgiveness and to play again. An adult dog might also bite a puppy to teach it proper manners. Forgiveness and reconciliation (as mutual forgiveness) may function to heal a relational breach that is felt communally.[18] This function may explain third-party reconciliation rituals as observed among chimpanzees.[19] It would be difficult to imagine one individual mediating between two other individuals unless their conflict had serious repercussion for the entire social group. In this context, the crime that shames or humiliates others (hubris) constitutes a relational breach that demands symbolic and material amends to the community (not mere character reform and, to be sure, not bare punishment as institutionalized in modern prisons) to restore the conditions for solidarity as mutual aid. We are acquainted with these healing scenes, perhaps in our lives, but centrally in the "happy endings" of the comic arts. In contrast, the shame of an unforgiven or unforgivable crime can infect a social milieu, sickening a society, and, tragically, transmit repercussions over generations.

The codes of a biosocial ethos, cultivated through comic play and violated in tragic breach, can be systematized in moral theories with sets of rules and universal laws. However, systematic moral theory risks overlooking the affect-laden communicative exchange that forms the motivating and intelligent ground for mutual response and responsibility, and, as a consequence, rituals of forgiveness and reconciliation may recede as remnants of premodern politics. Modern moral theories also miss the significance of the biosocial ethos as a habitat or home.

LAYER 3: THE BIOSOCIAL NETWORK AS A LIVABLE PLACE OR HOME

The sense of belonging to a community, or what is understood broadly and fluidly as a cluster in a biosocial network, as a living landscape, introduces a third layer of ethical life. Ultimately, multispecies alliances and not individuals saddled with principles may be the locus of social expectations and restraints. Pre-Socratic Greek and ancient African ethics warn of crime as the overstepping of limits, and threaten the offender with banishment or isolation. This ancient notion of communal justice invokes aspects of what is at stake for a biosocial ethos and some of its participants. Social animals live and breathe in the clustered networks that transmit layers of meaning and subjective intent. Multispecies networks require skills in friendly relations and the recognition of distinct niches in local habitats to avoid conflict and survive adversity through meaningful connection. Those who overstep boundaries or otherwise upset social expectations can elicit a chorus of outrage and this sense of fairness carries over to encounters across species. In Oromo culture, interspecies reconciliation ceremonies bring peaceful compromise and sacred places of refuge to baboons and humans competing for the same food sources (chapter 4). Dangers to communities may stem from individuals or from system functions. Sharply vertical biosocial gradients (including those of modern bureaucracies, such as neoliberalisms' education prison systems or factory farms and animal research labs) warp the social fabric before any rule-governed moral decision or negotiated relationship between individuals takes place. This warped system is home, and its disturbances and injustices can reverberate as pan-psychic trauma.

The elephants in Uganda's Queen Elizabeth National Park testify to the compelling drive for home through the traumatic symptoms of its destruction (introduction).[20] The need to cultivate thick relationships in an intimate weave of solidarity is not accounted for in the otherwise solicitous care given to the animal plus or minus a few friends in a cage or a zoo. Social bonds are interwoven not only between companions, but, more profoundly, in an affective field structured through biocultural matrices of transmitted meaning. It is telling that the first recorded human word for freedom, translated as "mother," seems to signal a yearning among ancient debtors exploited as slave laborers for this affective field.[21] Rupture in communal relationships may be passed down through generations as a sense of inhabiting a haunted landscape (as relayed in Toni Morrison's novel *Beloved* and in G. A. Bradshaw's poignant study, *Elephants on the Edge*). Intergenerational trauma can be passed down through gene expression, i.e., epigenetically, folding ruptured history into the biosocial network and into the punctured meaning of home (introduction).

LAYER 4: ANIMAL SPIRITUALITY AND COMPASSION

Transcendent encounters in sacred times or places are rare, but occur in multiple species as a vertical event of ecstatic uplift or enhanced tranquillity (chapter 4). Heightened moods or psychic states loosen the boundaries of ordinary subjectivity, with its particular attachments, and open up "oceanic" or holistic experiences of immersion in life and its revitalizing energies. The other end of the vertical vector, disgust, ripples across regions of the animal kingdom as well. Biosocial responses to a local niche or culture molds disgust as an expression of an ethical evaluation. Similarly, the sense of the pure and the elevated, for social creatures, can take on an ethical tone. This enlightened state is displayed in the moral beauty of an alpha male's unexpected adoption of an orphan, in the forgiveness and reconciliation ceremonies of Oromo communities, and in acts of consolation among primates proffered by a third party. At its height, this elevated sense manifests sublime compassion (agape) toward strangers. Mammals may not only protect the most vulnerable among themselves; at least in the case of some primates, good will may extend beyond any expectation for the rewards of communal attachment and reciprocity to concern for an outsider.[22] Compassion is the "ethical heart" of response ethics and moral theories of altruism. In our interspecies restaging, compassion is understood as a vertical dimension of a multilayered agential, affective, and communal ethics.[23] This ethics of compassion, which is developed systematically in Kant's notion of the "supererogatory" or Derrida's "hyperbolic," suspends ordinary moral judgment or social expectation and expands the sense of belonging beyond normal social attachments and identities.

Compassion, rare though it may be, calls into question the human versus animal binaries altogether. The moral beauty of generosity and the cosmic peace glimpsed in compassion's sublime register diminishes the ego and deflates ordinary social hierarchies, while dissipating negative energies and moods.[24] Forgiveness, seemingly exhibited in young elephants when they strive to heal a relational breach with humans after a transgression, may have for these elephants a spiritual as well as a communal element.[25] Forgiveness, if mutual and conciliatory, opens the promise of avoiding cascading cycles of violence and future tragedies. Gestures of repentance (the play bow in dogs or a look of regret rather than a smirk in humans) elicit forgiveness, but more than these gestures may be needed to begin the healing process in extreme situations. On occasion, some degree of punitive revenge is often an unavoidable part of the cathartic process for us animals. Vengeance, however, easily escalates to mutual destruction if not restrained and rechanneled into positive energies and affects by techniques and social rituals that we moderns know primarily and wistfully from the arts of comedy. Responsibility is like ourselves a collective enterprise.

In the most sublime register, an oceanic feeling—achieved through the repetitive gestures, breathing exercises, or social rituals that allow for a deep pause from ordinary activities and social norms—can generate an enlarged sense of belonging. Mystical experiences drawing upon refreshing agencies and energies in the life-world reboot the promise of an undivided earth and profound sense of home or what Lynn Margulis and Dorion Sagan venture to call Gaia (chapter 2), and Barbara Smuts may glimpse in baboon sangha (chapter 4).

This four-layered model of ethics entails affect attunement in horizontal relationships and culminates in an enlightened experience of worldly peace. These layers of engagement enjoin energies of agency and conviviality that humans understand through the quests of romance and comic eros, ancient political decrees of emancipation, and the subversive egalitarianism of the carnival (chapter 2).

The laughter provoked by the tickling of rodents, playful games of friendship among predators and their would-be prey, the chimpanzee mockery of alpha males, or the magical promise of a "green world" among baboons pausing by a stream—these comic reveries offer speculative insights for an interspecies flourishing (*eudaimonia*). The artistry of ethics is in the last analysis unanalyzable—it is a gift.[26] This gift in its regenerative force offers an alternative to J. S. Mill's pity for the lower pleasures of the pig and the common fool who would never know the higher life of reason. Logos can only judge. Eros is a festival.[27]

CRITICAL REFLECTIONS AND A DREAM

Only in large-scale human societies, where impersonal rules and atomistic modernism replace an age-old, trans-species anarchic communitarianism as the sole ground of ethics, do social exchanges take on a rationalistic or calculating function and irresolvable egoism versus altruism dichotomies punctuate the public sphere. As Jared Diamond suggests, elements of modern moral theories proliferate in the context where individuals live as strangers, and ties of obligation are shaped abstractly by institutions and bureaucracies.[28] Still, even in modern nation-states, pockets of an occasional small-scale community ethos sustain intimate social networks that are otherwise thinned out in hypermobile, and electronically mediated urban populations. The codes of playful encounter and mutual aid survive in neoliberalism's abstractly global and urban environment and conjure an alternative ideal.

Yet inequalities have increased geometrically as relatively egalitarian hunter-gather societies have yielded to the technologies and communication systems of large-scale agriculture, urban centers, the industrial revolution, and global finance capital. Anthropocene inequalities exacerbate tensions between groups and species. No doubt, social creatures are typically organized along social vectors of rank and status within and across species, and these social hierarchies and the alliances they sustain bend the social field of animal societies. The world abounds with predators.[29] However, the human predator has gained extreme technological advantages and created virtual and real societies unbound by any reliable ethics.[30] Small-scale society ethics seems more of a Paleolithic fantasy than a sustainable ground for the modern individual. The abstract moral rules constructed to relate the unrelatable require for their enforcement bureaucratic and governmental apparatuses, not the whimsical constraints of small-scale communities and social play. Even the sociopath, who lacks moral emotions such as shame and guilt, can function in the context of bureaucratic reason.[31] It is not surprising, then, that moral reason has been used by our predatory species to justify social gradients to the point of social misery and genocides. Sentimental appeals on behalf of animal welfare offer some relief and reform, but do not easily extend concerns beyond the humane treatment of those infantilized pets or primate cousins that solicit ordinary modes of sympathy. Yet, modern moral theories emerge from an older ethics of solidarity and mutual aid that continue to motivate social movements and that can in fact cross species lines. The aim of this book is to strengthen those movements by foregrounding layers of social attunement and ethical agency within and across species.

Compassion for strangers may be rare in humans or other animals and is not the everyday anchor of an interspecies ethics. Ordinarily, social animals attend to their own kin and kind, build political alliances, threaten to harm enemies, and ignore others. However, neoliberalism's escalating inequities fueled, if you like, by a Faustian gene, and threatening massive extinction, provoke some to wonder, with David Graeber, if we are not "long overdue for . . . Jubilee." "Jubilee" refers back to ancient carnivals, where servants and slaves reverse roles with their masters, debts to powerful elites are forgiven, and all reclaim freedom from bondage and return home.[32] Why not take Jubilee as the high point of ethics once again, but this time across species?[33] Could interspecies acts of compassion offer some rare glimpse of a cosmic peace? What other dream?

Yet predation and death are sewn into the fabric of life, leaving difficult questions unanswerable. How should we deal with the moments when death, tragedy, and unpardonable disgrace strike? How do we respond to violation and destruction when the gods are dead, the waters run dry, and life's laughter no longer seems relevant? The coda turns to a moment of breakage when the world threatens to lose its meaning and exposes bare life to the cold exile of the absurd. J. M. Coetzee portrays a scene of empty suffering in his novel *Disgrace*. From the raw edges of absurd existence, this novel offers a glimpse of humans and dogs, alike and together, searching for some minimal sense of regained connectivity. Perhaps the entrenched violence of our world, like that found in Coetzee's narrative, forecloses any sustained chance for a green world peace. Grave suffering threatens to close off pathways for forgiveness, salvation, or grace. But a bizarre final scene in Coetzee's novel speaks to the urgency of a call for grace from one disconnected creature for another. This urgency is expressed through a mournful musical note that relays an unrelenting need for attachment and belonging through a plea to a stranger. In this bare musical attunement, with its minimal sublime, pockets of life-giving meaning regenerate, holding out against time's entropic march and the relentless absurd.

Even in the wake of despair, waves of laughter and music weave necessary folds against the unraveling of disintegration and final darkness. Across species, these grace-giving blue notes offer a response to an erotic pulse that could be heard in the refrain of an orphan or a stranger—or, as Coetzee's bleak narrative insists, a random three-legged dog.

CODA; OR, THE SONG OF THE DOG-MAN

Mourning in J. M. Coetzee's *Disgrace*

"Perhaps that is what I must learn to accept. To start at ground level. With nothing. . . . Yes, like a dog . . .
Well, now he [Lucy's father] has become a dog-man."

—J. M. COETZEE, DISGRACE

SHARED LIFE IN SOUTH AFRICA

Gayatri Spivak praises South African writer J. M. Coetzee's *Disgrace* as an exemplary postcolonial text because of its refusal to impose a voice on the subaltern.[1] This praise by one of the leading postcolonial theorists may be surprising given that the African National Congress has condemned this novel for its seemingly blatant racist depiction of black men as the rapists of white women.[2] The Other that Spivak has in mind, however, does not refer to the black Africans who are depicted as dogs, nor, for that matter, to any of the dogs that populate the novel, but to Lucy, the white daughter of the protagonist. After a terribly brutal rape, the pregnant daughter decides to keep the child, and consents to a marriage (as a third wife) to a man who protects one of the rapists as part of his family. The daughter's response to the rape leaves the protagonist, and most likely the reader, utterly bewildered. The protagonist believes he can understand the motives of the men who did this to her. He is able to visualize how these men must have looked as they approached his daughter after having killed her guard dogs; how they "drank up her fear . . . [and] . . . heighten her terror. . . . *Call your dogs! They said to her . . . No Dogs? Then let us show you dogs!*" He suspects that the drives of these men—black men that he on occasion as well represents as dogs—are not different in kind from aspects of himself. Indeed, he views himself as a predator in the sexual liberties that he regularly takes with young women. "He can, if he concentrates, if he loses himself, be there, be the men . . ." Coetzee writes; "the question" is whether this male protagonist, a protagonist who can imagine in himself the pleasure of the savage male rapist, has "it in him to be the woman."[3]

For myself, however, perhaps in part as a female reader of this novel, the question is somewhat different yet. The ethical force of the novel is sufficiently enigmatic that it is not just difficult to grasp the decision of the daughter, a decision that she believes to be that of "a good mother and a good person"; it is even more difficult to understand the nature and basis for the various stages of ethical transformation undergone by the central protagonist. In fact, I would say that the primary subaltern of this postcolonial novel is the protagonist himself, at least if by subaltern one means a character that is opaque and whose suffering and ethical transformations resist our normal terms for understanding.

And yet the protagonist is clearly not a subaltern in any kind of political sense. To the contrary, as a white professor of English literature who makes casual sexual use of the young "colored" women of the novel, and who shows little concern for his students or his teaching except as an occasion for his own gain or pleasure, he represents aspects of what we could call the "colonial mindset." In the context of this novel, this mindset is linked to a range of transgressions from the casual sexual use of darker-skinned women and the economic exploitation of Africa through European colonialization to the cruel treatment of animals. Instead of prompting the reader to moral judgment against this mindset or its protagonist, the narrative presents through its central character a very strange and perhaps strangely compelling ethical transformation.

The treatment of animals poses for this novel an instance of the ease with which humans exploit others for their own use. Coetzee insists on analogies between factory farming and the genocide of the Holocaust in his speeches and in other literary contexts. *Disgrace* similarly makes use of this comparison, in what may well expose the very root of the colonial mindset, by troubling the relationship between humans and animals. Consider the trajectory of the narrative: The novel opens with a man who expresses little ethical regard for others, human or animal, and who, while not a vicious man, represents his own desires through animal imagery, typically of predator to prey. Amoral predation seems to be posited as the norm in human and animal behavior. Over the course of the novel, the protagonist finds himself forming bonds with random animals. Already in the middle of the novel, a peculiar "bond seems to have come into existence between himself and the two Persians [the ethnic name designates the breed of sheep about to be slaughtered for a feast].... The bond is not one of affection. It is not even a bond with these two in particular, whom he could not pick out from a mob in a field. Nevertheless, suddenly and without reason, their lot has become important to him."[4] By the end of the novel, this former university professor is volunteering to assist a veterinarian (who is a female friend of his daughter's) with euthanizing abandoned animals left at her clinic. The only stated motive for this odd behavior is to become "a good person."

The novel is compelling, and yet no moral theory that I know of explains its ethical force. At the juncture in the novel where the protagonist states his only aim is to be a good person, the stance of this former sensualist seems to take a turn toward what a Nietzschean frame of mind might cast as Kantian asceticism.[5] Kant famously argues that humans should treat animals well, not for their sake, nor for the sake of anyone's happiness, but for the sake of being a good person. The moral agent thereby distinguishes himself from the animal through a sublime mode of moral reason that is the source of moral law. According to this view, only human beings are worthy of respect for their own sake. However, despite clear Kantian moments in the narrative's ethics, neither self-respect nor rational law can capture the ethical force of the final and most bizarre task that this peculiar character chooses for himself: He insists on escorting euthanized dogs from the clinic to an incinerator in order to ensure that the corpses are not mishandled as they are placed on a conveyor belt. This care for the animal corpses teeters somewhere between the sublime and the ridiculous or absurd.

Whatever the novel's strange but compelling ethical force, perhaps no other contemporary literary author has received as much attention from U.S. philosophers in recent years as Coetzee, and much of this attention has been on the problem of how human beings ought to treat other animals. Yet, for many of the novel's readers, it is not clear if the strangely skewed ethical stance of the novel opens new ethical vistas or simply disturbs our normal ones. As I read the novel, the African National Congress may have been right to flag the images of black Africans portrayed once again as rapists and animals. And yet these images unfold in the context of a narrative that exposes the subtle ways in which the colonial mindset continues in South Africa and elsewhere and locates some basis for transforming this mindset where it is most easily dismissed, namely, in the relation of human beings to other animals. Certainly the novel disturbs any normal modern paradigm of ethics. But is there some other source for its compelling force? A minimal but suggestive glimpse into South African Ubuntu communal justice appears at the novel's end in the felt connectivity between the dog and the human protagonist.[6] Here the novel shifts from an aesthetics of alterity to an ethics of call and response. The end leaves us searching once again beyond modernity's sentiment and reason or Christianity's personal grace for the communal and multilayered sense of justice as shared suffering, reconciliation, and home. A significant feature of Ubuntu is its extension of the communal to ancestors. How far does this extension travel in Coetzee's transformative novel? Humans have coevolved with other species. Could a dog too be an ancestor?

HISTORICAL BACKGROUND TO THE NOVEL

Some background on the history of colonialism in South Africa provides insight into the power relations in the novel and so too into the puzzling nature of the novel's ethical force. Historian Clifton Crais traces colonialism through two main stages, both involving the imposition of a coercive labor system by white Europeans upon two groups of black people in southern Africa, the Khoikhoi and the less easily dominated Xhosa in the Eastern Cape.[7] The transfer of colonial power from the mercantilist Dutch East India Company to the industrializing and expansive British in the late eighteenth and the nineteenth centuries altered the economy as well as the system of thought of both the colonizer and the colonized. The British abolished the institution of slavery as practiced by the Dutch-speaking Afrikaners and replaced a premodern spectacle of excess and servitude with race-based capitalism, which rested on more strategically "rational" and less visible styles of coercion. As Crais explains,

> the colonial discourse of the black as Other . . . gradually informed . . . the important changes which were taking place in the composition and conduct of the colonial state. Less interested in the infliction of punishments, the state became preoccupied with institutions aimed at transforming the very inner character of the individual. Part of a much larger change in the way power was exercised, punishment became progressively "interiorized." Disorderly prisons were replaced by more "efficient" and systematically constructed buildings geared to reform and control.[8]

Crais's Foucauldian analysis juxtaposes two systems of power: 1) from the British, the utilitarian exercise of social engineering through bureaucratic rationalization in the service of capitalist growth; and 2) the precapitalist forms of servitude and slavery instigated by their continental predecessors. Two distinct colonial systems of thought, or mindsets, have developed from these two periods of colonization, the one Anglo and modern, the other continental and antimodern. The modern system brought biological racism, while the earlier system sustained a kind of cultural racism in South Africa well into the nineteenth century. Both systems of power continue to exert a force in the culture of contemporary South Africa and in the novel.

CODA; OR, THE SONG OF THE DOG-MAN

BEYOND GOOD AND EVIL

While teaching at a modern Anglo university in postapartheid Cape Town, the protagonist of *Disgrace* romanticizes an older style of privilege associated with the first wave of colonization. This romantic, antimodern posture estranges the protagonist from his university and modern forms of power that, if introduced by the British, have been intensified as neoliberal globalization replaces earlier forms of capitalist expansion. Early in the novel, the protagonist characterizes his sexual relations with young women through the image of a snake in a garden. Both the images of the snake and the garden play an important role in understanding the way in which power is understood in the novel. The metaphor of the garden recalls the image of precolonial South Africa that attracted Europeans and is used to portray a naïveté and lack of agency in the women whom the protagonist seduces. The image of the snake belongs to a cluster of images associated with Lucifer, the figure that is celebrated in a poem by Lord Byron that fascinates the protagonist. This Lucifer, Coetzee writes, could "resign his own for others' good but not in pity and not because he ought"; his "perversity of thought" and "pride" could lead just as readily to "crime."[9] This figure beyond good and evil reflects an aspect of that retro premodern colonial mentality, the Ueberman, who presumes that the Other, whether that Other is Africa or beautiful women, is there for the taking. In this "noble" cast of mind, such a figure may nonetheless, should he choose, and for whatever reason, exercise his power or privilege with generosity, but not because of any law or rule or other source of moral obligation. Such a skewed postmoral figure may aim, in short, to be a good man, and this aim has little to do with the ordinary obligations of morality. The protagonist betrays a sense of prerogative most provocatively and sinisterly when he asserts of his student's seductive beauty: "It is part of the bounty that she brings into the world. She has a duty to share it."[10]

The protagonist thinks of his unbridled erotic desires as natural, even at one point comparing his own irrepressible sexual urges with those of a dog in heat. The Foucauldian framework that proves useful for an analysis of colonial systems of thought should serve as well to remind us that the unbound will of the sensualist and predator this protagonist romanticizes in his erotic and aesthetic pursuits is no more natural and free than the social Darwinism of capitalism. Any particular colonial mindset has been trained by a complex mesh of economic forces, social systems, and biocultures; it does not express some quasi-natural desire of men when he reverts to the existence of a "wild animal." (Even the figure of Lucifer is not a natural creature but a mythic one.)

Yet key scenes in the novel do not merely draw on animal imagery, but point to the treatment of animals as central to the novel's ethical project. In fact, animals, and not human victims, seem to represent the ultimate targets of human arrogance in much of Coetzee's work. His 1997–98 Tanner Lectures at Princeton University (published as the *Lives of Animals* and reprinted in *Elizabeth Costello*) explicitly set up the parallel between the treatment of animals in factory farms and the European Holocaust.[11] Published in 1999, *Disgrace* refers to the incinerating of unwanted animals as a *Loesung* (the German word used for the Final Solution).[12] Yet the basis for an ethical concern with animals is never, in any of his writing, made clear. In *Disgrace*, the protagonist undergoes an ordeal of suffering that provokes some degree of sympathy for the wounded and the vulnerable, including random animals. But the protagonist also makes a point of mocking the moral sentiments of good-natured animal-welfare advocates early in the novel in such a way that it would be difficult to grant any easy retrieval of these sentiments at the end of the novel. As Coetzee writes, these people are a "bit like Christians of a certain kind. Everyone is so cheerful and well-intentioned that after a while you itch to go off and do some raping and pillaging. Or to kick a cat."[13] And later on in the novel: "He is not, he hopes, a sentimentalist," he thinks to himself as he "takes charge of disposing of their [the animal corpses] remains."[14] This bizarre scene hardly invokes sympathy of any kind. In short, the novel may well aim to expand our moral sentiments and, as it does so, at least by the end of the novel, call upon a duty toward animals, but no standard moral element (such as moral sympathy or rational moral law) accounts for the full ethical force of the novel.[15] It is too strange for that.

No doubt it is because this novel challenges our sensibilities with an ethical position that is virtually unreadable that it has emerged as such an important literary text for the ethics of alterity, a tradition of ethics that traces back to Emmanuel Levinas. In part, this appeal to a Jewish thinker could be fitting given that the brutal techniques of the Holocaust did in fact develop out of factory farms and industrial agriculture and that these modern techniques (used by both British and Continental wings of power) for the treatment of nonhuman as well as human animal species are central to Coetzee's larger ethical concerns. I think that this specific postmodern tradition of ethics sheds some light on aspects of this narrative's ethical force, but here too there are limits to what this tradition can explain. In much of the remainder of this coda, I examine aspects of an ethics of alterity in the novel and then turn to a more expansive basis for ethics in terms of what it means to live a life of meaning and connectivity in the face of brute suffering.

Before proceeding, we should acknowledge limits to drawing upon any moral tradition rooted in Jewish memories of the Holocaust for an ethics that addresses animal suffering. The Levinasian tradition emerged as a response to the horrors of the Holocaust, in particular the need to rethink European moral theory given the ease with which standard moral sentiments and principles (racially and culturally biased empathy and rational duty) can lend themselves to horrifying causes. Any appeal to a post-Holocaust ethics to interpret a novel that compares the treatment of animals to that of Jews in concentrations camps or even to that of black Africans in colonial society risks moral outrage unless we are very careful about respecting the differences.[16]

Yet, as mentioned earlier, many scholars interpret the enigmatic force of Coetzee's novel *Disgrace* along with much of the rest of his corpus through the postmoral framework of alterity ethics. Spivak develops her insights on *Disgrace* in this tradition through references to Derrida and Levinas; other scholars draw more from Deleuze, Lyotard, Agamben, and Adorno in the continental tradition or from Stanley Cavell in the American tradition.[17] These interpretations locate in Coetzee's narrative what Cora Diamond characterizes, with nuanced Old Testament undertones, as a psyche that is wounded through its exposure to the other, the sense of responsibility to the other that comes from this wounding, and a "moral inadequacy" that results.[18] Drawing upon Diamond's insight, one sees that the ethical force of Coetzee's novel begins from the brute fact of suffering and not, as does modern moral theory, from the always-too-late obligation to avoid suffering. Modern moral theories provide guides or principles for avoiding harm to others, but give little in the way of restoring communities, given the pervasive suffering that persists despite good intentions. It is with the fact of this suffering that this novel begins.

An ethics of response to alterity provides a good beginning point for understanding the solitary protagonist of this novel. Certainly, if not yet an ethics, an alterity abyss opens wide and in multiple places in this novel where, say in contrast with major characters found in the communitarian ethos of Africana writers such as Toni Morrison (one of the favorite writers of the student whom the protagonist seduces), Coetzee portrays the protagonist as an aesthete who aims to remain proudly aloof from others, who does not think of himself as dependent upon them, and who resolutely determines never to be subject to their views of him. Yet, as would accommodate an alterity ethics, this existential stranger, this uncommunal man, this serpent in the garden, undergoes a wounding that transforms him from serpent to outcast while rendering him open and exposed to others in ways that he had never expected to be. His ethical concern for others appears to emerge from this woundedness or incapacity and not from any rational agency or common moral sentiments. Moreover, as we would also find in an alterity ethics, the concern for others that emerges in the novel, a concern that this time centrally includes nonhuman animals, does not rest on understanding or judging those others, let alone on any presumption that those others are substantially and analogously like ourselves.[19]

Thus, while I am arguing that the ethical force of the novel, in the last analysis, carries us beyond alterity ethics to an ethics of call and response, there are very good reasons for approaching the novel from this post-Holocaust tradition. I draw upon the tradition as far as possible before finally suggesting some ways in which we could view the novel as oriented not toward otherness per se, but toward a primordial eros, in this case, as a calm passion, for a meaningful life shared with others.

In contrast with most other scholars who approach Coetzee through the tradition of alterity, I shall draw from a theorist of alterity who happens to be, not a man, but a woman—Julia Kristeva. This is because, unlike Levinas and other philosophers writing after the Holocaust, Kristeva locates the primary challenge of alterity first and foremost not in the alterity of the other person but in the need to come to terms with unclaimable elements within one's own self. This focus in Kristeva on the alterity of the self fits well with the strangeness that inhabits Coetzee's peculiar protagonist. Kristeva develops an ethics of alterity in *Strangers to Ourselves* based on layers of strangeness originally located within the self.[20] Critics (including myself and in part based on readings of Toni Morrison's novels) have argued that Kristeva's initial focus on alterity in the self rather than on a social eros falls short for ethics and for the development of the psyche and even for the representation of the mother and her agency. My concern is that the alterity of the self is more projected onto others than encountered and that Kristeva's theory of the psyche is finally anchored in a narcissistic rather than a sufficiently prosocial one.[21] For this very reason, Kristeva's theory of the psyche sheds a great deal of light on the narcissistic protagonist of Coetzee's novel. Modern moral theory begins from the assumption that harm can in most circumstances be avoided. Coetzee, like Kristeva, assumes that the situation in which we find ourselves is first of all one of woundedness, or disgrace, and that this situation renders us both abject and strange to ourselves. According to this view, this woundedness seems to fundamentally separate the human from other animals, for Kristeva, to be sure—perhaps, also, to some degree for Coetzee.

Yet, despite certain parallels between the ethical insights of Kristeva and Coetzee, and despite a pleasure I take in insisting that a male protagonist who never claims to understand women can himself best be approached, at least initially, through the conceptual net of a female psychoanalyst, we will see that he does finally elude full capture, at least in her terms. Perhaps the main indication that the ethical force in Coetzee's narrative will elude Kristeva's human-centered perspective is that the man who once viewed the dogs in the novel with indifference chooses to become, as he says near the end of the novel, a "guardian of animal souls." In the ethical idiom of

CODA; OR, THE SONG OF THE DOG-MAN

the novel, he will take upon himself the role of the "dog-man." This ethical idiom in Coetzee's novel introduces a unique dimension into alterity, a dimension that is postoedipal and nonhumanist in a way that takes us somewhere other and more enigmatic than even Kristeva. For a cynical era ever on the verge of nihilism, this novel brings us to the threshold of a near religious response to the life we share with other animals.

KRISTEVA'S RELEVANCE

As we have remarked, literary scholars have interpreted *Disgrace* (and, for that matter, much of the rest of Coetzee's literary work) through just about every major philosopher or theorist of alterity except for Kristeva.[22] Even though I will argue that the novel does not fully accommodate Kristeva's psychoanalytic approach, her contributions to an ethics of alterity give us rich insights into the novel's protagonist.

Psychoanalytic theory examines presumed drives at the core of our identities that are erotic and destructive, even incestuous, through a cluster of tragic myths tracing back to the Sophoclean story of Oedipus. These drives are said to render the core of the self opaque, and manifest themselves in unwanted tendencies or abject fantasies, like raping, pillaging, or even, I would think, kicking cats—drives that we cannot easily alter or control, but that these analysts dare us to fully deny. (Chapter 4's discussion of the plasticity of a rat's sexual drives should forewarn that we are eventually headed off course from the oedipal/antioedipal scenario.) However pervasive these drives may or may not be, a psychoanalytic approach offers a promising place to start, given that Coetzee's narrative suggestively sets up the protagonist in terms that invoke transgressions—"the rights of desire," as he says—with an explicitly antioedipal cast.

The protagonist describes himself as "a servant of Eros," seduces the student Melanie, who is young enough to be his daughter, and, just in case we miss the significance of this act, the narrator tells us that the seduction occurs on his daughter's bed. This rather desiccated and deluded middle-aged man, teacher of the romantic poets, is far from the Byronic character that he would like to be. A "great self-deceiver," as his ex-wife describes him, he lacks the panache of the great poet, and, regardless, the era of the Byronic man and all that he stands for is or should be long gone. A committee of peers at the university, characterized in terms that remind the reader of South Africa's Truth and Reconciliation committees, attempts to understand and then finally condemns him, while the student press ridicules him, for a harmful pattern of seductions that may or may not fall just short of rape and that he stupidly and arrogantly defends.[23] Coetzee's protagonist perceives this committee seeking repentance as a mere bureaucratic apparatus, and its pretense of restorative justice as a mask for resentment's drive to punish the superior man. The protagonist's refusal to admit to any moral error leads to his dismissal from the university and to his self-imposed exile. He chooses to live with his daughter on the frontier as a modern-day Oedipus and Antigone.

Kristeva's theory of the psyche (even if not as generalizable to all individuals and cultures as she might assume) provides a striking framework for understanding Coetzee's melancholic protagonist. In *Black Sun*, Kristeva diagnoses human subjectivity as melancholic by nature.[24] Her claim is that individuation differentiates humans from other animals through a process that begins with a traumatic separation from the abject body of the mother. (This image of the mother as agentless abject body may be fading from contemporary U.S. culture,[25] but is relevant for Coetzee's novel.) According to the separation narrative, an ontological gap or separation (an alterity abyss) registers in our psyche as an ill-defined but persistent sense of loss and incompleteness. We counter this melancholy through the compensation in meaning proffered by art. In maturation, the ontologically wounded subject finds meaning by developing not solely what the modern moral theorists would term agency, which seems to presuppose a higher degree of self-consciousness and self-control than possible for the melancholic or otherwise moody human psyche, but what literary scholars term a voice, or, more broadly, a sense of one's own style. The conceptless meaning embodied in singularity, i.e., the meaning expressed through the images, rhythms, and habits that sustain subjectivity, can (under certain conditions) ward off the

CODA; OR, THE SONG OF THE DOG-MAN

threat of nihilism. This threat was brought on by the solitude of individuation and by an acute awareness of one's own mortality. The separation narrative does not necessarily explain how human children mature, as Jared Diamond observes in his discussion of hunter-gatherer societies, and should not be treated as ontologically fixed even for modern humans.[26] Neither humans nor nonhumans need disconnect from their mothers to mature; mammals in general are born into extensive periods of dependency—indeed, they remain critically interdependent their entire lives. However, some basic existential quest for meaning in the face of an abyss is central to the ground zero ethics of Coetzee's novel.

For Kristeva, cultivating a sense of meaning for a singular life is an act of faith that requires the support of a loving father. (Here her psychoanalytic theory strays nicely from its fatherly Freudian legacy.) A loving father guides the emerging subject from a self-absorbed depressive state through images of forgiveness and reconciliation. "The 'primary identification' with the 'father in individual prehistory' would be the means, or the link that might enable one to become reconciled with the loss of the Thing," Kristeva explains, using the term 'Thing' to designate the maternal element. (Coetzee's protagonist associates this animal-like Thing at his core, his inner Lucifer self, with rogue dogs in heat and, indirectly, with the black rapists rather than with a maternal element. However, for both Kristeva and the protagonist, this undefinable "Thing" at the core of the self elicits "violent pleasures.") Kristeva insists: "Primary identification initiates a compensation for the Thing and at the same time secures the subject to another dimension, that of imaginary adherence, reminding one of the bond of faith."[27] Images of the loving father in Christian art assist one to sublimate erratic drives while offering some glimpse into the possibility of reconciliation and truth and of some meaning that survives death. While music provides a sense of reconnection with the primordial maternal ground of our being (a preoedipal Dionysian matrix), visual images (the calm Apollonian element) can generate a bond of faith not through a happy experience of reconciliation but through the difficult promise of reconciling with the irreconcilable. For Kristeva, this quasi-religious promise invokes an identification with the loving father from our childhood.

In *Strangers to Ourselves*, she moves beyond *Black Sun* to describe her project in terms of a distinctly cosmopolitan "ethics of the irreconcilable." While this project has a Kantian dimension, namely, the respect for the stranger outside of normal community or social bonds, the most sublime form of ethical response does not come from identification with a judging and law-bound father, associated with Kantian rationalism, but with a loving and forgiving one. This identification allows one to respond to the singularity of the other—the other, moreover, who is not necessarily either rational or an easy object of sympathy and who may register as abject. The ethical response occurs through a highly sublimated and sublime mode of eros that she calls love.

Kristeva's vision of ethics provides a half-way reliable guide for understanding the ethical development of Coetzee's melancholic protagonist, for he, likewise, attempts to deal with a prevailing sense of disconnection and devitalizing loss by searching for meaning in music, originally in a chamber opera that he is composing called "Lord Byron in Italy." His central interest in the musical composition eventually turns from the poet-seducer Byron to Byron's aging, abandoned, and unbeautiful lover, Teresa, and finally to Byron's abandoned child. At the end of the novel, he develops an ethical attentiveness to abandoned or otherwise abject others that is almost fatherly or, as he says—perhaps to distance himself, as does Kristeva, from the oedipal father—grandfatherly in its virtuousness, that is not at all judgmental, and that, as he says, one should call "by its proper name: love."[28] The novel leaves the reader with a bizarre image of the protagonist carrying a dog lovingly to the operating table for euthanizing. In accordance with a Kristevan psychoanalytic approach, the protagonist embraces his inner maternal (the aging and ever more abject Teresa) through music and identifies with the figure of the loving father, or grandfather, and does so only after suffering through an ordeal that brings him face-to-face with his own abject nature. He emerges from a journey of self-knowledge or rather from an acknowledgment of his own woundedness and incapacity, transformed by a need to tend lovingly to abject others.

It is sublime or at least kind of so. For Coetzee's fascination with the boundaries between the human and animal does not fit smoothly into either modern moral humanism or a Levinasian, Judaic-Christian alterity ethics or even their psychoanalytic redoing. The images and music that represent what the protagonist learns from the ordeal seem finally focused more on the relationship between a man and dog than on either the gods or the triangles of family romance that the psychoanalytic theorist draws from classical Greek tragedy. And, however ethically compelling, the images of the protagonist at the operating table in the clinic and at the incinerator are nearly absurd. It is not clear how Kristeva could account for an ethics that brings the sublime in proximity with the ridiculous.

I will quote fairly extensively from the first major passage in the novel in which Coetzee's protagonist ponders his unfathomable ethical compulsion to accompany the abject corpses of animals to the incinerator, because this passage is so very difficult to interpret:

> Why has he taken on this job? [the protagonist muses]. . . . For the sake of the dogs? But the dogs are dead. . . . For himself, then. For his idea of the world, a world in which men do not use shovels to beat corpses into a more convenient shape for processing. . . . The dogs are brought to the clinic because they are unwanted. . . . That is where he enters their lives. . . . He may not be their savior, but he is prepared to take care of them once they are unable, utterly unable, to take care of themselves. . . . A dog-man, Petrus [the daughter's former hired hand and soon-to-be husband] once called himself. Well, now he has become a dog-man: a dog undertaker, a dog psychopomp, a harijan.[29]

No ordinary moral concern, no rational sense of moral duty, no utilitarian calculus of happiness, not even ordinary sympathy accounts for the ethical stance of this character. He continues his musings: "Curious that a man as selfish as he should be offering himself to the service of dead dogs. There must be other, more productive ways of giving oneself to the world, or to an idea of the world. One could for instance work longer hours at the clinic. One could try to persuade the children at the dump not to fill their bodies with poisons. Even sitting down more purposefully with the Byron libretto might, at a pinch, be construed as a service to mankind."[30]

Do we have here in the Coetzee narrative what we could call an ethics of alterity? Perhaps. But if the novel exemplifies the ethics of alterity, as so many scholars claim, the ethical focus on the anonymous carcasses of dogs—dogs that he has put down—remains peculiar (if not demonically perverse). Surely any ethics of alterity would give prominence to the singularity of others. But the ethical bond that this protagonist feels toward animals—for example, toward the two Persian sheep earlier in the novel—has nothing to do with either their particularity or their singularity. He cannot tell one sheep from another.

At this point one could certainly understand a temptation to argue, in quasi-Deleuzian fashion, that this strange protagonist has blurred boundaries and become-animal.[31] And, in some respects, the Deleuzian interpretation also sheds light on a protagonist who calls himself a dog-man and who in scene after scene sees himself as akin to the dog or snake or other animal. However, something stranger yet is happening in this strange novel that cannot be captured in a Deleuzian conceptual net. For, while the narrative crisscrosses the boundaries between the human and other animal species, especially through representations of the protagonist as an animal like other predators, it does not blur them; on the contrary, the narrative maintains a sharp sense of ethical boundaries between the protagonist and the dogs he tends right through to the end. And these boundaries are significant. The protagonist does not feel any ethical compulsion to stop the *Loesung*, that is, the decision to euthanize and incinerate the abandoned animals at the clinic, which arguably he would do in the case of humans. Moreover, the narrative ends at the clinic with the protagonist reflecting upon the awareness that dogs have of their own mortality in contrast with humans: "What the dog will not be able to work out . . . what his nose will not tell him, is how one can enter what seems to be an ordinary room and never come out again."[32] The ethical treatment of various species doesn't seem to entail universal rules based on sameness.

So we are still left with the puzzle: can we account for the ethical force that lies behind this protagonist's concern to honor the corpses of animals, especially given that he fails to concern himself with more urgent moral problems, such as the children who live off the toxic garbage at the incinerator?

Perhaps Toni Morrison would not divert our attention from the children in this way, and, if so, for very good reason. His single-minded determination to focus his care on the corpses will undoubtedly strike many readers as bizarre, less ethical than pathological. And, certainly, the solicitude of whites toward animals over people of color remains politically suspect. In fact, one could easily argue that the protagonist's care for animal corpses is not ethical at all, that the narrative avoids important moral and ethical concerns and does not so much challenge our ordinary sensibilities as deviate from them. If so, this novel would offer less an ethical vision for melancholic modern human beings (and their separation narratives) than pathological symptoms of a postmodern disconnect from any salutary sense of ethical community, let alone moral law. Unless, that is, the stubborn determination to mourn creatures so abject as to have been abandoned entirely by any community or law represents ground zero for a postmoral ethics, and this time driven by a distinctly *social* eros.

DEVIANCE AND ANTIGONE

The Sophoclean themes in the tale proliferate. As we have said, the opening scene introduces these tragic themes fairly straightforwardly. We meet a man who is a modern-day agent of what the ancients took to be hubris (in the terms of classical tragedy, he is a *hybristae*; introduction, chapter 2). He is not a king or a tyrant, but he fancies himself among the aesthetic elite, a creature of eros, indulging as he does in the pleasures and passions of sex with younger women ("technically he is old enough to be [their] father") as well as dabbling in the arts of high culture. "Is he happy?" the narrative inquires, "By most measurements, yes, he believes he is. However, he has not forgotten the last chorus of *Oedipus*: Call no man happy until he is dead" (2). Elements of the oedipal saga continue after his affair with his student. If the protagonist takes on the role of the exiled transgressor, his alternately stubborn and yielding daughter and her unattractive veterinarian friend take on some of the features of Oedipus's two daughters, Antigone and Ismene.

Together, like Oedipus's daughters, they serve as guides for the outcast on the frontier. Or at least in part.

For, while the narrative positions the protagonist as the classical scapegoat, the sacrificed king-figure, the agent of hubris in Sophoclean tragedy, it also reminds us that we no longer live in those ancient communities. To the daughter's direct assertion that her father has been "exiled" like a "scapegoat" in "the wilderness," this cynical father, this father *qua* cynic, responds: "I don't think scapegoating is the best description. . . . Scapegoating worked . . . while we still had religious power behind it. You loaded the sins of the city on to the goat's back and drove it out and the city was cleansed. Then the gods died. . . . The censor was born, in the Roman sense. Watchfulness became the watchword" (91). The gods are dead, the religious "sacrifice" of random scapegoats is meaningless. The methods of surveillance and the normalizing codes of the bureaucratic state (that is, the work not of choruses but of committees in the university) have replaced the sacred communal rituals that gave meaning to pathos through cathartic violence. Of course, our current judicial processes express the aim not to scapegoat randomly but to respect moral and legal standards for determining responsibility and to punish accordingly. (The actual horror of the U.S. New Jim Crow prison system is another part of this story.) However, these modern means do not function in the South African frontier or in any liminal place where modern "rationality" is not the norm.

If the ethical force that Coetzee's novel relays through this modern-day *hybristae* is neither classical nor modern, neither religious nor utilitarian, and neither rational nor sentimental, then it is not going to be easy to determine what this force is. The protagonist may exhibit aspects of an Oedipus on the eastern frontier in modern South Africa, but, if so, it is not at all clear what role the partial disrupting of the boundaries between the human and nonhuman play, and yet this troubling of boundaries is central. Just after his exile to the frontier, where he learns that his daughter's friend runs the clinic for abandoned animals and he expresses his disdain for animal lovers, his daughter responds, "there is no higher life. This is the only life there is. Which we share with animals" (74). At this still early point in the narrative the father reacts the way any of us might, "As far as animals, by all means let us be kind to them. But let us not lose perspective. We are of a different order of creation from the animals. Not higher, necessarily, just different. So if we are going to be kind, let it be out of simple generosity" (74). Perhaps we could have found the protagonist repeating these same words at the end of the novel, where, reduced to an abject state of mind, he assists at the clinic and at the incinerator. But if these words do anticipate his perspective at the end of the novel, the tone and imagined meaning of these words is utterly transposed. As a result of his experience on the frontier, the tacitly arrogant tone of "different" vanishes. And while the daughter, perhaps like Antigone, may very well provide some guidance for her father in exile, her words fall short of the disturbing force conveyed by the final image of the father carrying a maimed dog to its death at the operating table. Something more bizarre is happening in this farcical scene than family romance doggie style.

Let's return to the middle of the novel to prepare for thinking about how the ethical import of the final scene diverges from any normal code of morality. After the exchange between the father and daughter regarding our shared life with animals, the protagonist undergoes a terrifying ordeal that transforms both him and his daughter in ways that are difficult to understand, although differently. Two black men and one black boy (referred to by the protagonist as "the jackal boy") rape the daughter after shooting her dogs and dousing her father with alcohol and setting him on fire. (Fire resonates as a symbol and a punishment for the violence of a man, or dog, in sexual heat; water is its attempted cure.) The instigators, the three black intruders, enter on stage as the classical nemesis, the agents of revenge for the father's thoughtless seduction of another man's daughter at the university and the larger violation of colonization and apartheid that white privilege represents.

The symbolic justice in the classical portrayal of ancient or archaic tragedy accounts for aspects of the daughter's perspective. Recall that in the ancient tragedy the protagonist, as the ignorant agent of hubris, whether by accident or not, violates human bonds that are sacred to community. The community heals as the exile of the protagonist brings about cleansing and atonement. The daughter's suggestion that her father is the (not entirely unmerited) sacrificial scapegoat points to a tragic sense of justice and provides some insight into her acceptance of a marriage alliance with the uncle of the jackal boy, the man who, as her former worker, once referred to himself as her dog-man. The father suggests that she has decided to lie down like a nun and accept violation as her share of the burden of the injustice of colonial Africa. "'How humiliating,' [he] says, and she agrees.... 'But perhaps it is a good point to start from again [she adds]. Perhaps that is what I must learn to accept. To start at ground level. With nothing.' ... 'Like a dog.' 'Yes, like a dog'" (205).

Lewis Gordon, in his essay "Tragic Revolutionary Violence," interprets what he believes to be the role of cathartic violence in the context of decolonization from the perspective of the colonized. He writes of those who "rise up against the privileged and the powerful and bring these people down to the level of the scapegoat" and he allows that "if [the powerless] cannot make a colonized or colored life as good as a white one, he can at least make a white one no more valuable than a colonized or a colored one; he can, that is, bring the white god down to humanity."[33] In the novel, acceptance of the conditions of rape may appear to the deeply traumatized daughter as an act of cleansing and atonement—cathartic justice—in postapartheid South Africa. Here "justice," however, may be a symptom of a continuing problem.

To be sure, her view is not shared by the protagonist, and it cannot be the ethical center of the novel. The protagonist insists that the gods are dead in modern South Africa and that his daughter's sacrifice contributes nothing to justice. To the extent that the idea of such a sacrifice strikes the reader as a pathological mix of white guilt and female masochism, as I think it should, her perspective cannot be what makes the novel ethically compelling. Nor can it capture what remains relevant and compelling in the communitarian ethos of ancient societies. At best we can say, drawing once again from Spivak, that the novel asks the generous reader to counterfocalize, to struggle to grasp an ethical perspective in this daughter that remains out of reach and unavailable in a narrative told from the point of view of the father. At worst, the rape of the female character serves as a vehicle for the moral or religious advance of a male perspective, and the colonial mindset is never fully disengaged. Not only does the male protagonist in the novel gain his enlightenment on the backs of women who are resigned to suffering and subordination; ANC representatives continue even today to excuse crimes of rape, which are out of control in postapartheid South Africa, as payback for colonization.[34] Yet, as South African historian Helen Moffett argues, rape is a crime that goes well beyond race; no ethical democracy can fail to respect women's most basic rights.[35]

Still, however, something of the daughter's self-abjection resonates with the final image of the father, and with the central ethical force of the novel, which we've yet to understand. The novel is in part a father-daughter story, as Spivak suggests, even if the final chapter, chapter 24, renders the daughter only a part of a larger vision that includes nonhuman animals. This last chapter contains three scenes and, accordingly, three key elements for ethics that are vital to the novel's vision.

Let's run quickly through the major parts of this last chapter. In the first scene, the father returns to composing his opera to Lord Byron, but he alters the opera's focus from Byron to Byron's abandoned and aging mistress, Teresa, and to their abandoned child. In the second scene, he visits his daughter, whom he finds out in the field near her home in the countryside. As he glimpses her pregnant and amidst the flowers, he envisions a "picture" of "*das ewig Weibliche* [or eternal feminine; . . . a] scene ready-made for a Sargent or a Bonnard" (218). He knows that his daughter is determined to love her child. This scene leads up to the final one, which is staged as a poignant scene of pathos or *pietà*. The protagonist, who declares that he intends to become a "loving father and grandfather," is posed, however, not with his daughter or any other human, but with a somewhat random dog, the twenty-fourth abandoned animal to be euthanized that day. What is the ethical meaning of these last three scenes of the novel?

The protagonist has known this twenty-fourth and last dog for the past some weeks and has come to feel a fondness for it. The dog, who is maimed, hangs around his feet after work, but, as the narrative emphasizes, this dog "is not 'his' in any sense" and "he has been careful not to give it a name (though [the veterinarian] refers to it as Driepoot)"; "nevertheless he is sensible of a generous affection streaming out toward him from the dog. Arbitrarily, unconditionally, he has been adopted; the dog would die for him, he knows" (215). If the protagonist's attempt to adopt the virtues of the "loving father and grandfather" prepares him to respond ethically to others, he has learned the virtues in part from his daughter, who is determined to love the child of her rape, and the friend, Bev, who tends abandoned or sick animals at the clinic. He finds the virtue again and completely in this limp dog who loves him "arbitrarily" and "unconditionally." He learns this sublime love (agape), in the last analysis, from the animal.

But why does this final scene insist upon a relation to this random dog—a dog that he will help to put down? Who is this Driepoot?

The Afrikaans' word *driepoot* signifies tripod or three-footed. In a narrative with Sophoclean themes, a dog with a maimed foot brings to mind the clubfooted king, Oedipus. Oedipus acquires his identity as king by puzzling out the answer to the riddle of the sphinx regarding the identity of a creature who walks on four legs, then two, and finally three in the humbled stage of old age. The answer is man, and this man, Oedipus, exemplifies the quest for the self-knowledge that seems to separate the human from the other animals. (Recall that the crimes of incest and murder Oedipus commits are said to exemplify the actions that would transgress against that same apparent distinction. In fact, as we now know, animals share similar codes.) The classic-era tragedy exemplifies the lot of the fallen man, the self-deceived transgressor, whose arrogance blinds him to what he does and who he is. The Coetzee tale alters the tragic scenario when it places, in the position of the classical protagonist and king, a random three-legged dog.

But then if the dog, not the aging man, takes the place of Oedipus, sacrificed for the functioning of the community, we might think again about the role of this narrative's human protagonist. Let's return to the protagonist's claims with regard to the animal corpses: "There must be other more productive ways of giving oneself to the world, or to an idea of the world. . . . But there are other people to do these things—the animal welfare thing, the social rehabilitation thing, even the Byron thing. He saves the honor of the corpses because there is no one else stupid enough to do it" (146). In the modern world, as defined in moral terms through rational laws of mutual respect, any kind of terrible harm inflicted upon fellow human creatures would count as a moral wrong. Euthanizing another rational creature without his full understanding and explicit consent is a scandal. But, in the context of modern moral philosophy, we may not find any clear moral law or rational principle that forbids humans from euthanizing suffering nonhuman species; certainly, the novel does not challenge modernist moral sensibilities on animal euthanization despite its faint echoes of the Holocaust. It does, however, aim to locate some ethical stance that would supersede our modern sensibilities. In this respect, the protagonist is a modern-day Antigone—an Antigone in an age when the gods are dead, and without any modern moral law or conventional sentiment for a guide.

For modern humanists and moral theorists, in principle every human life should be respected, even if political systems, through their systematic failures, fail to honor this principle. Kristeva's appeal to the gap between the human and the animal carries forward this same humanist moral focus. What modern humanism or even Kristeva's postmoral ethics cannot comprehend is that residual ethical force that disturbs ordinary moral sensibilities in even the most humane use of animal lives for the sake of human lives. The protagonist does not try to stop the euthanizing of any of the dogs; he does not depict their death as the same as murder; he even assists with the process. Yet the narrative does solicit a residual and deeply ethical lack of ease that acknowledges the deaths of animals as the profanely unintelligible sacrifice that persists—whether human animals eat nonhuman animals or simply euthanize and dispose of them. There is likely no way to eliminate predatory violence. But to this brute fact, the visceral conscience responds with disgust as a sense of life's absurdity wraps around the unclean and imperfectly ethical act. Life is not always a cooperative venture, and cosmic peace is but a dream. But that dream insists on limits to violence and violation and an acknowledgment of life's constitutive disgrace.

Kristeva draws our attention to images that endeavor to reconcile—to attend with compassion—the irreconcilable suffering of the abject and the abandoned. The strange images she finds in paintings and in novels establish what she believes to be the only basis we have for our faith in meaning. The final chapter of *Disgrace* likewise offers an image of the irreconcilable, the human and the abject, this time as the pathos of a man and a dog. A scene of *pietà*, the figure of the protagonist carrying the sacrificed animal, is of mourning for a creature without moral value by normal human standards. Compare the Sophoclean drama, where Antigone sanctions her final and peculiar show of respect for a brother who acted against the community and its laws, and, in their eyes, revealed himself to be a mere traitor, appealing to the gods. Her transgression against the community's tyranny is the act of burying her brother. The Christian portrayal of Mary holding her crucified son offers yet a similar appeal to the divine. The appeal to the gods for some ultimate forgiveness, however, is not likely to work in a secular if not cynical age—in an age when, as Coetzee reminds us, the sky gods are dead and "all things are permitted" (215). But if this strange scene of a man with a maimed animal suggests an inadequacy in our moral language and a failure of religion, it also gestures toward a ground zero for a postmoral ethics, one that lies at the threshold of traditional Judaic-Christian religion, but does not cross it. Our shameless protagonist, who flaunts conventions, will take his final ethical cues as did the ancient Cynics, those original so-called dog men, not from ordinary morality or institutionalized religion, but from animals. The irony for us is that it is not a god but the dog who calls this story's cynic back to ethical life.[36]

ATONEMENT AS ATTUNEMENT

The Coetzee narrative reasserts morally significant differences between humans and other animals. It doesn't have any real arguments against the inevitable uses that animals continue to fulfill for predatory species, the human animal among them. It doesn't insist upon bringing animals into a community of equality-as-sameness with humans. It certainly falls short of any utopian promise. However, the final image would lack ethical poignancy if it were not for the ethical crossing over of the boundaries between humans and other animals that occurs here and throughout the novel. In this last chapter, the protagonist turns away from the original project for his chamber opera, *Byron in Italy*, and toward a more "temperate" musical piece that is fitting for a man stripped bare of personal pride and normal laws. He plucks on his daughter's banjo, a simple instrument from her

CODA; OR, THE SONG OF THE DOG-MAN

childhood, and, significantly, a native instrument of Africa. He is searching on the banjo for what he describes as a "halting cantilena [he imagines might be] hurled by Teresa," the aging and abandoned lover, "into the empty air.'" In this polyphonic sound he is not seeking a complex layering of music, but just some one "authentic note of immortal longing."[37] Then, with nothing left of his life but a banjo and a vision of his daughter in the field—what he portrays as a calming image of the eternal feminine—he "hums Teresa's line." But this time, he does not hum this line entirely alone. The maimed dog by his side "smacks its lips and seems on the point of singing too, or howling. Would he dare to do that: bring a dog into the piece, allow it to loose its own lament to the heavens between the strophes of lovelorn Teresa?"[38]

This appeal to music for some elemental meaning appears centrally in Kristeva's theory of the psyche. Kristeva's melancholic, like Coetzee's protagonist, searches for meaning, not what moderns call happiness or rationality. Coetzee's protagonist finally grasps his transgressions, and music or art must provide whatever atonement is yet possible; amidst centuries-long ripples of trauma and pain, happiness or rationality can not provide the frame for what he does.[39] Kristeva, however, finds the self-transcending musical element not from any simple instrument or musical line but, on the contrary, as she explains in *Strangers to Ourselves*, in the European baroque. The polyvocal quality of Bach's Toccata and Fugue in D minor, best recognized perhaps by secular readers less as church music than as the vampire's theme in twentieth-century films, exemplifies the half-animal/half-human underside of our psyche, the underside that renders us the unknown knowers, strangers to ourselves. According to Kristeva, this abject elemental undead ground of the psyche threatens to consume the subject if we do not subdue its savage force and sublimate its energy into the mathematically constrained, multiple voices constructed in baroque music and drawn from our personal lives. Bach's baroque piece expresses through beauty what is strange and mysterious.

In contrast, the nearly ridiculous humming of the man and the dog to the African banjo is at its origin a shared, communal endeavor. Both Kristeva and Coetzee appeal to music in grounding a search for meaning in an experience that is elemental. For Kristeva, the sublimated emotions we find in Bach's toccata invoke a heightened degree of religious passion that is unambiguously sublime. In Coetzee's novel, the simple plucking of the banjo in a bare, desublimated style expresses a simple cry to the other not to be abandoned. This cry of the maimed and abandoned, unlike the unconscious voicing of violent pleasure, or conscious longing to live forever, offers a common ground, a call and response across two different but coevolved species, for a transcendent moment of a shared ethics.

Much is at stake for ethics in the different conceptions of what is elemental to the human soul. In her experimental prose style, Kristeva multiplies the voices within the psyche and fractures narrative unity to express what she believes to be the traumatic separation from the maternal Thing, something alleged to lie at the core of the human self. By the end of his journey, Coetzee's protagonist strains to find that one note that might resonate not only down into the depths of the human psyche, or even from psyche to psyche, but across cultural barriers of Afrikaans, English, or Xhosa and, finally, animal species—in "mother Africa." Here we may find some relevance in the fact that his daughter Lucy shares her name with the fossil remains of an Australopithecus in Africa, a creature who links the human and nonhuman, and that the note comes from his daughter's African banjo. It is on that musical instrument of conviviality that the protagonist searches for a "song . . . to fill . . . the overlarge and rather empty human soul" and finds a single note that is matched in the response of another.[40]

Kristeva and Coetzee both pose the search for ethical meaning in the context of a deep and troubling solitude, one that tracks the self as a stranger in the world. Dostoyevsky's melancholic search for an ethic of faith in the modern void, not say Toni Morrison's thick communal ethic, lurks in the background for both these authors. Ethics takes up the existential journey of the stranger, and that first stranger is not first of all the other; it is the self. Neither author finds the community. However, for both Kristeva and Coetzee, a troubled image of loving reconciliation enhanced by a mournful musical tone provides a glimpse into some odd leftover remainder of a brutal world. Here is a ground zero of ethics where the moral relevance of the outcast reemerges, but now on a frontier where the gods are dead.

CODA; OR, THE SONG OF THE DOG-MAN

But here on the frontier is a life we share with other animals. Coetzee goes deeper than Kristeva with regard to the human relation to other animals. Kristeva attends to music and image, not concepts and principles, as the basis for ethics, but fails to offer a means to reconcile the human with the nonhuman animal; in that direction lies, for her, the risk of psychosis. Unlike Coetzee, she poses the origin of meaning in high art's sublimation of eros and she frames the process of meaning making through the elements of a family romance that, for all its Sophoclean oddity, remains fully human.[41] The cultivation of the individual severs the human psyche from animality and its subhuman archaic past even as that past continues to fracture subjectivity and narrative meaning.

Coetzee's ethical narrative reverberates around tonal variations of an alternative thought, that "we are of a different order of creation from the animals . . . not higher, necessarily, just different." As predatory animals, humans continue to eat other species. Moral and legal codes may continue to permit the tempered killing of other species, for no other reason than that they are different. How they are different is of secondary concern, and everyone will have her theory about what that difference is. But when the protagonist of Coetzee's narrative recognizes some distant and deeper dimension of his ancestral self in the maimed dog, and specifically in the dog's ability to love arbitrarily and unconditionally, the narrative gives us a glimpse of an ethical force beyond normal moral codes, a force that we can learn from other animals. This ethical force brings the sublime into solidarity with the abject or ridiculous, as in the scenes of dog and man singing to the banjo and the mourning at the incinerator. This literature professor who sought the sublime through his eros and art proved to be blind to the collusion of his ideals with the privileges that configure an Afrikaner's colonial mindset. The novel will not present us with an alternative route to the European sublime. Instead, this novel reconfigures Europe's vertical vectors through what African cultures may hear, through an old solidarity chant, "I am because we are," as a call and a response.

As the last dog at the clinic signals some sign that he would sing along with the strumming of the banjo, we stumble with the protagonist onto this other origin for ethics. This origin is, perhaps as Kristeva suggests, found in music and image, but this time music and image are not simply of the loving father or of the violent maternal. This time, the abandoned dog guides the ethical response. This animal does not speak, and the novel does not give us in words what the dog's love might mean. Instead the dog leaves us with a bare assertion of faith: that in this world there must be meaning and that this holds for even those creatures that are abject or strange or otherwise beyond any ordinary moral concern. And that their deaths tear holes in this world of ours, holes that are also wounds, and that these deaths, this suffering, should not be left unobserved or unattended.[42] Ethics forbids allowing the other, this time an animal other, to die alone and unmourned. Philosophy without music and image as a testimony to shared pasts and futures loses not just a part of ethics, but its paleozoic ground.

— om —

ACKNOWLEDGMENTS

For this book, I am in debt to mixed communities of philosophers, scientists, activists, and friends, not all of whom are human. The project coevolved with my sister and historian Julie Willett's research on a different kind of animal, the chauvinist pig, and led to the opening coauthored chapter on subaltern laughter. (Any mistakes in that chapter are her fault.) In many ways, the project began even earlier with raising my children, Liza and Joe, together with our cats, as I came to discover the continued relevance of anarchy theory in new fields of application.

Local knowledge from scientists, humanists, and posthumanists at Emory lent vital support. The research grew out of readings on philosophy and the natural sciences (all the way to physics) with Stefan Boettcher, Deboleena Roy, Sean Meighoo, and Lynne Huffer. Coteaching with Deboleena Roy opened a world of ideas on posthumanism. Primatologist Malini Christine Suchak and neuroscientist Katherine Bryant augmented the manuscript with their own invaluable research and knowledge. During too many stages to count, David Peña-Guzman and Lauren Guilmette assisted with research and editorial suggestions.

Kelly Oliver and John Protevi offered invaluable encouragement as their own thought continues to challenge the boundaries of philosophy. I am grateful along with many others for Gary Steiner and Gary Francione's series at Columbia University Press. Wendy Lochner is an inspired editor

ACKNOWLEDGMENTS

and, happily, assisted by Christine Dunbar, as well as the copyediting services of Susan Pensak.

Christiane Bailey, John Sanbonmatsu, Ralph Acampora, Arnold Farr, Piers H. G. Stephens, Andrew Lamas, Dinesh Wadiwel, Mark Aghatise Igbinadolor, Kelly Ball, Eric Tafolla, Tracy Williams, Tara Doyle, Fereydoon Family, Tom Flynn, Michael Sullivan, Elissa Marder, Don Beith, Bret Buchanan, Bettina Bergo, Clifton Crais, Eduardo Mendieta, Pamela Scully, Sam Timme, Gail Presbey, Amy Coplan, JeeLoo Liu, Mark Causey, Russell Ford, Peter Steeves, Leonard Ortmann, Elizabeth Goodstein, Lisa Knisely, Todd May, Robert Frodeman, Emily Parker, Jeremy Lowe, Jim Winchester, Alison Suen, Mecke Nagel, Debra Bergoffen, Keith Nightenhelser, Marta Jimenez, Meghan Jordan, Christopher Long, Ian Werkheiser, Diane Michelfelder, Irene Klaver, Stephanie Rogers, Joseph Diaz, and Shannon Winnubst all offered rich hints or clarifying comments along the way. My deep heartfelt thanks to Duane Davis and to my colleague Noëlle McAfee and to Kelly Oliver for encouraging the better part of my thoughts, and much more.

I am grateful to audiences at the International Marcuse Society Meeting in Lexington, Kentucky, PhiloSOPHIA, Philosophy and the City in Brooklyn, the Society for Phenomenological and Existential Philosophy, Eastern American Philosophy Association, The Society for Existential and Phenomenological Theory and Culture at the University of Victoria, American Studies Conference, CREUM at the Université de Montréal, Pennsylvania State University, American Philosophy Forum, Southern Illinois University at Carbondale, University of New Mexico, De Paul University's "Why So Serious?" conference, Emory University, and to reading groups with Occupy activists in Atlanta.

An earlier version of chapter 3 was published by SUNY Press in *philoSOPHIA* 2, no. 2 (Summer 2012) as "Affect Attunement in the Caregiver-Infant Relationship and Across Species: Expanding the Ethical Scope of Eros." Springer published an earlier version of the coda in *Continental Philosophy Review* 45, no. 1 (March 2012) as "Ground Zero for a Post-moral Ethics in J. M. Coetzee's Disgrace and Julia Kristeva's Melancholic." *PhaenEx* published an abbreviated version of chapter 4 as "Water and Wing Give Wonder: Trans-Species Cosmopolitanism" vol. 8, no. 2 (December 2013).

NOTES

INTRODUCTION

1. Charles Siebert, "An Elephant Crackup?" *New York Times,* October 8, 2006. I thank Kelly Oliver for drawing my attention to this seminal article.
2. Dr. Evelyn Abe, June 11, 2012, http://blackstarnews.com/news/135/ARTICLE/8279/2012-06-11.html.
3. Dussel traces ethics' origins as far back as the Neolithic revolution. His liberatory aim of alternative communitarianisms is based on a critique of the current world system. See Enrique Dussel, *Ethics of Liberation: In the Age of Globalization and Exclusion,* trans. Eduardo Mendieta, Camilo Perez Bustillo, Yolanda Angulo, and Nelson Maldonado-Torres (Durham: Duke University Press, 2013), especially the introduction, 1–52. See also his critique of narrow North American renditions of communitarianism, 77–84.
4. G. A. Bradshaw, Allan N. Shore, Janine L. Brown, Joyce H. Poole, and Cynthia J. Moss., "Elephant Breakdown," *Nature* 433 (2005): 807; and G. A. Bradshaw, *Elephants on the Edge: What Animals Teach Us About Humanity* (New Haven: Yale University Press, 2009).
5. On the development of attachment theory through experiments on rhesus monkeys, see Bradshaw, *Elephants on the Edge,* 46–47.
6. Ibid., 86, xvi.
7. Ibid., 67.
8. Ibid., 67.
9. Bradshaw et al., "Elephant Breakdown," 4.
10. Ibid., 10.
11. Noëlle McAfee offers a psychoanalytic account of the impact of tragic trauma in the human public sphere and a basis for its repair in *Democracy and the Political Unconscious*

INTRODUCTION

(New York: Columbia University Press, 2008). Her account draws upon a notion of "working through" that could be expanded for cross-species ethics.

12. See also Barbara Smuts, "Encounters with Animals," *Journal of Consciousness Studies* 8 (2001): 302.

13. On the ethical significance of "ideals" in the context of poststructuralist skepticism, see Drucilla Cornell, *Defending Ideals* (New York: Routledge, 2004).

14. For the role of utilitarianism in animal rights movements, see Susan J. Pearson, *The Rights of the Defenseless: Protecting Animals and Children in Guilded Age America* (Chicago: University of Chicago Press, 2011), 9.

15. For Peter Singer's response to Frans de Waal and, in particular, his reemphasis of the role of reason, see Peter Singer, "Morality, Reason, and the Rights of Animals," in *Primates and Philosophy*, ed. Stephen Macedo and Josiah Ober (Princeton: Princeton University Press, 2006), 140–160.

16. John Stuart Mill, *Utilitarianism* (Chicago: University of Chicago Press, 1906).

17. In the poststructuralist or phenomenological traditions, see, for example, H. Peter Steeves, *Animal Others: On Ethics, Ontology, and Animal Life* (Albany: State University of New York Press, 2006), an anthology announcing that "the animal is 'first philosophy'" (ibid., 13); Ralph R. Acampora, *Corporal Compassion: Animal Ethics and Philosophy of Body* (Pittsburgh: University of Pittsburgh, 2006); Peter Atherton and Matthew Calarco, eds., *Animal Philosophy* (New York: Continuum, 2004); and see Matthew Calarco's *Zoographies: The Question of the Animal from Heidegger to Derrida* (New York: Columbia University Press, 2008); Kelly Oliver, *Animal Lessons: How They Teach Us to Be Human* (New York: Columbia University Press, 2009); and Sean Meighoo and Ted Toadvine's books in progress, among many others.

18. There is a vast body of literature documenting our injustice to other species not only in colonialization and its aftermath in Africa but also in our own backyard. See, for example, Michael Pollan, *The Omnivore's Dilemma* (London: Penguin, 2006); Eric Schlosser, *Fast Food Nation* (New York: Harper Collins, 2005); and Jonathan Safran Foer, *Eating Animals* (New York: Little, Brown, 2010).

19. Robert N. Bellah and Hans Joas, *The Axial Age and Its Consequences* (Cambridge, Harvard University Press, 2013).

20. For an account of the four traditions, and the significance and history of response ethics, see Francois Raffoul, *The Origins of Responsibility* (Bloomington: Indiana University Press, 2010). On response ethics as an ethics of *eros* and the significance of Luce Irigaray's work, see Tina Chanter, *Ethics of Eros* (New York: Routledge, 1995).

21. On Levinas, see Bettina Bergo, *Levinas Between Ethics and Politics* (Dordrecht: Kluwer, 1999), 108; and Claire Elise Katz, "Reinhabiting the House of Ruth: Exceeding the Limits of the Feminine in Levinas," in *Feminist Interpretations of Levinas*, ed. Tina Chanter (University Park: Pennsylvania State University Press, 2001), 145–170.

22. Oliver, *Animal Lessons*, 306.

23. Ibid., 6.

24. This receptivity provides a basis for overcoming systems of exploitation, which, Marcuse argues in *Eros and Civilization*, have since Plato defined reason in such a way that it func-

INTRODUCTION

tioned to block any ethical concern for allegedly irrational animals or cultures. Herbert Marcuse, *Eros and Civilization* (Boston: Beacon, 1974), 110.

25. Oliver, *Animal Lessons*, 6–7.
26. But for a defense of the Derridean critique of biosocial continuity, see Leonard Lawlor, *This Is Not Sufficient: An Essay on Animality and Human Nature in Derrida* (New York: Columbia University Press, 2007); on this question, see also Robert Vallier, "The Indiscernible Joining: Structure, Signification, and Animality in Merleau-Ponty's *La nature*," *Chaismi International* 3 (2001): 187–212.
27. Elisabeth de Fontenay, *Without Offending Humans: A Critique of Animal Rights*, trans. Will Bishop (Minneapolis: University of Minnesota Press, 2012), 9.
28. Oliver, *Animal Lessons*, 208. Robert Vallier's translator's introduction to the English translation of the *Nature* lectures indicates that the *Nature* notes comprise three lectures that were given by Merleau-Ponty at the College de France in 1956–1957, 1957–1958, and 1959–1960. They were published in France in 1995, 1996 and 1998.
29. See Renaud Barbaras, "Life and Perceptual Intentionality," *Research in Phenomenology* 33 (2003): 22–38; and David Abram, *Becoming Animal: An Early Cosmology* (New York: Vintage, 2011).
30. Maurice Merleau-Ponty, *Nature: Course Notes from the College de France*, trans. Robert Vallier (Evanston: Northwestern University Press, 2003); Ted Toadvine, *Merleau-Ponty's Philosophy of Nature* (Evanston: Northwestern University Press, 2009), 76–97; David Abram, *The Spell of the Sensuous* (New York: Random House, 1996); David Morris, "Animals and Humans, Thinking and Nature," *Phenomenology and the Cognitive Sciences* 4 (2005): 49–72; Elizabeth Behnke, "From Merleau-Ponty's Concept of Nature to an Interspecies Practice of Peace," in *Animals Others: On Ethics, Ontology, and Animal Life*, ed. H. Peter Steeves (New York: SUNY, 1999): 93–116; Vallier, "The Indiscernible Joining."
31. The phrase "melody singing itself" is borrowed from Jakob von Uexkull, "A Stroll Through the World of Animals and Men," *Instinctive Behavior: The Development of A Modern Concept*, trans. and ed. Claire H. Schiller (New York: International Universities Press, 1957), 5–15.
32. Merleau-Ponty, *Nature*, 225.
33. Daniel N. Stern, *The Interpersonal World of the Infant* (Mineola, NY: Basic Books, 1985). See also Susan Bredlau's work in progress on infants and phenomenology as "seeing with" another in her unpublished paper "Husserl's 'Pairing' Relation and the Initial Role of Others in Infant Perception," delivered at Emory Philosophy Department Colloquium, October, 2012.
34. Stern, *The Interpersonal World of the Infant,* 56–7.
35. For a fuller account of ethical attunement, see Cynthia Willett, *Maternal Ethics and Other Slave Moralities* (New York: Routledge, 1995). Eros as social attunement is useful for breaking out of mirroring and narcissistic conceptions of human subjectivity in psychoanalysis and empirical psychology.
36. A rich but, perhaps, problematic account of ontological alienation is explored by Judith Butler and Athena Athanasiou in *Dispossession: The Performative in the Political* (Malden,

MA: Polity, 2013). This dispossession would seem to affect only humans and thereby claim a radical discontinuity between nature and culture or animal and human realms. Research on affect attunement and some prosocial desires in children and social animals generally suggest that the moral subject or human self is not necessarily melancholic or otherwise alienated, and that the mother's bodily stuff is not or should not be necessarily figured as abject. Children, bodies, and situations vary. The originary dispossession thesis, I suspect, hinders attempts to carry through on Butler and Athanasiou's call for new idioms of community, which might make use of prosocial affirmations of community norms alongside critiques of existing authoritarian or inegalitarian norms.

37. In the emphasis on co-responding selves rather than agential dependency, my aim is to widen the ground of political ethics beyond modern liberal conceptions of autonomy and dependency even as richly developed as in Sue Donaldson and Will Kymlicka's notion of animal citizenship in *Zoopolis* (Oxford: Oxford University Press, 2011), 109. On this basis I would not approach the rights of animals through liberal conceptions of inviolable self-ownership, but, more broadly, with negative liberties grounded in social freedom (so that reconciliation, playful reciprocity, and solidarity decenter and recontextualze liberal notions of self-ownership and modern abstract formulations of obligations). I do not see how to avoid treating predatory and parasitic behavior as ordinary aspects of life rather than as emergency conditions; although, to be sure, factory farming and animal cruelty are not justifiable. Chapter 1 opens with a discussion of multispecies defiance and solidarity, not animal dependency, to acknowledge the full social agency of other species in the face of domination and exploitation.

38. Frans de Waal, "Are We in Anthropodenial?" *Discover* 18 (1997): 50–53.

39. Ralph Acampora argues that while Merleau-Ponty provides clues as to how to develop a multispecies ethics, he does not acknowledge or develop as fully as he could the fact that nonhuman animals can be sources of meaning in their own right. See Acampora, *Corporal Compassion*, 15. If finding overlapping sources of meaning across species resonates with the deeper if perhaps underdeveloped aims of Merleau-Ponty's phenomenology, then the kind of approach that I take in this book could be said to be phenomenological and aligned with Acampora's seminal work. A similar argument could be made regarding an alliance with other major traditions, notably the pragmatism of John Dewey and Marcusean critical theory as well as the work of contemporary feminist anarchists such as Donna Haraway.

40. Gilles Deleuze and Felix Guattari, *A Thousand Plateaus: Capitalism and Schizophrenia*, trans. Brian Massumi (Minneapolis: University of Minnesota Press, 1987), 233. On surplus in contrast with basic repression, see Marcuse, *Eros and Civilization*, 35. On "repressive desublimation" as an immediate gratification where the social use of libidinal energy reduces the erotic to the sexual in the interest of domination, see Herbert Marcuse, *One-Dimensional Man* (Boston: Beacon, 1964): "For example, compare love-making in a meadow and in an automobile. . . . In the former . . . the environment partakes of and invites libidinal cathexis and tends to be eroticized. Libido transcends beyond the immediate erotogenic zones—a process of nonrepressive sublimation. In contrast, a mechanized environment seems to block such self-transcendence of libido. Impelled in the striving to extend the field, or

INTRODUCTION

erotic gratification, libido becomes less "polymorphous," less capable of eroticisms beyond localized sexuality, and the latter is intensified.... Thus diminishing erotic and intensifying sexual energy" (73). While in this project, in contrast with Marcuse's pscychoanalytic approach, I draw on child development studies and left Darwinism, suggesting that infant eros is social at its origin, Marcuse's larger political project of social transformation remains deeply relevant.

41. Deleuze and Guattari, *A Thousand Plateaus*. See also Rosi Braidotti, *The Posthuman* (Malden, MA: Polity, 2013), for a reading of the nature-culture continuum along similar lines. While Braidotti lays out the need for a new idiom of community, she does not yet offer this idiom. Braidotti affirms intensities among living creatures and intelligent machines, but these intensities seem to speak more to energy levels than to ethical rapport and community.

42. Donna J. Haraway, *When Species Meet* (Minneapolis: University of Minnesota Press, 2008).

43. On a wave theory of affects, and their function as affect clouds, see Cynthia Willett and Julie Willett, "Going to Bed White and Waking Up Arab: On Xenophobia, Affect Theories of Laughter, and the Social Contagion of the Comic Stage," *Critical Race Theory* 2, no. 1 (2014) Penn Sate Press. For more on network theory, which is a key source for a notion of affect clouds, see Graham Harman, *Prince of Networks: Bruno Latour and Metaphysics* (Melbourne: re.press, 2009); Bruno Latour, *Reassembling the Social: An Introduction to Actor-Network Theory* (Oxford: Oxford University Press, 2005). See also Nicholas A. Christakis and James Fowler, *Connected* (New York: Little, Brown, 2009). And Levi Bryant, Nick Srnicek, and Graham Harman, eds., *The Speculative Turn* (Melbourne: re.press, 2011). While ethics has been less central to speculative realism, my project could be understood in kindred terms given the speculative turn's emphasis on speculation, affect, and biosocial networks.

44. www.nbcnews.com/health/humans-can-smell-fear-its-contagious-1C6927562 (accessed December 3, 2013)

45. Natalie Angier, "The Smell of Fear (No Tweets Necessary)," *New York Times*, August 13, 2012, www.nytimes.com/2012/08/14/science/for-birds-whose-odor-conveys-fear-no-tweets-necessary.html?_r=1&nl=todaysheadlines&emc=edit_th_20120814.

46. Oliver, *Animal Lessons*, xi.

47. According to neuroscientist Katherine Bryant (e-mail communication, April 2, 2013), pheromone research is still in its infancy; however, it is likely that humans share common fear-signaling molecules with other mammals (at least probably other primates). Some detailed research on insects and a few mammals show that pheromones work across multiple species. For research on pheromones that spread across insect species, see Richard E. Greenblatt, Wendell E. Burkholder, John H. Cross, Robert F. Cassidy, Jr., Robert M. Silverstein, A.R. Levinson, H.Z. Levinson, , "Chemical Basis for Interspecific Responses to Sex Pheromones of Trogoderma Species (Coleoptera: Dermestidae)," *Journal of Chemical Ecology* 3 (1977): 337–347; K. W. Vick, W. E. Burkholder, J. E. Gorman, "Interspecific Response to Sex Pheromones of Trogoderma Species (Coleoptera: Dermestidae)," *Annals of the Entomological Society of America* 63 (1970): 379–381; J. A. Byers and D. L. Wood,

INTRODUCTION

"Interspecific Effects of Pheromones on the Attraction of the Bark Beetles, *Dendroctonus brevicomis* and *Ips paraconfusus*, in the Laboratory," *Journal of Chemical Ecology* 7 (1981): 9–18; R. Andrzejewski, J. Babinska-Werka, Anna Liro, Edyta Owadowska, Jakub Szacki, "The Attractiveness of Conspecific and Interspecific Odour for Bank Voles Clethrionomys Glareolus," *Acta Theriologica* 42 (1997): 231–234; Hanna Zaytseva-anciferova and WojciecH noWakoWski, "The Reactions of the Common Dormouse (*Muscardinus avellanarius*) and the Yellow-Necked Mouse (*Apodemus flavicollis*) to the Odour of Nest," *PECKIANA* 8 (2012): 203–207; and J. P. Signoret, "Sexual Pheromones in the Domestic Sheep: Importance and Limits in the Regulation of Reproductive Physiology," *Journal of Steroid Biochemistry and Molecular Biology* 39 (1991): 639–645.

48. Bradshaw, *Elephants on the Edge*, 67–68.
49. Adolescent male elephants engage in greeting and sparring behaviors at different periods of their development, which appear crucial for normal social maturation (one could argue both are ritualistic). See Kate E. Evans and Stephen Harris, "Adolescence in Male African Elephants, *Loxodonta africana*, and the Importance of Sociality," *Animal Behavior* 76 (2008): 779–787. For matriarchal rituals such as leading groups to historic water holes, see Katy Payne, *Silent Thunder: In the Presence of Elephants* (New York: Simon and Schuster, 1999). Another example of animal ritual that has been proposed is the chimpanzee rain dance, first described in detail in Jane Goodall, *In the Shadow of Man* (Boston: Houghton Mifflin Harcourt, 2000). The idea of the rain dance as a chimpanzee ritual is elaborated further in Robert B. Graber, "Ritual, Consciousness, Belief: A Speculation on the Origin of Religion," *Anthropology of Consciousness* 4 (1993): 14–18.
50. On specific patterns of call and response between dominant females and their affiliates when the dominant approaches, see Joseph Soltis, "African elephant vocal communication I: antiphonal calling behaviour among affiliated females," *Animal Behaviour* 70 (2005): 579–587.
51. Jonathan Haidt, *The Happiness Hypothesis* (New York: Basic Books, 2006). For an apt critique of the happiness industry, see Sara Ahmed, *The Promise of Happiness* (Durham: Duke University Press, 2010). A critical appropriation of any work in positive psychology will have to confront Ahmed's concerns.
52. Frans de Waal points out that many animal societies, including human ones, are structured to prevent incest. See Frans de Waal, *The Bonobo and the Atheist* (New York: Norton, 2013), 71–72.
53. Siebert, "An Elephant Crackup?" 4.
54. See Haidt, *The Happiness Hypothesis*, 213–240.
55. Toni Morrison, "Unspeakable Things Unspoken: The Afro-American Presence in American Literature," in *The Black Feminist Reader*, ed. Joy James and T. Denean Sharpley-Whiting (Malden, MA: Blackwell, 2000), 24–56. Note the contrast with Marcuse, who insists on the liberatory power of somewhat "'asocial' autonomous Eros" (*Eros and Civilization*, xiv). For more on tragic hubris in relation to Morrison's novels *Beloved, Jazz*, and *Paradise*, and in relation to discourse ethics and social justice generally, see Cynthia Willett, *The Soul of Justice* (Ithaca: Cornell University Press, 2001).

INTRODUCTION

56. Morrison, "Unspeakable Things Unspoken," 25.
57. Patricia Hill Collins, *Fighting Words: Black Women and the Search for Justice* (Minneapolis.: University of Minnesota Press, 1998), 188.
58. Here we modify Marcuse's politics of eros to include the biosocial dimensions of agency and community; these dimensions are not developed in the neo-Marcusean politics of life that Roberto Esposito proposes against "thanatopolitics." See his *Bios: Biopolitics and Philosophy* (Minneapolis: University of Minnesota Press, 2008), 159–215. Esposito's work, along with that of other thinkers in the continental tradition, traces back to critical reflections on modern European totalitarianism and not to large-scale societies dating back to the Neolithic revolution or new world systems. Chiara Bottici offers a critique of the limits of Esposito's communitarianism in her *Imaginal Politics* (New York: Columbia University Press, 2014), chapter 3. My project recontextualizes Esposito's central notion of an obligation in the face of death as one aspect of a larger politics of biosocial eros that embraces rituals of friendship and playful social norms.
59. For more on pragmatic approaches to animal ethics, see Erin McKenna and Andrew Light, *Animal Pragmatism: Rethinking Human-Nonhuman Relationships* (Bloomington: Indiana University Press, 2004); Erin McKenna, "Charlotte Perkins Gilman: Women, Animals, and Oppression," in *Contemporary Feminist Pragmatism*, ed. Maurice Hamington and Celia Bardwell-Jones (New York: Routledge, 2012), 238–255; Heather E. Keith, "Natural Caring: A Pragmatist Feminist Approach to Ethics in the More-Than-Human-World," in *Contemporary Feminist Pragmatism*, ed. Maurice Hamington and Celia Bardwell-Jones (New York: Routledge, 2012). See also Clare Palmer, *Animal Ethics in Context* (New York: Columbia University Press, 2010). All these sources draw from and amplify care ethicists' attentiveness to relations of dependence and vulnerability; my critical pragmatic focus is on agency, subversion, and empowerment in the context of interdependence and solidarity. Note the term solidarity understood as mutual aid extends fraternity across species barriers (see chapters 1 and 2). For a compelling contribution to a pragmatic ethics of nature, see Piers H. G. Stephens, "Nature and Human Liberty" in *Organization & Environment* 17 (2004): 76–98, among his many other essays.
60. Audre Lorde, *Sister Outsider* (Freedom, CA: Crossing, 1984), 53–59. One dimension of Lorde's eros, in contrast with care ethics, might be found in Lorde having thought of herself as possessing a warrior's defiance against the abuses of power. Not content with an ethics of caring for vulnerable others, this warrior ethic is also one of empowerment. As a woman and mother, I like it.
61. Patricia Hill Collins, *Black Feminist Thought* (New York: Routledge, 1991), 182. Note that Bradshaw also draws upon Collins, in this case to describe the nurturing of female communities. See Bradshaw, *Elephants on the Edge*, 251.
62. Toni Morrison, *Beloved* (New York: Signet, 1987), 162, 275.
63. Collins, *Black Feminist Thought*, 166.
64. Lorde, *Sister Outsider*, 55.

INTRODUCTION

65. Toni Morrison, "Home," in *The House That Race Built*, ed. Wahneema Lubiano (New York: Random House, 1998), 7. See also Nkiru Uwechia Nzegwu, *Family Matters* (New York: SUNY Press, 2006) for an important study of social relations at the center of African ethics and its difference from Western individualism and freedom. Other important works on African ethics and philosophy include Emmanuel Chukwudi Eze, ed., *African Philosophy: An Anthology* (Malden, MA: Blackwell, 1998); and Barry Hallen, *The Good, the Bad, and the Beautiful: Discourse About Values in Yoruba Culture* (Bloomington: Indiana University Press, 2000). Gail M. Presbey has related personal accounts of attempts to understand traditional conceptions of human-nonhuman animal relationships by interviewing African sages (American Philosophy Association meeting; December 29, 2012); she recommends as an important source on Oromo environmental ethics, *Indigenous and Modern: Environmental Ethics*, by Workineh Kelbessa, published by the Council for Research in Values and Philosophy, see Workineh Kelbessa, "Indigenous and Modern Environmental Ethics: A Study of the Indigenous Oromo Environmental Ethic and Modern Issues of Environment and Development Ethiopian Philosophical Studies," last modified February 20, 2011, www.crvp.org/book/Series02/II-13/front.htm.

66. This conception of eros (as nonpossessive desire) provides a vital source of ethical orientation missing when only affects and not desires are considered. See Marcuse's critique of the neo-Freudians for lacking a theory of drive and a meaningful sense of political goals in *Eros and Civilization*, 15–18. He notes that Freud's view of drive shifted from an earlier focus on drive as blind, unconscious, and regressive to a later sense of drive as providing a sense of direction or orientation (ibid., 27). This latter sense is crucial for my project. But, whereas Freud's eros is oriented finally toward infantile gratification or death, I'm interested in the drive toward belonging, acknowlegment, and what Morrison signifies by the trope of home for the African diaspora. On the original etymology of freedom and its connection with home and mother, see David Graeber, *Debt: The First 5,000 Years* (Brooklyn: Melville House 2011), 214–217.

67. Willett, *Maternal Ethics*, 1–49, *Soul of Justice*, 31–100, and *Irony in the Age of Empire: Comic Perspectives on Democracy and Freedom* (Bloomington: Indiana University Press, 2008), 92–116.

68. For the seminal article on the contrast between analytic, individualistic Western conceptions of self and models that emphasize interdependence, see Hazel R. Markus and Shinobu Kitayama, "Culture and the Self," *Psychological Review* 98 (1991): 224–253.

69. Bradshaw, *Elephants on the Edge*, 68 (emphasis mine). Another example of the ancient social bonds and the courtesy and limits these bonds require can be found among the Ju/wa hunter gatherers in the Kalahari Desert and lions as reported in Elizabeth Marshall Thomas, *The Tribe of the Tiger* (New York: Simon and Schuster, 1994).

70. Black Star News, "Profile: Dr. Eve Abe, 1/1/07," www.blackstarnews.com/?c=122&a=2822

71. Bradshaw, *Elephants on the Edge*, 68.

72. On this paradigm shift, see Marc Bekoff, *The Emotional Lives of Animals* (Novato, CA: New World Library, 2007).

INTRODUCTION

73. For a report on the research, see Judith Shulevitz, "Why Fathers Really Matter," *New York Times*, September 9, 2012.
74. Haraway, *When Species Meet*, 79, 4.
75. Bekoff, *The Emotional Lives of Animals*, 88.
76. N. R. E. Fisher, *Hybris* (Warminster: Aris and Philips: 1992), 18. For the Aristotle reference, see *History of Animals*, 615b10.
77. For a comparison between nonstate and state societies, see Jared Diamond, *The World Until Yesterday* (New York: Viking, 2012), 70–119. Mediated conflicts in nonstate societies aim to heal interpersonal relationships rather than render moral judgments of blame and determinations of right and wrong, as occur more often in state societies; moreover, in nonstates communal bonds and emotional closure take precedence over restoring an individual to preinjury conditions, i.e., "making the plaintiff whole" (103). While the U.S. and other states cannot return to prestate conditions, a greater attention to prestate forms of settlement would be a greater advantage for reaching affective and effective resolutions of conflict than are judicial or legal contests because these prestate forms encourage cooperative over excessively self-interested ventures. In later chapters, Jubilee will be examined as among the oldest of symbolic and material practices in state societies for canceling debt and returning servants and slaves home.
78. In this book the focus is on understanding communal bonds that precede, or intertwine with, and sustain conceptions of political or universal rights. (The assumption is also that rights talk should expand beyond liberalism to include second and third generation rights asserted by labor and anticolonization movements; see Cynthia Willett, "Three Concepts of Freedom," in *Irony in the Age of Empire*). This social ethos could offer a ground for an alternative political ethics to that of modern rights talk and the rules and modes of moral cognition that grow out of bureaucratically organized societies. However, it is also true that these modern societies, based on atomistic individualism, will continue to remain central to moral and political conceptions of justice for now. My aim is to recontextualize these modern theories in a larger social ethos and political ethics. Hubris as a social crime, committed by elites, and not a vice, is missed without this larger context. On the meaning of the Greek term *hubris* as a social crime for the pleasure of superiority (typically involving the abuse of power by the powerful and wealthy), and offering a correction for nineteenth-century misinterpretations of hubris as a subjective attitude or character flaw, see Fisher, *Hybris*, 1. Along related lines, Weir offers an important rethinking of identities through communitarianism in Allison Weir, *Identities and Freedom* (Oxford: Oxford University Press, 2013), 57ff. Admittedly, I have been wary of interpretations of communitarianism through "relational autonomy" approaches; such models would seem to make it more difficult to think outside the box of human exceptionalism and modern individualism. Most mammals, including humans, do not live first and foremost as autonomous individuals, but as thoroughly biosocial creatures. For this reason, I take a step back from the autonomy/dependency discourse to refocus on the social drama of interdependence, with its ancient, old-world resonances. This is not to deny a multitude of cognitive or autonomous capacities

INTRODUCTION

in various creatures, but to radically resituate and reinterpret them in a context of biosocial norms of interdependence, alliance-building, and solidarity.

79. "Frans de Waal on Laughing Chimpanzees," https://soundcloud.com/bigpicturescience/frans-de-waal-chimps-laughing (accessed March 14, 2013).
80. Christie Nicholson, "The Humor Gap," *Scientific American Mind Special Report: His Brain Her Brain How We're Wired Differently* (2010), 24–31. See also Jaak Panksepp and Lucy Biven, *The Archaeology of Mind: Neuroevolutionary Origins of Human Emotions* (New York: Norton, 2012), 351–388.
81. Braidotti, *The Posthuman*, 166–167. Along with Braidotti, I am not ready to restrict ethics within the boundaries of a postmodern or poststructuralist rendition of antifoundationalism as we seek new idioms for an ethics based in multispecies communities; yet these philosophical movements' contributions to larger alliances for critical thought are crucial. Contrary to Braidotti, I do not restrict new idioms of anarchic communitarianism to positive affects or to joy. The full range of affects play a role in animal social life and meaning-making activities. Eros is of lack and plenty, not merely one or the other, as Plato argued a long time ago.

1. CAN THE ANIMAL SUBALTERN LAUGH?

1. For a discussion of the evolutionary basis for continuities, see Frans de Waal, "Appendix A: Anthromorphism and Anthropodenial," in Frans de Waal, *Primates and Philosophers: How Morality Evolved*, ed. Stephen Marcedo and Josiah Ober (Princeton: Princeton University Press, 2006), 59–68. And see Marc Bekoff, *The Emotional Lives of Animals* (Novato, CA: New World Library, 2007). For a rich discussion of culture and communication in birds, see Eugene Morton, "Culture Shapes Bird Communication, Too," *Duke Research Blog*, http://sites.duke.edu/dukeresearch/2012/06/19/birdculture (accessed June 19, 2012).
2. "Advertising to Monkeys," *Colbert Report*, June 28, 2011, www.colbertnation.com/the-colbert-report-videos/390870/june-28-2011/advertising-to-monkeys.
3. Rowan Hooper, "The First Advertising Campaign for Non-human Primates," *New Scientist*, www.newscientist.com/article/dn20618-the-first-advertising-for-nonhuman-primates.htm (last modified June 27, 2011).
4. De Waal, *Primates and Philosophers* and *The Age of Empathy: Nature's Lessons for a Kinder Society* (New York: Harmony, 2009); Donna J. Haraway, *When Species Meet* (Minneapolis: University of Minnesota Press, 2008); Kelly Oliver, *Animal Lessons: How they Teach Us to be Human* (New York: Columbia University Press, 2009); Cary Wolfe, *Animal Rites: American Culture, the Discourse of the Species, and Posthumanist Theory* (Chicago: University of Chicago Press, 2003). For the use of animal imagery in literature and media, see Susan McHugh, *Animal Stories: Narrating Across Species Lines* (Minneapolis: University of Minnesota Press, 2011).
5. See Cynthia Willett, *Irony in the Age of Empire: Comic Perspectives on Democracy and Freedom* (Bloomington: Indiana University Press, 2008), for the full argument.

1. CAN THE ANIMAL SUBALTERN LAUGH?

6. Primatologist Malini Suchak confirms that she has on many occasions had chimpanzees laugh at her. Malini Suchak, e-mail message to author, April 20, 2013.
7. Cynthia Willett, Julie Willett, and Yael Sherman, "The Seriously Erotic Politics of Laughter," *Social Research* 79 (2012); Cynthia Willett and Julie Willett, "Bitches, Whores, and Other Fumerists," in *Philosophical Feminism and Popular Culture*, ed. Joanne Waugh and Sharon Crasnow (Lanham: Rowman and Littlefield, 2013). See also Ranajit Guta, *Elementary Aspects of Peasant Insurgency in Colonial India* (Durham: Duke University Press, 1999) for an intriguing list of criteria for subalternity that includes alternative channels of communication. Among these channels, she mainly focuses on rumor, but her analysis might be extended to include laughter and mockery.
8. De Waal, *The Age of Empathy*, 47. For a study of laughter primarily among humans and primates, see Robert R. Provine, *Laughter: A Scientific Investigation* (New York: Penguin, 2000).
9. On the emergence of biopower and its relevance in neoliberalism, see Michel Foucault, "Society Must Be Defended," in *Lectures at the College de France, 1975–1976*, ed. Mauro Bertani and Alessandro Fontana, trans. David Macey (New York: Picador, 2003); and *Naissance de la biopolitique: Cours au Collège de France (1978–1979)* (Paris: Seuil, 2004); for a critical reappropriation, see Roberto Esposito, *Bios: Biopolitics and Philosophy*, trans. Timothy Campbell (Minneapolis: University of Minnesota Press, 2008); on infrapolitics, see James C. Stott, *Weapons of the Weak: Everyday Forms of Peasant Resistance* (New Haven: Yale University Press, 1987). Note that we are more comfortable than some poststructuralists with rights talk based on rich notions of agency and on the social movements that transformed the classic liberal notion of rights toward modes of social equality and alternative idioms of belonging. See Willett, *Irony in the Age of Empire*, 116–149. While we cannot argue extensively on this point here, we suspect that these transformations of the notion of rights allow for richer discussions of animal agency and interaction than discussions based solely on our human responsibility for protecting vulnerable animals. For a defense of this later claim though, see David Wood, "The Truth About Animals," *Environmental Philosophy* 9 (2012): 159–167.
10. *Rise of the Planet of the Apes* (DVD), directed by Rupert Wyatt (2011). On biopower, see Esposito, *Bios*.
11. Elizabeth Kolbert, "Annals of Evolution: Sleeping with the Enemy—What Happened Between the Neanderthals and Us?" *New Yorker*, August, 15, 2011.
12. Charles Siebert, "An Elephant Crackup?" *New York Times Magazine*, October 8, 2006; G. A. Bradshaw and Allan N. Schore, "How Elephants Are Opening Doors: Developmental Neuroethology, Attachment, and Social Context," *Ethology* 113 (2007): 426–436.
13. For a study that characterizes clusters among elephants as nodes of social networks, see Patrick I. Chiyo, Cynthia J. Moss, and Susan C. Alberts, "The Influence of Life History Milestones and Association Networks on Crop-Raiding Behavior in Male African Elephants," *PLoS ONE* 7 (2012), www.plosone.org/article/info%3Adoi%2F10.1371%2Fjournal.pone.0031382.
14. J. M. Coetzee, *The Lives of Animals* (Princeton: Princeton University Press, 1999); Jacques Derrida, "The Animal That Therefore I Am (More to Follow)," trans. David Wills, *Critical*

1. CAN THE ANIMAL SUBALTERN LAUGH?

Inquiry 28, no. 2 (2002): 369–418; Oliver, *Animal Lessons*; Chloe Taylor, "The Precarious Lives of Animals," *Philosophy Today* 52, no. 1 (2008): 60–73.

15. Susan J. Pearson, *The Rights of the Defenseless: Protecting Animals and Children in Guilded Age America* (Chicago: University of Chicago Press, 2011), 9.
16. Ruby Blondell, Mary-Kay Gambel, Nancy Sorkin Rabinowitz, and Bella Zweig, eds. *Women on the Edge: Four Plays (The Classical Canon) by Euripides* (New York: Routledge, 1999), 12.
17. E. P. Evans, *The Criminal Prosecution and Capital Punishment of Animals* (1906), cited in Jeffrey St. Clair's introduction to Jason Hribal, *Fear of the Animal Planet: The Hidden History of Animal Resistance* (Petrolia, CA: CounterPunch, 2010), 2.
18. Hribal, *Fear of the Animal Planet*, 7.
19. Ibid., 8.
20. Ibid., 4.
21. Michel de Montaigne, "On Cruelty," in *The Complete Essays of Montaigne* (Palo Alto: Stanford University Press, 1958). Much thanks to Joe Diaz for drawing our attention to this essay.
22. Pearson, *The Rights of the Defenseless*, 16.
23. On the importance of sympathy, see Martha Nussbaum, *Frontiers of Justice: Disability, Nationality, Species Membership* (Cambridge: Harvard University Press, 2007), 35.
24. Ibid., 409.
25. See Martha Nussbaum's "Beyond 'Compassion and Humanity'," in *Animal Rights: Current Debates and New Directions*, ed. Cass R Sunstein and Martha C. Nussbaum (Oxford: Oxford University Press, 2004), 299–320. Her aim is to move the compassionate consideration of other creatures from the private, moral realm into the realm of justice. Her approach remains, as she explains, paternalistic.
26. David Hume, *A Treatise of Human Nature* (Oxford: Clarendon, 1960); Jonathan Haidt, *The Happiness Hypothesis* (New York: Basic Books, 2006), 17.
27. De Waal, *Primates and Philosophers*, 65.
28. This section is largely borrowed from Cynthia Willett, *Maternal Ethics and Other Slave Moralities* (New York: Routledge, 1995), chapter 6, 129–156. For the key texts of Frederick Douglass, see *Narrative of the Life of Frederick Douglass, an American Slave*, ed. Houston A. Baker, Jr. (New York: Viking Penguin, 1982); "The Heroic Slave," in *Three Classic African-American Novels*, ed. William L. Andrews (New York: Mentor, 1990), 27–28.
29. See Willett, *Irony in the Age of Empire*, chapter 5, 116–148, for the three generations in the transformation of rights.
30. See Jacques Derrida, *The Animal That Therefore I Am*, ed. Marie-Louise Mallet (New York: Fordham, 2008), 80.
31. Walter Benjamin, "On Language as Such and on the Language of Man," *Selected Writings*, vol. 1, *1913–1926*, ed. Marcus Bullock and Michael W. Jennings (Cambridge: Harvard University Press, 1996); Derrida, "The Animal That Therefore I Am." See also Jacques Derrida, "And Say the Animal Responded?" in *Zoontologies: The Question of the Animal*, ed. Cary Wolfe and trans. David Wills (Minneapolis: University of Minnesota Press, 2003), 121–146.

1. CAN THE ANIMAL SUBALTERN LAUGH?

32. On the relevance of Merleau-Ponty's term, see Oliver, *Animal Lessons*, 9.
33. Derrida, "The Animal That Therefore I Am," 19.
34. Elizabeth de Fontenay, *Without Offending Humans: A Critique of Animal Rights*, trans. Will Bishop (Minneapolis: University of Minnesota, 2012), 9.
35. Derrida, "The Animal That Therefore I Am," 48.
36. Oliver, *Animal Lessons*, 21.
37. Derrida, "The Animal That Therefore I Am," 27.
38. Alison Suen, however, points out the significance of Derrida's radical stance in her response to this chapter as presented at the American Studies Association Conference, in San Juan, Puerto Rico, November 15–18, 2012. Her argument is that there is a type of power in the radical incapacity of the vulnerable. We return to reclaim aspects of alterity ethics in chapter 4 in the context of animal compassion.
39. Oliver, *Animal Lessons*, 8.
40. Kelly Oliver makes clear that this biting back is to be understood as a type of agency in her response to critics, "Love Bites! Or Taking Ethics to Heart," *Environmental Philosophy* 9 (2012): 187–199. She develops a critique of the overemphasis on vulnerability in ethics in her *Women as Weapons of War* (New York: Columbia University Press, 2007). For a critique of postmodern theorists, see Gary Steiner, *Animals and the Limits of Postmodernism* (New York: Columbia University Press, 2013); but note too that Steiner doesn't critique the implicit human exceptionalist biases in claims that animals lack language and reason and fail as moral agents (ibid., 176–177). Our argument is that both human and nonhuman animals have communicative agencies and affective cognition that enable degrees and kinds of ethical interaction.
41. This would be Levinas's point, as Francois Raffoul observes in *The Origins of Responsibility* (Bloomington: Indiana University Press, 2010), 128. Our interest, with Levinas, is with language as a communicative vehicle for ethical comportment. Much attention has been given as well to technical dimensions of language as a recursive phenomenon. Those who claim that only human language is recursive overlook its role in music, which, as Steven Mithen explains, provides an evolutionary origin for human and nonhuman language; see *The Singing Neanderthals: The Origins of Music, Language, Mind, and Body* (Cambridge: Harvard University Press, 2006), 17.
42. Gayatri Spivak, "Can the Subaltern Speak?" in *Marxism and the Interpretation of Culture*, ed. C. Nelson and L. Grossberg (Bassingstoke: McMillan Education, 1988). See also Spivak's response to interpretations and a revision of the essay in Rosalyn Morris, *Can the Subaltern Speak: Reflections on the History of an Idea* (New York: Columbia University Press, 2010). Admittedly, Spivak's own approach remains within alterity ethics. While we respect Spivak's deconstructive strategies for exposing imperialistic impositions of meaning onto the subaltern, our own attention to the communicative patterns of nonhuman animals takes a turn that emphasizes their agency and our capacities for responding to their "speech." Here we do not assume that they share the same capacities for discourse (with syntax), but that they can communicate otherwise.
43. H. Peter Steeves, in *The Things Themselves: Phenomenology and the Return to the Everyday* (Albany: State University of New York Press, 2006), writes of language as creative mimicry

1. CAN THE ANIMAL SUBALTERN LAUGH?

in all animals, human and nonhuman. See especially "Monkey See" (ibid., 1–15). He wonders if "human language is derivative of and inferior to the animal language that surrounds us" (ibid., xv).
44. Nancy Hewitt, *No Permanent Waves: Recasting Histories of U.S. Feminism* (New Brunswick, NJ: Rutgers University Press, 2010).
45. De Waal, *The Age of Empathy*, 106–7.
46. See Paola Cavalieri, with Matthew Calarco, John M. Coetzee, Harlan B. Miller, and Cary Wolfe, *The Death of the Animal* (New York: Columbia University Press, 2009). Cavalieri terms this use of human standards for measuring animal "inferiority," "perfectionism" (3).
47. See Con Slobodchikoff, *Chasing Doctor Dolittle: Learning the Language of Animals* (New York: St. Martin's, 2012) for the argument that many other species communicate and that human language is not an exception in the animal world.
48. *Ape Genius* (DVD), directed by John Ruben (2009), http://video.pbs.org/video/1200128615.
49. Michael Tomasello, *Why We Cooperate* (Cambridge: MIT Press, 2009), 19.
50. Malini Suchak confirms this via e-mail communication to the author, April 20, 2013.
51. G. A. Bradshaw, *Elephants on the Edge* (New Haven: Yale University Press, 2009), 29.
52. Ibid., 11. The primary source on elephant hippocampus morphology is Atiya Hakeem, P. R. Hoff, C. C. Sherwood, R. C. Switzer, L. E. Rasmussen, and J. M. Allman, "Brain of the African Elephant (*Loxodonta africana*): Neuroanatomy from Magnetic Resonance Images," *Anatomical Record Part A* 287a (2005):1117–1127. The elephant hippocampus pretty much puts the primate brain to shame in terms of proportional size and structural complexity, according to neuroscientist Katherine Bryant (e-mail correspondence, April 2, 2013.) She would amend Bradshaw's statement to say that the hippocampus is responsible for mediating long-term memory, and especially the spatial organization of things ("place cells") but also social memory. On the hippocampus and "place cells," see Elizabeth Marozzi and Kathryn J. Jeffery, "Place, Space and Memory Cells," *Current Biology* 22 (2012): 939–942. Bryant notes that it is difficult to distinguish social information from other kinds of information and that there may be no such thing as nonsocial information. And she adds the caveat that the exact function of the hippocampus probably varies from species to species and it's likely that the elephant hippocampus might focus on social memory. For a link to discussion of whether the hippocampus encodes only spatial information or also social relationships, see Dharshan Kumaran and Eleanor A. Maguire, "The Human Hippocampus: Cognitive Maps or Relational Memory?" *Journal of Neuroscience* 3 (2005): 7254–7259.
53. Tomasello et al., *Why We Cooperate*, 63, 72.
54. Zanna Clay and Frans de Waal, "Bonobos Respond to Distress in Others: Consolation Across the Age Spectrum," *PLoS ONE* 8 (2003), www.plosone.org/article/info%3Adoi%2F10.1371%2Fjournal.pone.0055206.
55. Malini Suchak reports that this interpretation occurred in the United States. In the United Kingdom, the press had no trouble saying that the chimpanzees outperformed the humans and demonstrated a causal knowledge that either the children did not have or did not demonstrate. E-mail communication to author, April 20, 2013.

1. CAN THE ANIMAL SUBALTERN LAUGH?

56. This evidence that chimpanzees understand causal relations seems to be at odds with some claims that chimpanzees have poor understanding of causal properties of objects, and little capacity for deducing unobservable properties; see Daniel Povinelli, *Folk Physics for Apes* (New York: Oxford University Press, 2001).
57. Suchak, e-mail communication.
58. See Friedrich Nietzsche, "A Critical Backward Glance" in *Birth of Tragedy and the Genealogy of Morals,* trans. Francis Golffing (New York: Random House, 1956), 3–17.
59. Jaak Panksepp and Lucy Biven, *The Archaelogy of Mind: Neuroevolutionary Origins of Human Emotions* (New York: Norton, 2012), 371.
60. Tomasello et al., *Why We Cooperate,* 116.
61. Stefan Lovgren, "Animals Laughed Long Before Humans, Study Says," *National Geographic,* March 31, 2005 (accessed July 21, 2012), http://news.nationalgeographic.com/news/2005/03/0331_050331_animallaughter.html.
62. Jesse Bering, "The Rat That Laughed: Do Animals Other Than Humans Have a Sense of Humor? Maybe So," *Scientific American* 307 (July 2012): 76.
63. Ibid., 76.
64. Ibid., 44.
65. Ibid., 60.
66. Vicki Hearne, *Adam's Task* (New York: Vintage, 1986), 62.
67. Provine, *Laughter,* 94–95.
68. Bekoff, *The Emotional Lives of Animals,* 87.
69. Ibid., 89.
70. De Waal, *The Age of Empathy,* 198. Jean-Jacques Rousseau, *On the Social Contract,* trans. Donald A. Cress (Indianapolis: Hackett, 1987), book 3, chapters 12–18, 49–79.
71. E-mail communication, April 20, 2013. This is in contrast with "despotic" rhesis monkeys, where a higher-ranking individual will take the food right out of the mouth of a lower-ranking individual, a behavior that would violate social norms of chimpanzees.
72. De Waal, *The Age of Empathy,* 199, 161, 24.
73. Ibid., 47.
74. Ibid., 99.
75. This statement by George Orwell is found in Sonia Orwell and Ian Angus, eds., *The Collected Essays, Journalism, and Letters of George Orwell,* vol. 3: *As I Please, 1943–1945* (New York: Godine, 1969), 184. This citation is referred to in Sandra Swart's rich article, "The Terrible Laughter of the Afrikaner—Towards a Social History of Humor," *Journal of Social History* 42 (2009): 899.
76. De Waal, *The Age of Empathy,* 8. See also Charles Darwin, *Descent of Man and Selection in Relation to Sex* (New York: Hurst, 1878), especially chapter 3.
77. Bradshaw, *Elephants on the Edge,* 14.
78. De Waal, *Primates and Philosophers,* 44–45.
79. Todd M. Preuss, e-mail to author, July, 14, 2011.
80. De Waal, *The Age of Empathy,* 187.
81. Ibid., 59.

1. CAN THE ANIMAL SUBALTERN LAUGH?

82. Ibid., 61.
83. This quotation is from the Spanish writer Oriol Pi-Sunyer's "Political Humor in a Dictatorial State: The Case of Spain," *Ethnohistory* 24 (1977): 179–190. This citation is found in Swart, "The Terrible Laughter of the Afrikaner," 899.
84. De Waal, *The Age of Empathy*, 72.
85. Barbara Kingsolver, *Animal, Vegetable, Miracle: A Year of Food Life* (New York: Harper Collins, 2007), 90.
86. Ibid., 95.
87. There is quite a bit of nature writing in the United States with animals (Farley Mowat), and all the boy-and-dog books like *Where the Red Fern Grows, Old Yeller*, etc., and then Jack London's books written from the point of view of a dog (*Call of the Wild, White Fang*). For a study of the role of horse in urban America, see Clay McShane and Joel A. Tarr, *The Horse in the City: Living Machines in the Nineteenth Century* (Baltimore: John Hopkins, 2007).
88. Bekoff, *The Emotional Lives of Animals*, 57.
89. Hribal, *Fear of the Animal Planet*, 11.
90. See Philip Caputo, "Maneless Lions," in *National Geographic*, http://ngm.nationalgeographic.com/ngm/0204/feature2/fulltext.html; we owe this observation to a member of our audience at the October 2012 meeting of the American Studies Conference in Puerto Rico.
91. Hribal, *Fear of the Animal Planet*, 25–26
92. Vicki L. Ruiz, *From Out of the Shadows: Mexican Women in Twentieth-Century America*, 10th ed. (New York: Oxford University Press, 2008); Annelise Orleck, *Storming Caesar's Palace: How Black Women Fought Their Own War on Poverty* (Boston: Beacon, 2006).
93. Eileen Boris and Rhacel Salazar Parrenas, eds., *Intimate Labors: Cultures, Technologies, and the Politics of Care* (Stanford: Stanford University Press, 2010).
94. Alexander Saxton, *The Indispensable Enemy: Labor and the Anti-Chinese Movement in California* (Berkeley: University of California Press, 1975).
95. See, for example, David R. Roediger, *The Wages of Whiteness: Race and the Making of the American Working Class* (New York: Verso, 2007), *Working Toward Whiteness: How America's Immigrants Became White: The Strange Journey from Ellis Island to the Suburbs* (New York: Basic Books, 2006), *History Against Misery* (Chicago: Kerr, 2006).
96. Vijay Prashad, *Everybody Was Kung Fu Fighting: Afro-Asian Connections and the Myth of Cultural Purity* (Boston: Beacon, 2001).
97. See, for example, Calvin Martin, *The Way of the Human Being* (New Haven: Yale University Press, 2000), *In the Spirit of the Earth: Rethinking History and Time* (Baltimore: Johns Hopkins University Press, 1993), *Keepers of the Game: Indian-Animal Relationships and the Fur Trade* (Berkeley: University of California Press, 1982); Howard Harrod, *The Animals Came Dancing: Native American Sacred Ecology and Animal Kinship* (Tucson: University of Arizona Press, 2000); and Joel Martin, *The Land Looks After Us: A History of Native American Religion* (New York: Oxford University Press, 1999).

98. Upton Sinclair, *The Jungle* (Hollywood, FL: Simon and Brown, 2012); *Modern Times* (DVD), directed by Charles Chaplin (1936; Santa Clarita, CA: Charles Chaplin Productions, 1936).
99. Donna Haraway, *When Species Meet* (Minneapolis, University of Minnesota Press, 2008).
100. Thomas G. Andrews, *Killing for Coal: America's Deadliest Labor War* (Cambridge: Harvard University Press, 2008), 134.
101. Ibid., 130.
102. Susan Orlean, *Rin Tin Tin: The Life and the Legend* (New York: Simon and Schuster, 2011), 52. Another apparently true animal story turned into a movie tells of two lions who worked together against the British attempt to build a railroad across their territory in Africa at the end of the nineteenth century. See *The Ghost and the Darkness* (DVD), directed by Stephen Hopkins (1996).
103. Haraway, *When Species Meet*, 21.

2. PALEOLITHIC ETHICS

1. *New York Post*, "Occupy Wall Street Animals Go Wild ZOO-COTTI" (accessed November 4, 2011).
2. See Russell Simmons's letter to the *New York Post* objecting to their misrepresentation of Occupy Wall Street. Russell Simmon, "Russell Simmons Calls Out the *NY Post* for Misrepresenting Occupy Wall Street," *Untitled Flow* (accessed November 4, 2011).
3. Donna Haraway, *When Species Meet* (Minneapolis: University of Minnesota Press, 2008).
4. Peter Kropotkin, *Mutual Aid as a Factor of Evolution* (London: Heinemann, 1904).
5. For a pre-Foucauldian critique of the social control of desire through the "apparti" of capitalism, see Hebert Marcuse, *Eros and Civilization* (Boston: Beacon, 1966), xviii.
6. Marc Bekoff, *The Emotional Lives of Animals* (Novato, CA: New World Library, 2007).
7. One key way to approach this eros is through a notion of friendship as solidarity. Todd May develops such a notion in his "Friendship as Resistance," in *The Anarchist Turn*, ed. Jacob Blumenfeld, Chiara Bottici, and Simon Critchley (London: Pluto, 2013), 59. This chapter too borrows from Cynthia Willett, *Irony in the Age of Empire* (Bloomington: Indiana University Press, 2008), 143–147. Todd May's discussion assumes that reciprocity is interpreted economically as in a capitalist or neoliberal frame; hence he rejects reciprocity as an element in friendship; in my various discussions, here and elsewhere, I borrow from alternative conceptions of reciprocity as friendly play rather than flat equivalence.
8. Henri Bergson, "Laughter," in *Comedy*, ed. Wylie Sypher (Baltimore: Johns Hopkins Press, 1956), 72–73.
9. On the comic as a moment in the ascetic training of the Cynics in plain living and, in particular, the lessons they learned from animals, see Julie Piering, "Cynic Ethics: Lives Worth Examining," *Grundlagen der Antiken Ethik/Foundations of Ancient Ethics*, ed. Jörg Hardy and George Rudebusch (Goettingen: Vandenhoeck and Ruprecht, forthcoming).

2. PALEOLITHIC ETHICS

10. Eva Jablonka and Marion J. Lamb, *Evolution in Four Dimensions* (Cambridge: MIT Press, 2006).
11. See Foucault's 1967 lecture "Different Spaces," in the *Essential Works* volume *Aesthetics, Method, and Epistemology*, ed. James D. Faubion (New York: New Press, 1998), 175–185. Thanks to Lauren Guilmette for this reference.
12. In *Debt: The First 5,000 Years* (New York: Melville House, 2011), David Graeber takes his political ethics of mutual aid from Kropotkin's alternative to Marx's revolutionary theory (see especially 404*n*9).
13. Lynn Margulis and Dorion Sagan, *Acquiring Genomes: A Theory of the Origins of Species* (New York: Basic Books, 2003), 32.
14. Ibid., 19, 70.
15. Frans de Waal, *Primates and Philosophers: How Morality Evolved*, ed. Stephen Marcedo and Josiah Ober (Princeton: Princeton University Press, 2006), 15.
16. E-mail to author, April 2013.
17. Elizabeth Wilson, *Psychosomatic* (Durham: Duke University Press, 2004), 90. See also Jane Bennett, *Vibrant Matter* (Durham: Duke University Press, 2010).
18. Jablonka and Lamb, *Evolution in Four Dimensions*, 237.
19. Ibid.
20. Regarding the relevance of more ancient philosophy for the new science, Christopher Long also has remarked that Aristotle claims in *De Anima* that flourishing is appropriate for understanding animal life. See Christopher Long, "Anarchy and Animals," Digital Dialogues@Penn State with Cynthia Willett, Shannon Winnubst, and Christopher Long, no. 59 (December 2012), www.personal.psu.edu/cpl2/blogs/digitaldialogue/2012/12/digital-dialogue-59-anarchy-and-animal-humor.html.
21. De Waal, *Primates and Philosophers*, 20.
22. Barbara Smuts, "Encounters with Animals," *Journal of Consciousness Studies* 8 (2001): 5.
23. Margulis and Sagan, *Acquiring Genomes*, 46.
24. Ibid., 49.
25. Haraway, *Where Species Meet*, 3–4.
26. Ibid., 3.
27. Ibid.
28. Margaret McFall-Ngai et al., "Animals in a Bacterial World, a New Imperative for the Life Sciences," *Proceedings of the National Academy of Sciences of the United States of America* (110): 3229–3236.
29. Jacques Derrida, *The Animal That Therefore I Am*, trans. Gary Wills (New York: Fordham Press, 2008).
30. Haraway, *When Species Meet*, 22.
31. Ibid., 83, 220.
32. Ibid., 83, 237. Haraway refers to Isabelle Stengers, *Power and Invention: Situating Science*, trans. Paul Bains (Minneapolis: University of Minnesota Press, 1981). See also Isabelle Stengers, "The Cosmopolitical Proposal," in *Making Things Public: Atmospheres of Democracy*, ed. Bruno Latour and Peter Weibel (Cambridge: MIT Press, 2005), 995. See also

2. PALEOLITHIC ETHICS

Carol Adams, *The Sexual Politics of Meat: A Feminist-Vegetarian Critical Theory* (New York: Continuum, 1990); and David Nilbert, *Animal Rights/Human Rights* (Lanham, MD: Rowman and Littlefield, 2002).

33. Mechthild Nagel, *Masking the Abject: A Genealogy of Play* (New York: Lexington, 2002).
34. Judith Butler, "Bodies in Alliance and the Politics of the Street," *EIPCP Multilingual Webjournal*, www.eipcp.net/transversal/1011/butler/en (accessed 5 November 2011).
35. Bekoff, *The Emotional Lives of Animals*, 17.
36. Ibid., 24.
37. Ibid., 107.
38. Jared Diamond, *The World Until Yesterday* (New York: Viking, 2012).
39. Bekoff, *The Emotional Lives of Animals*, 32; Kropotkin, *Mutual Aid as a Factor of Evolution*, 58.
40. Bekoff, *The Emotional Lives of Animals*, 86; de Waal, *Primates and Philosophers*, 174–175, who yields some ground in the debates to Singer, Korsgaard, and others who emphasize the unique capacities of the human animal for moral reasoning.
41. Bekoff, *The Emotional Lives of Animals*, 86.
42. Cf. Paola Cavalieri's argument in *The Death of the Animal*, with Matthew Calarco, John M. Coetzee, Harlan B. Miller, and Cary Wolfe (New York: Columbia University Press, 2009). Cavalieri defends an attention to the suffering of passive creatures as a central moral concern. Following Schopenhauer, she is critical of reciprocity as ultimately egoistic (ibid., 20). Via Bekoff's study of social carnivores, I am arguing that "the golden rule" need not be reduced to an egoistic exchange and that it can account for the ethics of a profoundly egalitarian and playful exchange, also referred to as generalized reciprocity.
43. Bekoff, *The Emotional Lives of Animals*, 89.
44. Ibid., 95.
45. Ibid., 101.
46. Mikhail Bakhtin, *Rabelais and His World*, trans. Helene Iswolsky (Bloomington: Indiana University Press, 1984), 9. Bakhtin's study of carnival is restricted to Europe. On the African carnival during the period of American slavery, regarding some aspects of its potential as a drum and dance call for what the slavers perceived as dangerous uprising in Congo Square, New Orleans, see Ned Sublette, *The World That Made New Orleans: From Spanish Silver to Congo Square* (Chicago: Lawrence Hill, 2009).
47. Herbert Marcuse, *Eros and Civilization* (Boston: Beacon), xxv.
48. Bakhtin, *Rabelais and His World*, 10.
49. Ibid., 78.
50. Northrop Frye, *Anatomy of Criticism: Four Essays* (Princeton: Princeton University Press, 1957), 236.
51. Haraway, *When Species Meet*, 240.
52. Bakhtin, *Rabelais and His World*, 82.
53. Bekoff, *The Emotional Lives of Animals*, 96.
54. Malini Suchak, e-mail to author, April 25, 2013.

2. PALEOLITHIC ETHICS

55. For more discussion of the wave and particle models of affect, see Cynthia Willett and Julie Willett, "Going to Bed White and Waking Up Arab" *Critical Race Theory* 2: no. 1 (2014).
56. Micah White, "From KillCap to WikiSwarms,"*Adbusters America*, July/August 2012.

3. AFFECT ATTUNEMENT

1. Jürgen Habermas, *The Theory of Communicative Action* (Boston: Beacon, 1981).
2. Iris Young, *Inclusion and Democracy* (Oxford: Oxford University Press, 2000); Noëlle McAfee, *Democracy and the Political Unconscious* (New York: Columbia University Press, 2008).
3. Frans de Waal, *Primates and Philosophers: How Morality Evolved*, ed. Stephen Marcedo and Josiah Ober (Princeton: Princeton University Press, 2006), 30. There de Waal gathers together highly persuasive evidence for the major argument of this chapter.
4. Frans de Waal, *The Age of Empathy: Nature's Lessons for a Kinder Society* (New York: Harmony, 2009), 73.
5. Barbara Smuts, "Encounters with Animals," *Journal of Consciousness Studies* 8 (2001): 293–309; and see her interview on "Holy Baboon! A 'Mystical' Moment in Africa," Robert Krulwich, National Public Radio, December 22, 2009 (storyId=121713610), where she describes her encounter with baboons who pause by a stream in a moment of silence. I return to this encounter in the next chapters.
6. Marc Bekoff, *The Emotional Lives of Animals* (Novato, CA: New World Library, 2007). Much of his work moves on to explore the origin of ethics in intersubjective behavior and hence is the basis for more complex layers of ethical life than we are dealing with in this chapter.
7. De Waal, *Primates and Philosophers*, 173–175.
8. Our use of language lights up areas of motor and visual areas of the brain so that we can actually feel a rough texture when we hear or say the phrase "rough day"; see John Hamilton, "Imagine a Flying Pig: How Words Take Shape in the Brain," www.npr.org/blogs/health/2013/05/02/180036711/imagine-a-flying-pig-how-words-take-shape-in-the-brain (last accessed April 15, 2013).
9. I use the term *postlapsarian* to indicate that, from a post-Nietzschean genealogical perspective, animals and humans are not innocent objects, but often complicated moral and ethical subjects implicated in a world of work, culture, power, and technology. For a related discussion of Nietzsche's environmentalism, see Mark Causey, "Nietzsche's Hyperanthropocentrism" (unpublished manuscript). J. M. Coetzee's novel *Disgrace* characterizes this postlapsarian world alternatively, through quasi-religious images of a fall from grace or as a state of disgrace (we return to his specific imagery in the coda). My study's assumption is that, from the perspective of post-Nietzschean multispecies eros ethics, there never has been a "golden age," that is, no state of nature where humans and other animals lacked knowledge of good and evil. This assumption is not however meant to preclude times and

3. AFFECT ATTUNEMENT

places where a more peaceful coexistence or egalitarian societies can be found. Nor is it meant to rule out a rhetorical appeal to a golden age, or green world, as an ethical ideal. (For more on romantic ideals and vertical experiences, see chapter 4). On Hesiod and Ovid's myths of a golden age in which humans and animals shared a peaceful existence, see Gary Steiner, *Animals and the Limits of the Postmodern* (New York: Columbia University Press, 2013), 168. Mostly, we live in a world of predatory violence, and thus my book begins not with golden ideals or even affect attunement and discourse ethics, but with animal dissent and an appeal to solidarity.

10. Isabelle Stengers, *Cosmopolitics I*, trans. Robert Bononno (Minneapolis: University of Minnesota, 2010), 33.
11. Mary Catherine Bateson, "The Epigenesis of Conversational Interaction: A Personal Account of Research Development," *Quarterly Progress Report of the Research Laboratory of Electronics* 100 (1979): 170–176; Colin Trevarthen, "Descriptive Analysis of Infant Communication Behavior," *Studies in Mother-Infant Interaction*, ed. H. R. Schaffer (London: Academic, 1984), 227–270; Daniel N. Stern, *The Interpersonal World of the Infant* (Mineola, NY: Basic Books, 1985); *The Forms of Vitality* (Oxford: Oxford University Press, 2010); Constantina Papoulias and Felicity Callard, "Biology's Gift: Interrogating the Turn to Affect," *Body Society* 16 (2010): 29–56; Cynthia Willett, *Maternal Ethics and Other Slave Moralities* (New York: Routledge, 1995); Anna Gibbs, "Contagious Feelings: Pauline Hanson and the Epidemiology of Affect," *Australian Humanities Review* (March-May 2002) no. 25, www.australianhumanitiesreview.org 2001 (accessed November 12, 2013), and "Panic! Affect Contagion, Mimesis and Suggestion in the Social Field," *Cultural Studies Review* 2008 14 (2): 130–145.
12. Willett, *Maternal Ethics and Other Slave Moralities*.
13. Smuts "Encounters with Animals"; Erica Fudge, *Animal* (Trowbridge: Reaktion, 2002), 26–27; Malini Suchak, e-mail to author, April 27, 2013; Franz de Waal, *The Age of Empathy* (New York: Random House, 2009); Bekoff, *The Emotional Lives of Animals*; Donna Haraway, *When Species Meet* (Minneapolis: University of Minnesota Press, 2008).
14. See also John Protevi, *Political Affect* (Minneapolis: University of Minnesota Press, 2009) for an interesting view of other dimensions of a Deleuzean-influenced affect theory fully developed for a political ethics. On affect theory, see Teresa Brennan, *The Transmission of Affect* (Ithaca: Cornell University Press, 2004), especially 12. See Ralph R. Acampora, *Corporal Compassion: Animal Ethics and Philosophy of Body* (Pittsburgh: University of Pittsburgh Press, 2006) for a defense of a phenomenological trans-species ethics. This chapter develops the passing suggestion that infant experiences can provide insights for a trans-species embodied ethics (ibid., 36). A complementary critical project to the project in this chapter would treat political ethics within a critique of forms of captivity and other uses of power that obscure and distort animal sociality (ibid., 95–115).
15. Here I draw on language that resonates with Megan Craig's "pragmatic phenomenology" of sense-giving experiences and immersion in life. See Megan Craig, *Levinas and James: Toward a Pragmatic Phenomenology* (Bloomington: Indiana University Press, 2010).
16. In order to negotiate between the views of whether or not there is some sense of self in the first weeks of life, I have described the first period of infancy as "subjectless sociality";

3. AFFECT ATTUNEMENT

see Willett, *Maternal Ethics and Other Slave Moralities*, 1995. The account of early infancy reflects less the theoretical debates and positions of Stern, Shaun Gallagher, and Colin Trevarthen, who posit an infant subjectivity, than those who think that infants are coaxed into subjectivity. Shaun Gallagher, *How the Body Shapes the Mind* (Oxford: Oxford University Press, 2006); Colin Trevarthen, "Descriptive Analysis of Infant Communication Behavior," *Studies in Mother-Infant Interaction*, ed. H. R. Schaffer (London: Academic, 1977), 227–270.

17. Smuts, "Encounters with Animals," 302.
18. Humberto Maturana and G. Verden-Zoller, *The Origins of Humanness in the Biology of Love* (Exeter: Imprint Academic, 2009). Maturana has moved beyond his earlier model of life as autopoiesis, or self-organizing.
19. Charles L. Raison, Christopher A. Lowry, and Graham A. W. Rook, "Inflammation, Sanitation, and Consternation: Loss of Contact with Coevolved, Tolerogenic Microorganisms and the Pathophysiology and Treatment of Major Depression," *Archives of General Psychiatry* 67 (2010): 1211–1224.
20. Ibid., 1211.
21. Ibid. This work converges with other research on the gut brain. For a discussion from a psychologist of what Montaigne identifies as our second brain, see Jonathan Haidt, *The Happiness Hypothesis* (New York: Basic Books, 2006), 5.
22. Nicholas A. Christakis and James H. Fowler, *Connected: The Surprising Power of Our Social Networks and How They Shape Our Lives* (New York: Hachette, 2009), 108.
23. Ibid., 108.
24. Ibid., 116.
25. Ibid., 120.
26. Ibid., 133.
27. Karen Barad, *Meeting the Universe Halfway: Quantum Physics and the Entanglement of Matter and Meaning* (Durham: Duke University Press, 2007), 71–96.
28. Walt Whitman, "Song of Myself" in *Leaves of Grass* (New York: Signet Classics, 1980).
29. Stern, *The Interpersonal World of the Infant* and *The Forms of Vitality*. References to the former work are included in the text. Some of the ethical and political implications of the research on affects between caregivers and infants are explored in Willett, *Maternal Ethics and Other Slave Moralities*, especially 1–10, and Willett, *The Soul of Justice*, especially 1–30.
30. Shaun Gallagher observes this phenomenon as well in *How the Body Shapes the Mind* (Oxford: Oxford University Press, 2006).
31. Bateson, "The Epigenesis of Conversational Interaction."
32. Stern, *The Interpersonal World of the Infant*, 56–57, expanded in Stern, *The Forms of Vitality*.
33. Sometimes affect theories subsume hedonic affect into the category of emotion, which assumes a sense of self (I often use the terms *self* and *subject* interchangeably as I work across traditions of thought). Stern allows for hedonic tone to function at the level of subjectless sociality. Affect theories are indebted to Deleuze and Guattari, though they seem to prefer mostly to focus on what Stern terms vitality affects and vitality contours. For a

3. AFFECT ATTUNEMENT

broad sample of essays that tend to follow the vitality affects and consign hedonic affects to emotion, see Melissa Gregg and Gregory Seigworth, *The Affect Theory Reader* (Durham: Duke University Press, 2010).

34. Willett, *Maternal Ethics and Other Slave Moralities*, 31–47.
35. Gregg and Seigworth, *The Affect Theory Reader*, 199.
36. Stern, *The Interpersonal World of the Infant*, 139.
37. Steven Mithen, *The Singing Neanderthals: The Origin of Music, Language, Mind, and Body* (Cambridge: Harvard University Press, 2006), 110. See Bruce Richman, "Rhythm and Melody in Gelada Vocal Exchanges," *Primates* 28 (1987): 199–223. See also Katy Payne, *Silent Thunder: In the Presence of Elephants* (New York: Penguin, 1998).
38. E-mail communication, May 14, 2013.
39. Lea Leinonen, I. Linnankoski, M. L. Laakso, R. Aulanko, "Vocal Communication Between Species: Man and Macaque" *Language Communication* 11 (1991): 241–262. Cited in Mithen, *The Singing Neanderthals*, 111.
40. Ibid., 121.
41. Robert R. Provine, *Laughter: A Scientific Investigation* (New York: Penguin, 2000), 93.
42. Haraway, *When Species Meet*.
43. Ibid., 30.
44. Gilles Deleuze and Felix Guattari, *A Thousand Plateaus: Capitalism and Schizophrenia*, trans. Brian Massumi (Minneapolis: University of Minnesota Press, 1987), 233.
45. Ibid., 240.
46. Haraway, *When Species Meet*, 30.
47. Ibid., 29.
48. Ibid.
49. Deleuze and Guattari, *A Thousand Plateaus*, 258, 274.
50. Stern, *The Forms of Vitality*.
51. Ibid., 20, 22.
52. Bruce Wexler, *Brain and Culture* (Cambridge: MIT Press, 2006). Wexler's general thesis, though, emphasizes the political, social, and psychological disasters of cognitive dissonance, or the mismatch of internal frameworks and environment for adults, who have lost the plasticity of the cognitive functioning that is found in children.
53. For a discussion of the basis for ethical responses to animals that are not cute or otherwise attractive objects of sentiment, or do not invoke any ordinary form of sympathy or attachment, see chapter 4 and the coda.
54. Recall that a healthy 90 percent of the body's "cells are filled with the genomes of bacteria, fungi, protists, and such," shaking up our commonsense notion of personal identity; Haraway, *When Species Meet*, 3.
55. Raison et al., "Inflamation."
56. Cf. Fudge, *Animal*, 26–27; and as clarified by Suchak, e-mail to author.
57. J. Poole, *Coming of Age with Elephants* (New York: Hyperion, 1996).
58. Sarah Bakewell, *How to Live—Or—A Life of Montaigne* (New York: Random House, 2010), 129. An ethics of social eros has for its aim the enhancement of social bonds and

3. AFFECT ATTUNEMENT

meaningful attachments in contrast with various practices and techniques of detachment in the Hellenistic traditions, including Stoicism.

59. Haraway, *When Species Meet*.
60. Todd M. Preuss, Evolutionary Theory Workshop, personal conversation, May 28, 2011.
61. Ibid., and quoted from e-mail correspondence, July 14, 2011. See Todd M. Preuss, "The Human Brain: Rewired and Running Hot," *Annals of the New York Academy of Sciences* 40 (2011) 929; E1–E10.
62. Bekoff, *The Emotional Lives of Animals*, 1–2, 59–60.
63. The argument from "parallel evolution" is already found in Henri Bergson's *L'Evolution créatrice*, published in 1907, for which he received the Nobel Prize in Literature exactly two decades later. In that text, Bergson argues that instances of parallel evolution (such as the appearance of the eye in species that split before the eye was formed in either) problematizes the two dominant strands of evolutionary thinking: mechanism and finalism. He writes: "pure mechanism then would be refutable and finality, in the special sense in which we understand it, would be demonstrable in a certain aspect, if it could be proved that life may manufacture the like apparatus, by unlike means, on divergent lines of evolution; and the strength of the proof would be proportional both to the divergence between the lines of evolution thus chosen and to the complexity of the similar structures found in them." See Henri Bergson, *Creative Evolution* (New York: Dover, 1998), 55. Much thanks to David Peña-Guzman for this reference.
64. Smuts, "Encounters with Animals," 294.
65. Ibid., 295.
66. With some hesitation, I align pragmatic critical theory with Habermasian discourse ethics for the shared emphasis on communication. Habermas overemphasizes the role of reason and argument in ethics-oriented communication and deemphasizes the political weight of dissent and solidarity among oppressed groups.
67. De Waal, *The Age of Empathy*, 5.

4. WATER AND WING GIVE WONDER

1. Barbara Smuts, "Encounters with Animal Minds," *Journal of Consciousness Studies* 8 (2001): 293–309.
2. Ibid., 301.
3. Ibid. JeeLoo Liu cautions that the use of this Buddhist term in this context may be experienced as insulting or wrong to those who cultivate meditative communities and practices after years of effort. I risk leaving Smuts's language in this chapter with the hope that it will open up spiritual practices to a larger world rather than harming these practices or their reputation.
4. The approach here does not focus on naturalizing the human so much as demonstrating the capacities for technology, knowledge, and ethical comportment in other species, although I do not aim to exclude the former. On renaturalization, see Hasana Sharp, *Spinoza and the*

4. WATER AND WING GIVE WONDER

Politics of Renaturalization (Chicago: Chicago University Press, 2011); and Elizabeth Grosz, *Time Travels: Feminism, Nature, Power* (Durham: Duke University Press, 2005).

5. Tara Doyle, Buddhist scholar and director of Emory University's Tibetan Studies Program, clarifies (e-mail communication, April 22, 2013) that, in Buddhism, enlightenment is the ultimate spiritual attainment, not a precursor to that attainment, and the term is typically used only when discussing that highest state, where no more suffering or negative emotions exist. Words such as states, realizations, attainments, perfections, etc., would feel more accurate, in a Buddhist sense, for the ethical and spiritual phenomenon this chapter describes. Many Buddhists would also be uncomfortable with assertions that nonhuman animals can be fully enlightened (although they agree that some might and do demonstrate what are typically considered advanced, wholesome mental states). When the Buddha was, in a past life, a rabbit or elephant, he still wasn't seen as fully "enlightened," more like highly realized. This chapter's challenge to the human exceptionalism that lingers in this tradition as well as in modern Western enlightenment traditions aims to open up the term to new meanings, while retaining from the term the verticality of an expansive awareness of self and world.
6. Jared Diamond, *The World Until Yesterday* (New York: Penguin, 2012), 49–54.
7. Frans de Waal, "The Cosmopolitan Ape Primatology: Empathy, Morality, Community, Culture—Apes Can Have It All!" (interview), *Nautilus* 1, http://nautil.us/issue/1/what-makes-you-so-special/the-cosmopolitan-ape (accessed November, 15, 2013).
8. Stephen Dubner, "The Monkey Economy: Freakonomics Radio Live in St. Paul," www.youtube.com/watch?feature=player_embedded&v=J8449HgS3FM (accessed March 23, 2013).
9. Elizabeth Kolbert, "Annals of Evolution: Sleeping with the Enemy—What Happened Between the Neanderthals and Us?" *New Yorker*, August 15, 2011.
10. Plato, *Symposium*, trans. Robin Waterfield (Oxford: Oxford University Press, 1994), 210D–211B.
11. See Immanuel Kant, "Perpetual Peace: A Philosophical Sketch," in *Classics of International Relations*, ed. A. Vasquez (Upper Saddle River, NJ: Prentice-Hall, 1996); Tom Regan, *The Case for Animal Rights* (Berkeley: University of California, 2004).
12. Peter Singer, *Animal Liberation* (New York: Avon, 1990).
13. Antonio R. Damasio, *Descartes' Error: Emotion, Reason, and the Human Brain* (New York: Putnam, 1994).
14. On implicit bias, see Jennifer Saul, "Implicit Bias and Philosophy," www.biasproject.org (accessed November 15, 2013).
15. I owe the suggestion to name a narcissus gene to David Peña-Guzman. The Faustian and monkey narcissus genes in effect serve to reinterpret Marcuse's sharp contrast between the Promethean myth and narcissistic eros, which we return to later in the chapter.
16. Frans de Waal, *Primates and Philosophers: How Morality Evolved,* ed. Stephen Macedo and Josiah Ober (Princeton: Princeton University Press, 2006), 161–181.
17. Anthony J. Steinbock, *Phenomenology and Mysticism: The Verticality of Religious Experience* (Bloomington: University of Indiana Press, 2009.

4. WATER AND WING GIVE WONDER

18. Jonathan Haidt, *The Happiness Hypothesis* (New York: Basic Books, 2006), 201.
19. "But do we really know whether these animals like the psychoactive effects of the drug, or are they just willing to put up with them as a side effect of consuming a valuable food source? After all, fermented fruit is a tasty and nutritious meal. While it's hard to dissociate these motivations in animals, many cases suggest that the psychoactive effect is the primary motivator for consumption. Often, only a tiny amount of plant or fungus is consumed, so while its nutritional effect is minuscule its psychoactive effect is large." David Linden, *The Compass of Pleasure* (New York: Viking Penguin, 2011), 38.
20. Steinbock, *Phenomenology and Mysticism*, 13.
21. John M. Coetzee, "Notes on Issues Raised by Matthew Calarco," in Paola Cavalieri, *The Death of the Animal* (New York: Columbia University Press, 2009), 89.
22. Haidt, *The Happiness Hypothesis*, 184.
23. Sophia Yin, "The Dominance Controversy," http://drsophiayin.com/philosophy/dominance/?/dominance.php.
24. On amused contempt and pity, see W. E. B. Du Bois, *The Souls of Black Folk* (New York: Bantam, 1989), 3.
25. De Waal, "The Cosmopolitan Ape Primatology."
26. Frans de Waal, *Chimpanzee Politics* (Baltimore: Johns Hopkins University Press, 2007).
27. Malini Suchak, e-mail to author, April 30, 2013.
28. See also de Waal, *Chimpanzee Politics*, especially his account of styles of leadership. De Waal explains, citing Machiavelli, that chimpanzees who rule by fear rather than respect, and who have the support of the males of high rank but not the females and children, are less likely to fare well (ibid., 149).
29. For a stunning indictment, see the documentary *Food, Inc* (DVD), directed by Robert Kenner, Magnolia Pictures Participant Media and River Road Entertainment (2008).
30. Paul Rozen, "Disgust," in *Handbook of Emotions*, 2d ed, ed. M. Lewis and J. M. Haviland-Jones (New York: Gilford, 2000), 637–653. See also Haidt, *The Happiness Hypothesis*, 185.
31. Judith A. Tornchuk and George F. R. Ellis, "Disgust: Sensory Affect or Primary Emotional System," *Cognition and Emotion* 21 (2007): 1799–1818.
32. Charles Darwin, *The Expression of the Emotions in Man and Animals* (London: John Murray, 1972).
33. Martha Nussbaum, *Hiding from Humanity: Disgust, Shame, and the Law* (Princeton: Princeton University Press, 2004), 89.
34. Cf. Julia Kristeva, *Powers of Horror: An Essay on Abjection*, trans. Leon S. Roudiez (New York: Columbia University Press, 1982), 60–70, for whom the purification rites separate not only the sacred from the abject or filthy but also humans from animals. Sara Beardsworth provides a clear comparison of alternative theories of purification in *Julia Kristeva: Psychoanalysis and Morality* (New York: SUNY Press, 2004), 125.
35. Bruce Wexler, *Brain and Culture* (Cambridge: MIT Press, 2008).
36. Toronchuk and Ellis, "Disgust." For the other side, see J. Panksepp, "Criteria for Basic Emotions: Is Disgust a Primary 'Emotion'?" *Cognition and Emotion* 21 (2007): 1819–1828. See also I. Veissier, A. Boissy, L. Désiré, L. Greiveldinger, "Animals' Emotions: Studies

in Sheep Using Appraisal Theories," *Animal Welfare* 18 (2009): 347–354. This article "concluded that sheep are able to experience emotions such as fear, anger, rage, despair, boredom, disgust and happiness because they use the same checks involved in such emotions as humans." For instance, despair is triggered by situations evaluated as sudden, unfamiliar, unpredictable, discrepant from expectations, and uncontrollable, whereas boredom results from an overly predictable environment; all these checks have been found to affect emotional responses in sheep. Matias Lopez, Patricia Gosalla, Mercedes Vega et al., "Latent Inhibition of Conditioned Disgust Reactions in Rats," *Learning and Behavior* 38 (2010): 77–186. This article reports that animals can be conditioned to experience disgust due to controlled changes in their environment. The results demonstrate that the expression of both conditioned taste avoidance and conditioned disgust reactions depends critically on a common method of flavor exposure during preexposure and testing. And see C. M. Sherwin, C. M. Heyes, C. J. Nicol, "Social Learning Influences the Preferences of Domestic Hens for Novel Food," in *Animal Behaviour* 63 (2002): 933–942. This article "attempted to confirm that birds can develop socially learnt aversions to unpalatable foods." But it argues that the data is inconclusive. "The results provide no evidence that adult hens learn aversions through observing disgust reactions, but show that hens are sensitive to the extent of demonstrating preferences for palatable food."

37. Larry Young and Brian Alexander retell the story of the Pfaus experiment in *The Chemistry Between Us: Love, Sex, and the Science of Attraction* (New York, Penguin, 2012), 83. See J. Pfaus, "Pathways of Sexual Desire," *Journal of Sexual Medicine* 6 (2009): 1506–1533, and "Conditional and Sexual Behavior: A Review," *Hormones and Behavior* 40 (2001): 291–321.

38. Haidt, *The Happiness Hypothesis*, 187.

39. For photos of a dog expressing disgust with sensations of coldness combined with wetness, see "The Other End of the Leash," www.patriciamcconnell.com/theotherendoftheleash/yup-dogs-can-be-disgusted (last accessed January 22, 2013). For an article on disgust in dogs, see R. H. Gunlach, "An Anecdote Illustrating 'Disgust' in a Dog," *Journal of Genetic Psychology* 44 (1934): 253–254. See also Paul H. Morris, Christine Doe, and Emma Godsell, "Secondary Emotions in Non-primate Species? Behavioural Reports and Subjective Claims by Animal Owners," *Cognition and Emotion* 22 (2008): 3–20. In this article, the authors argue that disgust is a primary emotion, but they also make the claim that it is the primary emotion least likely to be observed by humans in animals. They did a sociological study of pet owners, and, compared to other primary emotions, disgust is the emotion that pet owners reported the least in their animals. This article does conclude, though, that even "secondary emotions" can be found in nonhuman animals. I wonder if disgust is missed in pet owners in part because other species do not share the same targets of disgust. For example, as we shall see shortly, dogs are attracted to their own urine smell, as well as the urine smell of others, all of which would disgust humans. Humans may conclude that dogs lack a disgust response rather than just differ in their responses and targets. Note that in Daniel Kelly, *Yuck! The Nature and Moral Significance of Disgust* (Cambridge: MIT Press, 2011) the author proposes to explain the moral significance that disgust can acquire through the evolution of tribal cultures. The violation of tribal norms, which coordinate a

4. WATER AND WING GIVE WONDER

group, can co-opt the disgust mechanism from its original repulsion to poisons and parasites to the violation of social norms, and this begins with norms that regulate behavior closely related to intrinsically disgusting phenomena, such as rotting corpses and bodily wastes (ibid., 119ff). He doesn't believe that there is evidence for a disgust mechanism for parasites with nonhuman animals, however; nonhuman animals would seem to be limited to intrinsic disgust reactions only to poisons. In fact, there is evidence for a wider range of disgust reactions in animals and some evidence for disgust functioning there too as a primary emotion that can expand to include social and cultural phenomena.

40. Hasana Sharp brought out the significance of visceral conscience in her response to a presentation based on this chapter at philoSOPHIA, in Banff, Canada, May 2013. Her helpful comments have led me to add emphasis to the use of this term in the argument.
41. Donna J. Haraway, *When Species Meet* (Minneapolis, Minnesota: University of Minnesota Press, 2008), 285–302. Katherine Schweitzer wrote a seminar paper for a course I cotaught with Deboleena Roy that has prompted me to return to this topic.
42. See Haidt, *The Happiness Hypothesis*, on gut brain, 5–6.
43. Elizabeth Wilson, *Psychosomatic* (Durham: Duke University Press, 2004), 45.
44. Marc Bekoff draws upon multiple sources to argue that given the evidence suggesting that various mammals share neural circuits for complex secondary emotions, including guilt, pride, and shame, there is reason to believe that dogs also experience these emotions, but not necessarily in ways easy for humans to detect. See www.psychologytoday.com/blog/animal-emotions/201303/can-dogs-experience-guilt-pride-and-shame-why-not.
45. Frans de Waal, *The Bonobo and the Atheist: In Search for Humanism Among the Primates* (New York: Norton, 2013), 155.
46. Ibid., 158
47. Ibid., 162.
48. On the SS officer, see www.jewishvirtuallibrary.org/jsource/Holocaust/himmler.html.
49. Malini Suchak's dissertation, "Chimpanzees Cooperate in a Competitive World" (Emory University, 2013) finds that some species are able to self-monitor social-norm following apparently apart from external threats of punishment.
50. *The Bonobo and the Atheist*, 154.
51. Suchak, e-mail communication, April 30, 2013.
52. Haidt, *The Happiness Hypothesis*, 8 and 63; on "constitutional ignorance," see Robert Wright, *The Moral Animal* (New York: Vintage, 1994).
53. Simon Critchley, *On Humour* (New York: Routledge, 2002), 29.
54. Stephen Colbert, "Whales Aren't People," *The Colbert Report,* number 08011, October 26, 2011.
55. For a development of Plessner's thesis, see Critchley, *On Humour,* 29. For Helmuth Plessner, see *Laughing and Crying: A Study of the Limits of Human Behavior*, trans. James Spencer Churchill and Marjorie Grene (Evanston, Ill: Northwestern University Press, 1970).
56. Critchley, *On Humour,* 28.
57. Ibid., 94–95.

4. WATER AND WING GIVE WONDER

58. Animal Planet, "Apes and Other Primates," http://animal.discovery.com/video-topics/wild-animals/apes-and-other-primates-videos/jane-goodall.htm (accessed February 22, 2013).
59. Henri Bergson, "Laughter," in *Comedy*, ed. Wylie Sypher (Baltimore: Johns Hopkins University Press, 1956).
60. Lorenz argues that laughter strengthens group affinity and promotes aggression against outsiders: "laughter forms a bond and simultaneously draws a line." See Konrad Lorenz, *On Aggression*, trans. Marjorie Kerr Wilson (Orlando: Harcourt Brace, 1966), 3. In egalitarian societies, this expulsion may be of the dangerous *hubristai*.
61. On humor as strengthening the immune system along with morale, see K. M. Dillon et al., "Positive Emotional States and Enhancement of the Immune System," *International Journal of Psychiatry in Medicine* 15 (1985): 13–15; R. A. Martin and J. P. Dobbin, "Sense of Humor, Hassles and Immunoglobulin," *International Journal of Psychiatry in Medicine* 18 (1988): 93–105; N. Cousins, "Why Laughter Is Good Medicine," in *The Study of Humor*, ed. H. Mindess and J. Turek (Los Angeles: Antioch University Press, 1979). On disgust as performing a similar function see Toronchuk and Ellis, "Disgust."
62. Marc Bekoff, *The Emotional Lives of Animals* (Novato, CA: New World Library, 2007), 39.
63. Malini Suchak explains that "dogs have a capability we don't have—we can't distinguish individuals by their urine. It's the same reason why they stick their nose in human's crotches when they greet them, it's a way of identifying an individual. It serves a very real function. We just have different, more visually oriented mechanisms for doing this." Suchak, e-mail communication, April 30, 2013.
64. Ibid.
65. On the baboon, see de Waal, *Primates and Philosophers*, 30.
66. Ibid., 174.
67. Ibid., 168.
68. www.radiolab.org/2010/feb/19/. Much thanks to Swasti Bhattacharyya for this source. The story is from the Great Ape Trust in Iowa; see www.iowaprimatelearning.org/.
69. Sue Savage-Rumbaugh, "Sibling Rivalry," in Marc Bekoff, ed., *The Smile of a Dolphin* (New York: Discovery, 2000), 175.
70. Ibid., 174.
71. Ibid.
72. Bekoff, *The Emotional Lives of Animals*, 86.
73. 5:161.33–6; tr. Guyer 1992, 1
74. John Sanbonmatsu develops Marcuse's and other Frankfurt theorists' critiques of Western exploitation of animals and alienation of humans from their own animal natures in the introduction to his edited collection, *Critical Theory and Animal Liberation* (Lanham: Rowman and Littlefield, 2011), 1–32.
75. Herbert Marcuse, *Eros and Civilization* (Boston: Beacon, 1966), 210.
76. Haidt, *The Happiness Hypothesis*, 236; Andrew Newberg, E. D'Auili, and R. Rause, *Why God Won't Go Away: Brain Science and the Biology of Belief* (New York: McGraw-Hill, 2001).

4. WATER AND WING GIVE WONDER

77. Northrop Frye, *Anatomy of Criticism* (Princeton: Princeton University Press, 1957), 183; Stanley Cavell, *Pursuits of Happiness* (Cambridge: Harvard University Press, 1981).
78. Jane Goodall, "Primate Spirituality," in *The Encyclopedia of Religion and Nature*, ed. B. Taylor (New York: Thoemmes Continuum, 2005), 1303–1306. See also Jane Goodall's *In the Shadow of Man*" (Boston: Houghton Mifflin Harcourt, 2000); pdf here: http://ftp.beitberl.ac.il/~bbsite/misc/ezer_anglit/klali/05_87.pdf).
79. "A Gentle Heart," in Bekoff, *The Smile of a Dolphin*, 173.
80. Katy Payne, www.onbeing.org/, aired originally on March 21, 2013.
81. Smuts, "Encounters with Animal Minds," 306.
82. De Waal, *Primates and Philosophers*, 31.
83. Compare the prophetic thoughts of Frederick Douglass on freedom in chapter 1 and see *Narrative of the Life of Frederick Douglass, an American Slave*, ed. Houston A. Baker Jr. (New York: Viking Penguin, 1982); "The Heroic Slave," in *Three Classic African-American Novels*, ed. William L. Andrews (New York: Mentor, 1990), 27–28.
84. See Ernst Cassirer, *Philosophy of Symbolic Forms*, vol. 3 (New Haven: Yale University Press, 1965).
85. Haidt, *The Happiness Hypothesis*, 195–197.
86. Ibid., 197.
87. On differences between xenophobic chimpanzees and bonobos, who demonstrate altruism toward strangers, see Sindya Bhanoo, "Milk of Human Kindness Also Found in Bonobos," *New York Times*, www.nytimes.com/2013/01/08/science/the-unexpected-altruism-of-bonobos.html?_r=0. On Dame Daphe Sheldrick's observations on compassion in elephants, see G. A. Bradshaw, *Elephants on the Edge: What Animals Teach Us About Humanity* (New Haven: Yale University Press, 2009), 24.
88. Immanuel Kant, *Critique of Judgement*, trans. James Creed Meredith (Oxford: Oxford University Press, 1973).
89. Haidt, *The Happiness Hypothesis*, 203.
90. William James, *Varieties of Religious Experience* (New York: Macmillan, 1961).
91. Here's a significant point where I would aim to allow for a step further for the relational ethics approach that I share with Elizabeth Anderson's "Animal Rights and the Values of a Nonhuman Life," in *Animal Rights: Current Debates and New Directions*, ed. Cass R. Sunstein and Martha C. Nussbaum (Oxford: Oxford University Press, 2004), 284; and with Sue Donaldson and Will Kymlicka's *Zoopolis: A Political Theory of Rights* (Oxford: Oxford University Press, 2011), among many others. Anderson bases social membership on discipline enforced by commands (authoritarian models of dog and horse training via Vicki Hearne in this case) rather than egalitarian play (see Smuts, "Encounters with Animal Minds," 303). On ethical wonder in the context of human compassion toward nonhumans, see also Martha Nussbaum, "Beyond 'Compassion and Humanity'" in Cass and Nussbaum, *Animal Rights*, 306.
92. See discussion of Levinas in Matthew Calarco, *Zoographies: The Question of the Animal from Heidegger to Derrida* (New York: Columbia University Press, 2008), 55–77, where Calarco

aims to reinterpret what is at stake in Levinas in order to allow for compassion or other forms of ethical encounter across species barriers.

93. Workineh Kelbessa, *Indigenous and Modern: Environmental Ethics, Council for Research in Values and Philosophy*, www.crvp.org/book/Serieso2/II-13//front.htm (accessed December 14, 2012).

94. Workineh Kelbessa, "Indigenous and Modern Environmental Ethics: A Study of the Indigenous Oromo Environmental Ethic and Modern Issues of Environment and Development," *Cultural Heritage and Contemporary Lifeseries I*, vol. 1, *Culture and Values*, www.crvp.org/book/Serieso2/II-13//front.htm (accessed January 13, 2013).

95. Term borrowed from Marc Bekoff and Jessica Pierce, *Wild Justice: The Moral Lives of Animals* (Chicago: University of Chicago Press, 2010).

96. Don José Campos, *The Shaman and Ayahuasca*, trans. Alberto Roman (Studio City, CA: Divine Arts, 2011). Thanks to Anthony Bisignano for this reference. Shamanism is the oldest religious complex and involves a visionary transformation that conflates human and animal selves and a trance or dual consciousness of spiritual and terrestrial worlds; animals also were thought to experience these transformations; see Rebecca Stone, *The Jaguar Within* (Austin: University of Texas Press, 2011). See also Alphonso Lingis, *Excesses: Eros and Culture* (Albany: SUNY Press, 1983), where trance experiences, as "compassionate no-self, eyes open upon the universal impermanence," are explored in Sri Lanka (ibid., xi).

97. Rupert Gethin, *Foundations of Buddhism* (London: Oxford University Press, 1998).

98. Smuts, "Encounters with Animal Minds," 299.

99. Aristotle, *On the Soul*, 405a 19. Thales and the other Ionian sages seem to have fused what Aristotle calls natural philosophy with shamanism and mythmaking and thus experienced nature as what reveals itself rather than as physical object; see Chiara Bottici, *A Philosophy of Political Myth* (Cambridge: Cambridge University Press, 2007), 27–28.

5. REFLECTIONS

1. Barbara Smuts, "Encounters with Animal Minds," *Journal of Consciousness Studies* 8 (2001): 299. Here, in this culminating chapter, Smuts's essay serves as a key source for rethinking traditional models of ethical development. Smuts herself offers a model for rethinking the nature of interspecies encounter and friendship, from which I draw inspiration for my model, directed specifically at ethical ideals. I discovered as well Chi Yuan's poem from Smuts's article.

2. Ibid., 299–300.

3. For a critique of the use of human standards for reason, intelligence, and intentionality in arguments for human exceptionalism, see Gary Steiner, *Animals and the Moral Community* (New York: Columbia University Press, 2008), where Steiner also engages the Humean tradition in productive ways; and Paola Cavalieri, *The Death of the Animal* (New York: Columbia University Press, 2009). Cavalieri terms this use of human standards for

5. REFLECTIONS

measuring animal "inferiority" "perfectionism" (ibid., 3). She also provides an excellent argument for eschewing the dogmatism of unscientific metaphysics (ibid., 9); this argument leaves open the kind of speculative ethics that would learn from the sciences. A speculative ethics for interspecies living is based not on character ideals of classic virtue ethics (which are too oriented toward individual character and are perfectionist), nor on moral theory (which emphasizes the role of imperfect duties not to harm); cf. Cavalieri where this traditional division between virtue ethics and moral theory is stated (ibid., 9). Cavalieri's moral concern is with the obligation to prevent harm, including against those creatures that suffer and lack all agency (ibid., 18–19). While our own approach emphasizes unexpected ethical agency in a range of creatures, Cavalieri's utilitarian concern for the dependent and vulnerable, like that of response ethics, has significance for a Stage 4 of ethical interaction, based on compassion.

4. On technical and linguistic human advantages, see Jane Goodall, "What Separates Us from the Chimpanzees?" *TED Talk*, May 16, 2007, www.youtube.com/watch?v=5Iz7WRDjOjM.
5. An example of the use of modernist sentimentalism (in particular Hume) is found in Jess Prinz, "The Emotional Basis of Moral Judgments," *Philosophical Explorations* 9 (2006): 29–43. Here again my starting point is with Hegelian *sittlichkeit*, or small-scale communal and social networks, in contrast with the binaries of classic modern individualism. Ontologically, post-Hegelian philosophies begin with relationality rather than with early modernism's properties and things. This ontological difference has political repercussions as well. For example, the political notion of right does not turn on property or self-ownership, but ultimately freedom as belonging.
6. The realms and layers of ethical concern are expanded to include subjectless agencies and hence beyond respect for the "subject-of-life." Tom Regan, *The Case for Animal Rights* (Berkeley: University of California, 2004).
7. Robert R. Provine, *Laughter: A Scientific Investigation* (New York: Penguin, 2000), 114.
8. On concerns with the social media, see William Deresiewicz, "Faux Friendship," *Chronicle of Higher Education*, December 6, 2009. Social media need not weaken real friendships, but social networking can be co-opted into the utilities of the entrepreneurial self, which is one of the clear risks of neoliberalism.
9. Matthew Calarco expands upon a Levinasian approach in the context of what he calls an "agnostic ethics," which is open to creatures that are not subjects and who therefore cannot make a claim (and establish a right); see his response, "Toward an Agnostic Animal Ethics," in Cavalieri, *The Death of the Animal*, 79. The assumption I begin with here differs in emphasis: ethics as well as a political notion of rights originate in the encounters of social animals and not as the interruption of an isolated creature, propelled by appetite and egoism and experiencing the other as a radical alterity. This Levinasian view does come close to characterizing, however, the ethical awakening of the narcissistic protagonist of Coetzee's *Disgrace* (see the coda). But here our approach begins with the work of Donna Haraway, which is where Calarco ends his earlier book, *Zoographies: The Question of the Animal from Heidegger to Derrida* (New York: Columbia University Press, 2008), 148–149. Our approach here also is similar to J. Baird Callicott, "Animal Liberation

5. REFLECTIONS

and Environmental Ethics: Back Together Again" in *The Animal Liberation/Environmental Ethics Debate: The Environmental Perspective*, ed. Eugene Hargrove (Albany: SUNY Press, 1992), 249–262. Callicott develops the idea that humans form social bonds with other animals in communities and thus have obligations to them from Mary Midgley. See Mary Midgley, *Animals and Why They Matter* (Dexter, MI: Thomson-Shore, 1983). I agree that these bonds can be understood more fully through the affective communication within and across species, but also think that these bonds are the source of not just a Humean notion of sympathy but also a meaningful life. In this respect, I take a post-Heideggerian perspective that begins, as Calarco so well explores, with the exposure of one creature to another, rather than a modern philosophy of the subject; however, my stages locate sociality deeper down and in communicated affects and in this way diverge from the starting points of Levinas or other response ethicists. For a critique of Callicott, see Jennifer Welchman, "Hume, Callicott, and the Land Ethic: Problems and Prospects," *Journal of Value Inquiry* 43 (2009): 201–220; Welchman uses virtue ethics, which unfortunately diminishes what Callicott understands as the holistic approach of a communal ethic and what I aim to capture through biosocial networks, culminating in a sense of home. See also Clare Palmer, *Animal Ethics in Context* (New York: Columbia University Press, 2010), 51–57, for a critique of Callicott and for a relational ethics that emphasizes causal connections rather than affective ones for moral responsibility. Given my commitment to a larger communitarian project, affect-based communication remains central, although not to the exclusion of cognition. In primary and secondary emotions, cognitions are intertwined with affects. Causal interactions, I would think, acquire moral meaning and urgency through social bonds and so rely on these sources for their ethical valence.

10. Daniel Kelly, *Yuck! The Nature and Moral Significance of Disgust* (Cambridge: MIT Press, 2011), 67–68. Kelly's focus is on a complex of disgust mechanisms (against poison and parasites) that he theorizes as unique to the human species; however, his more general remarks on disgust transmission should apply to any species that experiences this affect.
11. On regional accents in songbirds, see BBC News, "Birds Have Regional Accents According to Scientists," www.bbc.co.uk/news/science-environment-16154490 (accessed March 2, 2013). For a similar claim in relation to whales, see Jenny Allen et al., "Network-Based Diffusion Analysis Reveals Cultural Transmission of Lobtail Feeding in Humpback Whales," *Science* 340 (2013): 485–488.
12. Here I borrow Daniel Kelly's aptly descriptive term, "sentimental signaling system," but without Kelly's unnecessary restriction of the very phrasing to instances of mere emotional contagion; see Kelly, *Yuck!* 68. Kelly's purpose, however, is quite distinct from mine. He aims to explain the signalizing of disgust as useful information serving to warn against poisons and parasites, uniquely paired in humans. My concern here is to develop an expansive social ethics. His analysis seems to allow my more liberal use of his phrasing here to indicate social exchanges based on affects and to allow for affects to have some cognitive components.
13. Provine, *Laughter*, 113.

5. REFLECTIONS

14. On the importance of touching and swaddling in Paleolithic societies, see Jared Diamond, *The World Until Yesterday* (New York: Viking, 2012), 173–209.
15. Provine, *Laughter*.
16. Eva Jablonka and Marion J. Lamb, *Evolution in Four Dimensions: Genetic, Epigenetic, Behavioral, and Symbolic Variation in the History of Life* (Cambridge, MIT Press, 2006).
17. For a review of the literature on laughing as a signal that animals are not in danger and of nonaggression, see Matthew M. Hurley et al., *Inside Jokes: Using Human to Reverse-Engineer the Brain* (Cambridge: MIT Press, 2011), 259–263. The authors speculate that tickling and chasing function as proto-humor in species without theory of mind and that humor in our ancestors is coextensive with play. Based on comic theory, we add to this claim that self-irony (or self-humbling of the play bow and "admitting mistakes") is also a key part of both play and humor as well as of social ethics (see chapter 4). My project isn't focused on information-based modeling but on community building.
18. For these themes of forgiveness and reconciliation interpreted in a Kantian frame, rather than from ancient cultures, see Linda Radzik, *Making Amends* (Oxford: Oxford University Press, 2009). The ancient references to tragedy and comedy are aimed to capture the communal and secular importance of social bonds, relationships, and their violation. Instead of Kantian autonomy and rational choice or judgment, eros as heteronomy is central. Social bonds shift from the background to the foreground in this philosophical analysis, as they do in comic and tragic drama. On the evolutionary value of forgiveness in the context of elephant/human interactions, see G. A. Bradshaw, *Elephants on the Edge* (New Haven: Yale University Press, 2009), chapter 8, 129–146.
19. Malini Suchak, e-mail communication, May 15, 2013.
20. A neurobiological analysis of the interweaving of the individual in an environment is developed in Bruce E. Wexler, *Brain and Culture* (Cambridge: MIT Press, 2006), especially in part 2, 139ff.
21. See David Graeber, *The First 5,000 Years* (Brooklyn, NY: Melville House, 2011), 65, where Graeber claims that the Sumerian word *amargi* is the first recorded word for freedom, literally meaning to "return to mother," presumably the return home of debtors taken as slave laborers in the establishment of the first state governments some five thousand years ago.
22. Frans de Waal, *The Bonobo and the Atheist* (New York: Norton, 2013), 78. Malini Suchak demonstrates that capuchin monkeys, for example, exhibit other-regarding actions toward out-group individuals in her dissertation, "Chimpanzees Cooperate in a Competitive World" (Emory University, 2013).
23. Kelly Oliver, *Animal Lessons: How They Teach Us to Be Human* (New York: Columbia University Press, 2009), 18.
24. This quest for cosmic peace echoes Gary Steiner's "cosmic justice;" see his *Animals and the Limits of Postmodernism* (New York: Columbia University Press, 2013), 175ff.
25. Bradshaw, *Elephants on the Edge*, 129–146.
26. On the "gift" of "unanalyzable" jokes and art, see Hurley et al., *Inside Jokes*, 277.

27. On eros as a festival or an original celebration of sociality, see Cynthia Willett, *Maternal Ethics and Other Slave Moralities* (New York: Routledge, 1995), 31–47, which offers an interpretation of Enrique Dussel's remark "proximity is a festival" in his *Philosophy of Liberation* (Maryknoll, NY: Orbis, 1985), 17.
28. Diamond, *The World Until Yesterday*, 92ff.
29. Even "make love, not war" bonobos prey on other primates. See the report of Gottfried Hohmann and Barbara Fruth's observations in David Quammen, "The Left Bank Ape: An Exclusive Look at Bonobos," *National Geographic*, March 2013, http://ngm.national geo-graphic.com/2013/03/125-bonobos/quammen-text.
30. For Jane Goodall on technical and linguistic human advantages, see Goodall, "What Separates Us from the Chimpanzees?" 1.
31. R. J. R. Blair, E. Colledge, L. Murray, and D. G. Mitchell, "A Selective Impairment in the Processing of Sad and Fearful Expressions in Children with Psychopathic Tendencies," *Journal of Abnormal Child Psychology* 21 (2001): 491–498.
32. See Graeber, *The First 5,000 Years*, 390.
33. Patrick McDonnell's children's storybook about a young Jane Goodall names her toy chimpanzee, symbol of the wonder of nature, and her dream of "living with, and helping, all animals," Jubilee. *Me . . . Jane* (New York: Little, Brown, 2011). Thanks to Megan Craig for this reference.

CODA; OR, THE SONG OF THE DOG-MAN

1. Gayatri Chakravorty Spivak, "Ethics and Politics in Tagore, Coetzee, and Certain Scenes of Teaching," *Diacritics* 32 (2002): 17–31.
2. For a discussion of this issue, see David Attwell, "Race in Disgrace," *Interventions* 4 (2002): 331–41; and Peter McDonald, "Disgrace Effects," *Interventions* 4 (2002): 321–30.
3. J. M. Coetzee, *Disgrace* (New York: Penguin, 1999), 160.
4. Ibid., 126.
5. See Friedrich Nietzsche's "Third Essay: What Do Ascetic Ideals Mean?" in *Genealogy of Morals* in *The Birth of Tragedy and The Genealogy of Morals*, Frances Golffing, trans. (New York: Doubleday, 1956), 231–299.
6. On Ubuntu justice, see Mechthild Nagel, "An Ubuntu Ethic of Punishment," in *The End of Prisons*, ed. Mechthild E. Nagel and Anthony J. Nocella II (Amsterdam: Rodopi, 2013), 177–186. Nagel highlights the difficulties with Ubuntu ethics, including its speciesist and patriarchical aspects, and she warns against romanticizing it. Here I aim to redirect its communitarianism beyond speciesism, thus offering, as Nagel recommends, at least one corrective. Nagel mentions the Ubuntu emphasis on restitution over revenge and punishment, and its historical significance for forming and justifying the Truth and Reconciliation Commission, as the most promising component of this African ethic. As Nagel argues, in the neoliberal or neocolonial context of gross inequities, a transformational as well as restorative component of justice is required—Jubilee (chapters 2 and 4).

7. For an understanding of the history of race and frontier in white supremacist South Africa, see Clifton C. Crais, *The Making of the Colonial Order: White Supremacy and Black Resistance in the Eastern Cape, 1770–1865* (Johannesburg: Witwaterstrand University Press, 1992).
8. Ibid., 126–127.
9. Coetzee, *Disgrace*, 33.
10. Ibid., 16.
11. J. M. Coetzee, *The Lives of Animals* (Princeton: Princeton University Press, 1999), and *Elizabeth Costello* (New York: Penguin, 2003).
12. Coetzee, *Disgrace*, 142.
13. Ibid., 73.
14. Ibid., 143–144.
15. Cf. Alice A. Kuzniar, *Melancholia's Dog: Reflections on Our Animal Kinship* (Chicago: University of Chicago Press, 2006) for a reading of the novel that emphasizes the importance of sympathy and empathy. In this chapter, I am interested in what kind of ethics might open up beyond the limits of any ordinary conception of empathy, sympathy, or normal social bond for characterizing the ethical concern that Coetzee's protagonist develops for the abject and unsympathetic. Here we assume first that our cultural or subjective associations as well as our resentments, identifications, and other sources of motives and images inform empathy. Empathy is not direct from one person to another and so is never free from associations or otherwise unmediated by culture. Consider an example from *Disgrace* of the mediated and convoluted associations that inform any kind of empathy that works in the novel: the protagonist associates the abandoned pit bull, Katy, with the veterinarian, Bev, and with Lord Byron's abandoned lover, Teresa. This association composes the basis for a strange empathy that will later include the maimed dog in the final chapter. Second, as Kantians have long held, any ordinary moral sentiment is challenged by creatures who are viewed as abject and whose experience is beyond our ordinary imagination. Martha Nussbaum, who requires curiosity and imaginative identification with the other in sympathy in order to overcome disgust and respond, does not address the Kantian critique; see her *From Disgust to Humanity* (Oxford: Oxford University Press, 2010), xviii. Our approach is neither to return to the Kantian appeal to reason, which, as Nussbaum points out, lacks a clear motivating force, nor to appeal to any ordinary conception of empathy. See also Judith Butler, *Precarious Life: The Powers of Mourning and Violence* (London: Verso, 2004), 150. For this chapter, I assume that only minimally adequate communication is possible between the dog and the protagonist, and yet that this minimal communication generates an ethical sense of respect for the dog.
16. Cf. Heidegger's infamous parallel between the Holocaust and the mechanized food industry; cited in Tom Rockmore, *Heidegger and French Philosophy* (New York: Routledge, 1995), 150. On a related note, the film *Downfall* (directed by Oliver Hirschbiegel, 2005) portrays Hitler as concerned about his secretary and his dog, as well as a vegetarian, in contrast with his lack of concern for the fate of his fellow German citizens at the end of the Second World War. For a discussion of this contrast, see María Pía Lara, *Narrating Evil* (New York: Columbia University Press, 2007), 8.

17. See also Chloe Taylor, "The Precarious Lives of Animals: Butler, Coetzee, and Animal Ethics," *Philosophy Today* 52 (2008): 60–73; Taylor draws upon Coetzee's novel to extend Bulter's Levinasian ethics of nonviolence to animals. Here I am assuming a world in which violence is ineradicable.
18. See Cora Diamond's essay, "The Difficulty of Reality and Difficulty of Philosophy," in *Philosophy and Animal Life*, ed. Stanley Cavell, Cora Diamond, John McDowell, Ian Hacking, and Cary Wolfe (New York: Columbia University Press, 2008), 71–72. For an extensive reading of Coetzee's Elizabeth Costello novels from this tradition, see Stephen Mulhall, *The Wounded Animal: J. M. Coetzee and the Difficulty of Reality in Literature and Philosophy* (Princeton: Princeton University Press, 2009).
19. See Diane Perpich, *The Ethics of Emmanuel Levinas* (Stanford: Stanford University Press, 2008); and Claire Katz, *Levinas, Judaism, the Feminine* (Indianapolis: University of Indiana Press, 2003). See also Kelly Oliver, *Animal Pedagogy and the Science of Kinship* (New York: Columbia University Press, 2009) for the role of animals in the assertion of the human for Derrida, Freud, Kristeva, and other major figures in continental ethics.
20. Julia Kristeva, *Strangers to Ourselves*, trans. Leon Roudiez (New York: Columbia University Press, 1991). See Sara Beardsworth, *Julia Kristeva: Psychoanalysis and Modernity* (Albany: SUNY Press, 2004) for a compelling reading of Kristeva's work through her response to modern nihilism and the loss of meaning.
21. Richard Kearney, *Strangers, God, and Monsters: Ideas of Otherness* (New York: Routledge, 2003). And, for my similar concerns with the representation of the mother in Kristeva, Cynthia Willett, *Maternal Ethics and Other Slave Moralities* (New York: Routledge, 1995), 19–23.
22. For an interpretation of earlier novels through Kristeva's theory of the semiotic, see Benita Parry, "Speech and Silence in the Fictions of J. M. Coetzee," in *Critical Perspectives on J. M. Coetzee*, ed. Graham Huggan and Stephen Watson (New York: St. Martin's, 1996), 37–65. Parry discusses Coetzee's use of female narrators in various novels and the notion of the body as progenitor of woman's language as a language of the heart. She argues that these narratives remain sealed from the heterology of other voices, and in this respect is critical of Spivak (see note 1, this chapter).
23. Leigh M. Johnson provides a philosophical framework for understanding justice claims (including the role of forgiveness and personal grace) in the South African Truth and Reconciliation Commission in "Transitional Truth and Historical Justice: Philosophical Foundations and Implications of the Truth and Reconciliation Commission," *International Studies in Philosophy* 38 (2006): 69–105. Derek Attridge reads the novel as the search for grace, understood as a receiving of external beneficence; see his "Age of Bronze, State of Grace," in *J. M Coetzee and the Ethics of Reading* (Chicago: University of Chicago Press, 2004), 162–191. My aim joins with Johnson's deconstructive analysis in its aim to reconnect the personal (and religious or spiritual) meaning of grace with a communal and multilayered sense of justice. A minimal but suggestive glimpse into South African Ubuntu communal justice reemerges at the novel's end in the felt connectivity between the dog and the human protagonist. Individualistic conceptions of justice occlude communal elements of

tradition a African justice and consign reconciliation and grace to narrowly personal and modernist religious spheres.

24. Julie Kristeva, *Black Sun: Depression and Melancholia*, trans. Leon Roudiez (New York: Columbia University Press, 1989).

25. Oliver points out that the *Vanity Fair* cover shot of the pregnant Demi Moore in August 1991 marks a shift in attitudes toward the pregnant female body. For more on pregnancy and the female body, see Kelly Oliver, *Knock Me Up, Knock Me Down: Images of Pregnancy in Hollywood Films* (New York: Columbia University Press, 2012). My concern with this imagery in Kristeva traces back to this time, and no doubt follows the change in cultural imagery; see my *Maternal Ethics and Other Slave Moralities*, 19–23.

26. Jared Diamond, *The World Until Yesterday* (New York: Penguin Viking, 2012), 173–209.

27. Kristeva, *Black Sun*, 13–4.

28. Coetzee, *Disgrace*, 219.

29. Ibid., 146.

30. Ibid.

31. Paul Patton, "Becoming-Animal and Pure Life in Coetzee's *Disgrace*," *Ariel* 35 (2004): 101–112.

32. Coetzee, *Disgrace*, 219.

33. Lewis R. Gordon, "Tragic Revolutionary Violence," in *Fanon and the Crisis of European Man: An Essay on Philosophy and the Human Sciences* (New York: Routledge, 1995), 76. My concern here is the reduction of the crime of rape to the politics of race.

34. See Helen Moffett, "Rape as Narrative of Social Control," *Journal of Southern African Studies* 32 (2006): 129–144. In the context of discussing the current high crime rate, and especially the crime of rape, as a legacy of apartheid in postapartheid South Africa, Moffett explains the "tacit social understanding that certain kinds of white-on-black violence were 'necessary' as a kind of oil that kept apartheid hierarchies running smoothly" (ibid., 140). At the same time, she points out the possible political damage of Coetzee's representation of blacks as the rapists of white women and thus as "barbarians" (ibid., 135). The novel accounts for that political legacy in such a way as to contribute to a posthumanist ethics. It does not claim to tell its story from the positions of white women or black Africans, and it, in fact, fails to do so. Again Moffett: "South African women are sick of hearing that apartheid is to blame for the brutality that men mete out to them" (ibid., 143). The protagonist has difficulty finding a role for himself other than as predator or protector of women. He does, though, identify with women through his relation with dogs. Hence the radical and progressive element of the novel is the relation with dogs, not women, which remains problematic.

35. Ibid., 137.

36. On the importance of the seriocomic, the Cynic as dog men, their shameless disregard for conventions, and the learning of ethics from animals, see R. Bracht Branham and Marie-Odile Goulet-Gaze, eds., *The Cynics: The Cynic Movement in Antiquity and Its Legacy* (Berkeley: University of California Press, 1996). As we've argued in the previous chapters, actual animals such as dogs are hardly shameless or without their own sense of disgust.

37. Coetzee, *Disgrace*, 214.
38. Ibid., 215.
39. For a discussion of the role of race in the selective punishment of rape in South Africa, see Pamela Scully, "Rape, Race, and Colonial Culture," *American Historical Review* 100 (1995): 335–359. Scully explains how race figures in the view that male sexuality is a result of uncontrollable passions and female seduction in South Africa.
40. Coetzee, *Disgrace*, 4. Note that African music, unlike European, primarily serves for communicative purposes and hence is not commonly considered, by traditional European standards, as "art."
41. Kristeva stays close to Freud, who argues that the oedipal complex lies at the beginning of religion, morality, culture, and society, even as she modifies his claim to include the preoedipal phase. See Sigmund Freud, *Totem and Taboo*, trans. James Strachey (New York: Norton, 1913), 156.
42. For a discussion of Husserl's ethics as an idea of a world with numerous origins and distinct subjects, see Jacques Derrida, "Violence and Metaphysics," in *Margins of Philosophy*, trans. Alan Bass (Chicago: University of Chicago Press, 1982), 125–126. See Perpich, *The Ethics of Emmanuel Levinas*, 71–72, for an elaboration of Derrida's critique of Levinas and the latter's response with regard to the difference between having meaning in the world and having a world; she also discusses the tensions in Levinas due to the need to represent oneself in this world rather than appearing out of the blue unmediated by any mode of representation.

INDEX

Abe, Evelyn, 2, 23
Abram, David, 17, 179*n*29
Acampora, Ralph, 17, 178*n*17, 180*n*39, 197*n*14
Acholi, the, 2, 23–24
affect, 3, 12, 18–21, 64, 94–105, 132–50, 181*n*43, 198*n*33, 208*n*9; attunement, 12–15, 80–101, 121, 132–43, 170, 176–80; across species, 15–16, 25, 71, 79, 115, 120, 179*n*36
Africa, African societies, 1–5, 13–15, 21–23, 28, 39, 74, 81, 128, 148–73, 182
agape, 124–28, 142, 168; *see also* spirituality; transcendence
Ahmed, Sarah, 182*n*51
alterity ethics, 9–15, 34, 39–40, 128, 155; *see also* Levinas, Emmanuel
altruism, 46, 65, 128, 143, 206*n*87; *see also* reciprocity; Darwin, Charles
anarchism, anarchy, 5–6, 22, 33, 50–51, 60–63, 72–77, 95, 108, 175
Angier, Natalie, 18
anthropocene, 134, 144
anthropocentrism, 16
anthropomorphism, 27
Antigone, 158, 163–70
Ape Genius (film), 44

Aristotle, 9, 12, 24–25, 85, 100

Bakhtin, Mikhail, 77, 195*n*46
Barad, Karen, 86, 135
Bekoff, Mark, 1, 24, 49–50, 54, 62, 71–79, 196*n*6, 204*n*44
Benjamin, Walter, 40–42
Bentham, Jeremy, 7, 9, 34–36, 42, 72
Bergson, Henri, 62, 119, 200*n*63
bonobos, 44–50, 102, 132–33, 206*n*87, 211*n*29
Bradshaw, G. A., 4–5, 19, 23, 33, 45, 51, 67, 141
Braidotti, Rosi, 17, 23, 26, 181*n*41, 186*n*81
Bryant, Katherine, 66, 181*n*47, 190*n*52
Byron, Lord, 152, 158–61, 167–70

Calarco, Matthew, 17, 178*n*17, 190*n*46, 195*n*42, 206*n*92, 208*n*9
call and response, 1, 11, 13–5, 58, 88–93, 99, 112–14, 134, 150–60, 172–73, 182*n*50
Callicott, Baird, 208*n*9
carnival, carnivalesque, 53, 77–78, 109, 143, 145, 195*n*45
cats, v, 81, 153, 157, 175
Cavalieri, Paola, 190*n*46n, 195*n*42, 207*n*3
Cavell, Stanley, 154

Chanter, Tina, 178*nn*20, 21
chimpanzees, 5, 16, 26, 44–53, 79, 93–97, 115–19, 126–33, 139, 190*n*55, 191*n*56, 202*n*28, 206*n*87
Coetzee, J. M. 28, 106, 124, 145–74
Colbert, Stephen, 29–30, 44, 59, 118–19
comedy, 27, 50–59, 70–71, 77–78, 109, 117–18, 140–43, 210*n*18; *see also* joy; laughter
communication: animal, 8, 12–16, 41–47, 58, 80–90, 125; across species, 29, 42, 58, 71, 80–90; across sensory modalities, 88–101, 132; origins of, 48
communitarianism: and ethics, 2, 13, 21–5, 94–96, 143, 155, 177*n*3, 183*n*58, 185*n*78, 186*n*81, 211*n*6; across species, 2, 21–26, 94–96, 211*n*6; and anarchism 6, 60–61, 72–77, 94–96; and music, 16
community selection hypothesis, 66–77
Cornell, Drucilla, 178*n*13, 182*n*55, 197*n*14
cosmopolitan, cosmopolitanism, 2, 6, 9, 16, 72–73, 94, 104, 160
Critchley, Simon, 118–19
Cynics, the, 31, 63, 113, 164, 170, 193, 214*n*36

Darwin, Charles, 51, 75, 111, 132; Darwinism, 61–65, 120, 153, 180*n*40
de Fontenay, Elisabeth, 42
de Waal, Frans, 16, 25, 29, 37, 50–53, 60, 64–66, 81, 99, 102, 116, 120–27, 132
death and mortality, 4, 18–20, 66, 112, 118–19, 159, 162, 145, 169–74; drive, 69–70, 77, 95, 112–13; fear of, 125
Deleuze, Gilles, 17–18, 21, 23, 94, 95, 154, 180, 181, 198*n*33
Derrida, Jacques, 8, 11–12, 34, 39–41, 58, 71–72, 142
Diamond, Jared, 143, 185*n*77
disgust, 18, 27, 85, 97, 109–41, 202*n*36, 203*n*39, 209*n*10, 212*n*15; *see also* affect
domestication, 8, 34
Donaldson, Sue and Will Kymlicka, 7, 180*n*37
Douglass, Frederick, 38–39, 64, 84
Dussel, Enrique, 82, 177*n*3, 211*n*27

elephants, 1–5, 12–17, 24–25, 33, 44–45, 52, 67–68, 97, 102, 121, 128, 133–34, 137–38, 141–42, 177*n*4, 182*n*49
entropy, 69–70, 145
eros, 4, 9–13, 17–26, 38, 44, 62, 73, 77–83, 87, 91, 94–96, 103–4, 125, 128, 133–34, 143, 155–57, 160, 163, 173, 180*n*40, 183*nn*58, 60; *see also* affect; *agape*
extinction, 1, 33, 145, 154–62

farming, factory, 4, 106, 110, 149, 153–54, 180*n*37
Foucault, Michel, 8, 187*n*9
Freud, Sigmund, 18–20, 70, 82, 104, 111, 113, 119, 159, 184*n*66; *see also* death drive; Oedipus complex

Gaia, 64, 66, 70, 143
Gallagher, Shaun, 197*n*16, 198*n*30
genes, genetics, 24, 31–33, 36, 65–68, 103–5, 110, 131–41, 145, 121, 132
golden rule (See also "reciprocity") 50, 75–6, 83, 124, 139, 195*n*42
Goodall, Jane, 100, 119, 126, 132, 182, 205*n*58, 206*n*78, 208*n*4, 211*nn*11, 33
Gordon, Lewis, 166, 214*n*33
Graeber, David, 63–64, 145, 184*n*66, 194*n*12, 210*n*21
Greek: philosophy, 3, 8, 10–12, 63, 103, 113, 194*n*20; drama and tragedy, 5, 20–5, 114–16, 161, 165, 76–78; culture, 5, 20, 34, 70, 125, 140, 185*n*78
gut brain, 84, 113–17, 198*n*21; *see also* parasites

Habermas, Jürgen, 80–81, 200*n*66
Haidt, Jonathan, 19–21, 37, 106, 113, 127, 198*n*21
Haraway, Donna, 17–18, 24, 27, 57–63, 66, 70–73, 78, 94–96, 114
Heidegger, Martin, 208*n*9, 212*n*16
Hewitt, Nancy, 43, 190*n*44
Hill Collins, Patricia, 21–23
Holocaust, the, 9, 41, 149, 153–56, 169, 212*n*16
Hribal, Jason, 55, 188*n*17

INDEX

hubris, 3, 20, 24–25, 33, 61, 76, 102, 112–16, 120, 139, 163–65, 185*n*78; *see also* Greek culture
humor, 30, 32, 48–51, 55, 59, 79, 98, 109, 117–25, 210*n*17; and satire, 77, 118, 139; *see also* comedy; joy; play

industrial revolution, the, 35–36, 51, 144
Irigaray, Luce, 82, 178*n*20

Jablonka, Eva and Marion Lamb, 67
Johnson, Leigh, 213*n*23
joy, 18, 48–62, 68, 136, 186 (f81); *see also* humor; play

Kant, Immanuel, 9, 76, 85, 101, 104–6, 124–25, 131, 142, 149, 160, 210*n*18, 212*n*15
Katz, Claire, 178*n*21, 213*n*19
Kearney, Richard, 213*n*21
Kelly, Daniel, 209*nn*10, 12; 213*n*39
Kingsolver, Barbara, 53, 96
Kristeva, Julia, 9, 111, 156–61, 169–76, 213*n*22, 215*n*41
Kropotkin, Peter, 61–64, 70, 73, 133

Latour, Bruno, 181*n*43, 194*n*32
Laughter, 25–26, 30–31, 48–55, 59, 62, 77–79, 93, 109, 112, 117–20, 134–49; *see also* comedy; joy
Lawlor, Leonard, 17, 179*n*26
Levinas, Emanuel, 9–10, 154, 161, 189*n*41, 208*n*9; *see also* alterity ethics
logos, logocentrism, 9–11, 20, 73, 81, 90, 105, 133, 143
Lorde, Audre, 22–23

madness, 23, 32–33, 58, 103–4
Marcuse, Herbert, 17, 22, 44, 73, 77, 81, 125, 178*n*24, 180*n*40, 182*n*55, 183*n*58, 184*n*66, 201*n*15
Margulis, Lynn, 64, 66, 69, 71, 143
Massumi, Brian, 180*n*40, 199*n*44
Maturana, Humberto, 84
McAfee, Noëlle, 80. 177*n*11, 196*n*2
Mendieta, Eduardo, 17, 177*n*3
Merleau-Ponty, Maurice, 12, 16, 180*n*39

Mill, J. S., 1, 7, 9, 26, 36, 85, 143
mirror neurons, 6, 120–21, 137
Moffett, Helen, 167, 214*n*34
Morrison, Toni, 21–23, 74, 141, 155–56, 163, 172
mother, maternal, 23, 89, 93, 96, 123, 137, 141, 148, 156–72, 179*n*36, 210*n*21
music, 12–13, 15, 26, 89–92, 135, 145–46, 159–61, 171–74, 179*n*31, 189*n*41, 215*n*40; and metaphor, 12, 16

Neanderthals, 31–32, 92
Neolithic revolution, 2, 3, 12, 51, 177*n*3, 183*n*58
Nussbaum, Martha, 36–37, 111, 188, 206*n*91, 212*n*15

Occupy movement, 27, 44, 52, 60–62, 73, 79, 176; *see also* anarchism
Oedipus complex, 18–19, 95, 157, 159, 163–64, 168, 215*n*41; *see also* Freud, Sigmund; Kristeva, Julia
Oliver, Kelly, 10, 17, 42, 175, 189*n*40, 214*n*25
Oromo, the, 128–29, 140–42, 184*n*65

Pääbo, Svante, 31–33, 103, 105
Panksepp, Jaak, 48–49
parallel evolution, 82, 97–98; *see also* Darwin, Charles
parasites, 76, 84, 109, 112, 204, 209; *see also* gut brain
pathos, 5, 39–40, 68, 115, 164, 167
Pearson, Susan, 34–35
Perpich, Diane, 213*n*19, 215*n*42
PETA (People for the Ethical Treatment of Animals), 118–19
phenomenology, 12–17, 105–6, 118–19, 125, 178*n*17, 179*n*33, 180*n*39, 197*n*15; and Hegel, 124; *see also* Merleau-Ponty, Maurice; Steinbock, Anthony
pigs, 1, 7, 34, 78, 110–11, 117, 175
Plato, 20–21, 103–5
play, 3, 15–17, 44–96, 102, 107–15, 120–34, 137–52, 164; *see also* joy
Plessner, Helmuth 118–19, 125, 204

219

INDEX

poststructuralism, 8–11, 13, 15, 17, 34, 40, 42, 72, 94, 178*nn*13, 17, 186*n*81, 187*n*9
pragmatism, 12, 17, 21–22, 180*n*39, 183*n*59, 197*n*15, 200*n*66
Preuss, Todd, 97
primates, 16, 28–31, 44–50, 65–75, 92–116, 142, 181*n*47, 211*n*29
Protevi, John, 197*n*14
Provine, Robert, 48–50, 93

Raffoul, Francois, 178*n*20, 189*n*41
rats, rodents, 48, 58, 111–13, 143, 202*n*36
reciprocity, 3, 5, 13–14, 38, 50, 65, 75–76, 89, 90, 101, 132–33, 137–39, 193*n*7, 195*n*42; *see also* altruism
reconciliation and forgiveness, 17, 25, 30, 129–32, 139–40, 158–59, 172, 180*n*37, 210*n*18, 123*n*23
rhesus monkeys, 4, 16, 97, 177
ridicule, ridiculous, 27, 30, 106–20, 134, 139, 150, 161, 173
rights: animal, 7, 34–42, 119, 129, 180*n*37; human and civil, 7, 10–11, 21, 34–42, 167, 185*n*78, 187*n*9
Rise of the Planet of the Apes (film), 31, 44
Rockmore, Tom, 212*n*16

sacred, the: 27, 81, 102, 104–13, 129, 140–41, 164–65, 170, 202*n*34; *see also* transcendence; *sangha*
Sagan, Dorian, 64, 69, 71, 143
sangha, 3, 101, 105, 126, 130, 143; *see also* transcendence; sacred, the
scapegoat, scapegoating, 86, 164–66
Scottish enlightenment, 34, 37, 64
self-handicapping, 75–78, 90, 139
selves-in-communities, 66–76

shame, 20, 109, 113–17, 123, 139–40; *see also* affect
Siebert, Charles, 1, 4, 5
Singer, Peter, 36, 44, 104, 178*n*15
Smith, Adam, 34–35, 65, 68
Smuts, Barbara, 5, 27, 68, 83, 98, 100–1, 105, 126, 130–32, 132, 143
spirituality, spiritualism, 6, 12, 27–28, 70, 101–8, 125–30, 141–42, 201*n*5, 207*n*96; *see also* agape; *sangha*; transcendence
Spivak, Gayatri, 43, 147, 154, 167, 189*n*42
Steeves, Peter, 17, 178*n*17, 179*n*30, 189*n*43
Steinbock, Anthony, 106
Steiner, Gary, 175, 189*n*40, 196*n*9, 207*n*3
Stengers, Isabelle, 72, 82
Stern, Daniel, 14, 88, 90, 95, 136, 198*n*33
Suchak, Malini, 47, 50, 79, 93, 108, 122, 175, 187n6, 190n55, 204n49
superorganism(s), 84–87

Taylor, Chloë, 17, 187*n*14, 213*n*17
Toadvine, Ted, 17, 178*n*17, 179*n*30
Tomkins, Silvan, 14, 90
transcendence, 13, 107–8, 124–26, 141, 172, 180*n*40; *see also* spirituality; *sangha*; agape

visceral conscience, 113–17, 180, 204*n*40; *see also* gut brain

water, 26, 32, 34, 52, 100–45, 182*n*49
Wilson, E. O., 66
Wolfe, Cary, 17, 186*n*4, 188*n*31, 195*n*42, 213*n*18

Yerkes National Primate Center, 25, 52
Young, Iris, 80, 196*n*2

GPSR Authorized Representative: Easy Access System Europe, Mustamäe tee
50, 10621 Tallinn, Estonia, gpsr.requests@easproject.com

www.ingramcontent.com/pod-product-compliance
Lightning Source LLC
Chambersburg PA
CBHW021944290426
44108CB00012B/959